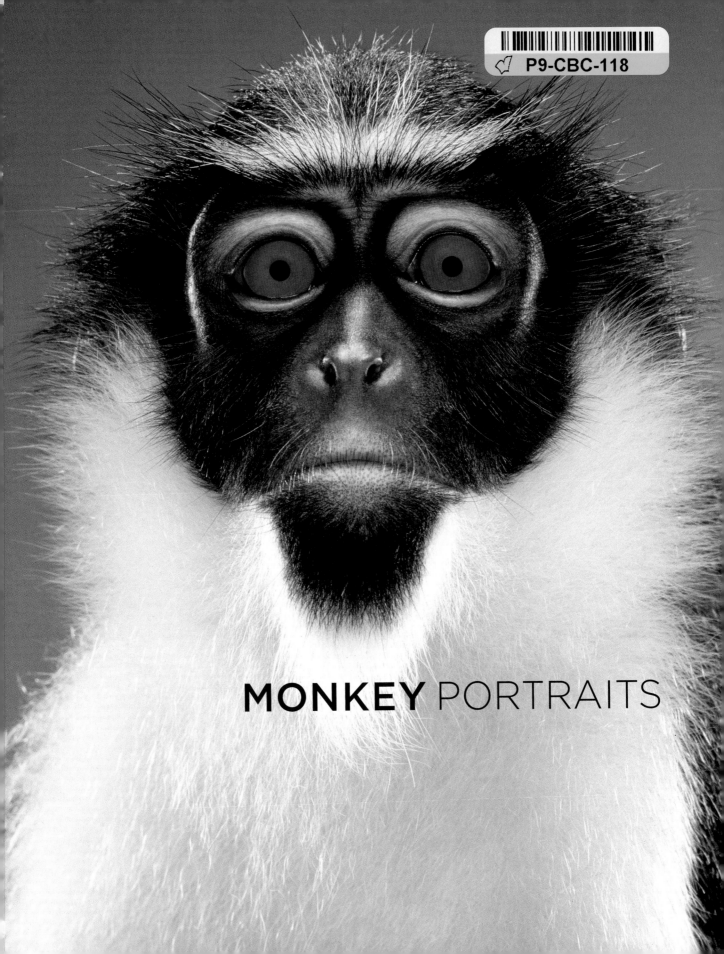

MONKEY PORTRAITS

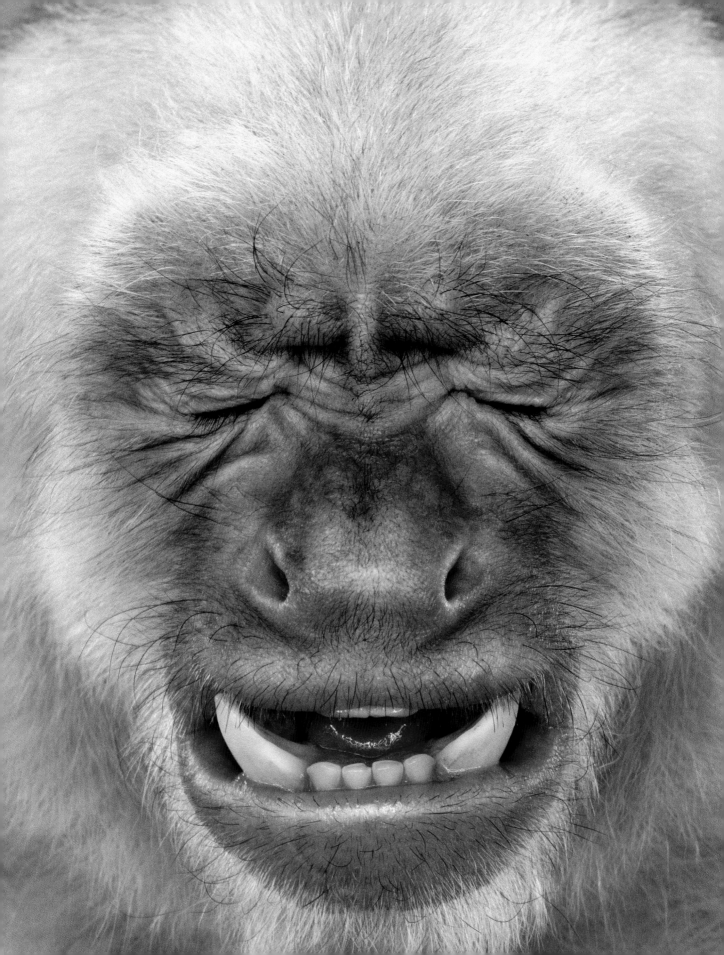

Photographs by
Jill Greenberg

Foreword by
Paul Weitz

Afterword by
Paul Myoda

MONKEY PORTRAITS

Little, Brown and Company
NEW YORK · BOSTON · LONDON

Little, Brown and Company
Hachette Book Group USA
237 Park Avenue, New York, NY 10017
Visit our Web site at www.HachetteBookGroupUSA.com

First edition: September 2006
First paperback edition: October 2007

Library of Congress Cataloging-in-Publication Data

Greenberg, Jill.
    Monkey portraits / Jill Greenberg. — 1st ed.
        p. cm.
HC ISBN 0-8212-5755-2 / 978-0-8212-5755-5
PB ISBN 0-316-00512-6 / 978-0-316-00512-8
1. Photography of primates. 2. Apes — Pictorial works. 3. Monkeys — Pictorial works. I. Title.

TR729.P74G57 2006
779'. 3298 — dc22   2005037068

Design by Gary Tooth / Empire Design Studio
Printed in Singapore

To my little monkeys, Violet and Zed,
and my great ape, Rob

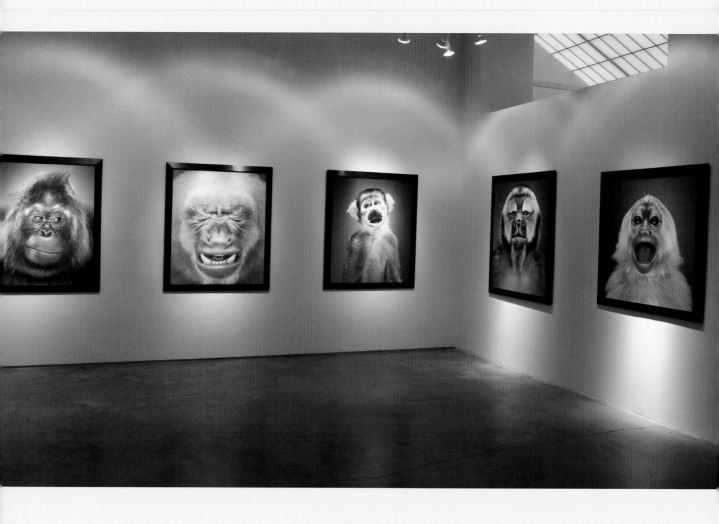

ClampArt, New York City, 2006

FOREWORD

I attended an exhibit of Jill Greenberg's monkey portraits a couple of years ago. Although I had met Jill socially before, I didn't put two and two together. I just went because I was attracted by the photo on the postcard invitation. So I was surprised to see a number of people I knew at the exhibit, many of whom I hadn't seen in years. As more and more old friends and acquaintances entered the gallery, plastic wine cups in hand, I had a feeling of discomfort and dread. I had changed a lot since I last saw most of them. They seemed as nice and as intelligent as ever, but they made me think of a weird, often unhappy guy I used to know – myself.

That was the perfect state of mind to be in while I looked at Jill's monkey and ape photos. The neutrality of the backgrounds allowed me to focus on their faces and their body language. There was a temptation to anthropomorphize them, but I don't think that is what drew me to the photos. I think it was the way the images held up a mirror to my own confusion. There is a degree to which our own humanity is comprehensible, and a degree to which our movement through time and toward death simply doesn't jibe with our attempts to be presentable.

These pictures make sense and they don't. They are beautiful and grotesque. They resonate with exploitation and respect. They're funny and sad. I like them a lot.

I bought a couple of huge prints that night, one for myself and one for my brother, with whom I share the superstition of always putting a monkey in any film I'm working on (it has devolved to a sock monkey in my current film). I'm relieved to find that the print I bought for myself is simply titled "The Monkey." The subject's name is apparently Katie, and she has starred in *Bruce Almighty, Friends*, and an Excedrin commercial. While I can't comprehend it, her worried, intense expression is extremely familiar.

Paul Weitz
filmmaker

INTRODUCTION

I began photographing monkeys and apes by accident. I had booked a small white capuchin named Katie for an advertising job. She was supposed to be having a tea party with two little girls in a pink room, standing on the table banging pots and wearing pink striped bloomers. For other assignments, I had shot penguins, lions, and albino pythons, but this was the first time I had photographed a monkey. Since I had a bit of extra time and a nice client, I decided to do a portrait of Katie.

When I got the contact sheets back, the images startled and amused me. Katie's expressions were so human and her intelligence seemed so obvious. I realized I had discovered a new subject—one perfect for social commentary. Since this work happened to commence in October 2001, just after the tragic events of 9/11, I was discovering my own sociopolitical awareness of the world. These animals' expressions allow an interpretation that can be perceived as passing judgment on the behavior of their genetic cousins. Ultimately I ended up having to reshoot the ad with a toy poodle, since the client decided the monkey looked too menacing—not quite the effect that they wanted to sell to moms in the Midwest.

I photographed more monkeys and apes whenever I had a chance or felt financially free enough to lay out the funds for these animal actors, with their attendant trainers and handlers. The project has taken about five years to complete, and the subjects were photographed at my studios in New York and Los Angeles, as well as at Parrot Jungle in Miami. In all, I have photographed more than thirty different primates, about twenty different species: marmosets, mandrills, capuchins, macaques, orangutans, and a chimpanzee, to name but a few. They all have resonated with me in different ways. I love the wisdom in the face of Jake, the older orangutan. He is only five years old but looks like an old man. Another favorite is Josh, the celebes macaque, who is on the cover. His black hair, amber-colored eyes, and long face make him look almost unreal, like a cartoon character.

What became apparent as I was making my selections after each shoot was that I was attracted to the images where the subjects appeared almost human, expressing emotions and using gestures I thought were reserved only for people. The formal studio portrait setting adds an air of both seriousness and humor. Some people have commented that the animals resemble friends or relatives. Sharon Stone remarked as I was shooting her, that she has "sat in studio meetings with guys like that," referring to "Haughty." Indeed, monkeys are not as high maintenance as many of the subjects I regularly photograph, albeit markedly more difficult to communicate with and give direction to. Of course, with primates, I don't have to be concerned with making sure they look "beautiful" or retouching them to appear flawless. They are us and the opposite of us at the same time since they share none of our cultural constraints on behavior or appearance. They seem to be looking back at us, sometimes judging, sometimes in shock. Is it something we've done? Maybe it is just that some of us are trying to pretend we aren't related. For anyone who doubts Darwin (ahem, Mr. President), look in the monkey mirror and think again.

Jill Greenberg

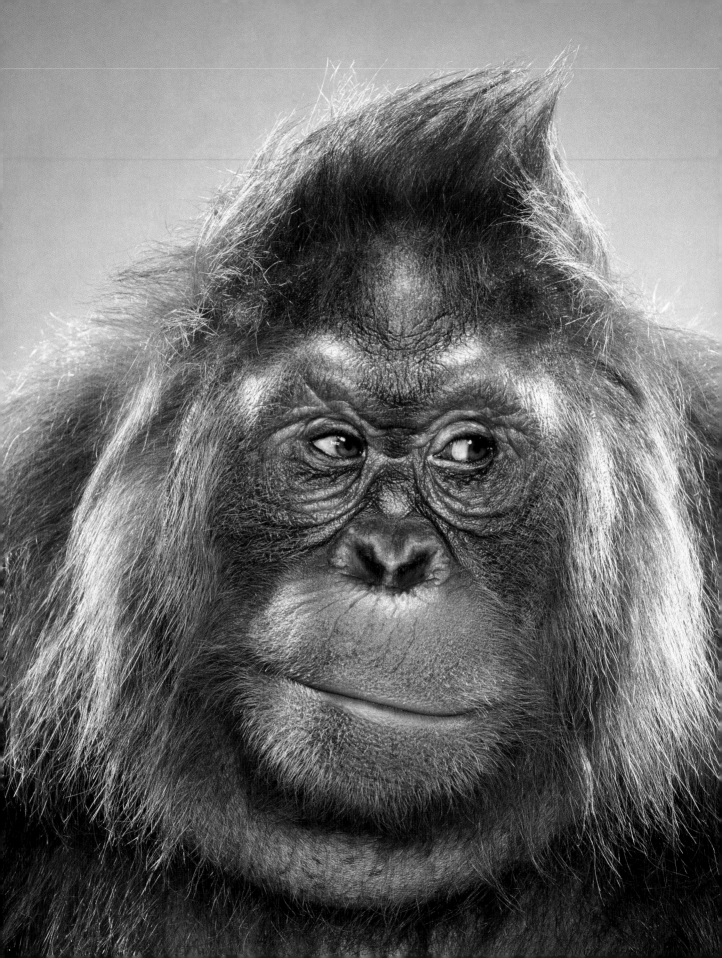

THE **PORTRAITS**

Heatmiser

Often I have gazed into a chimpanzee's eyes and wondered
what was going on behind them.
JANE GOODALL

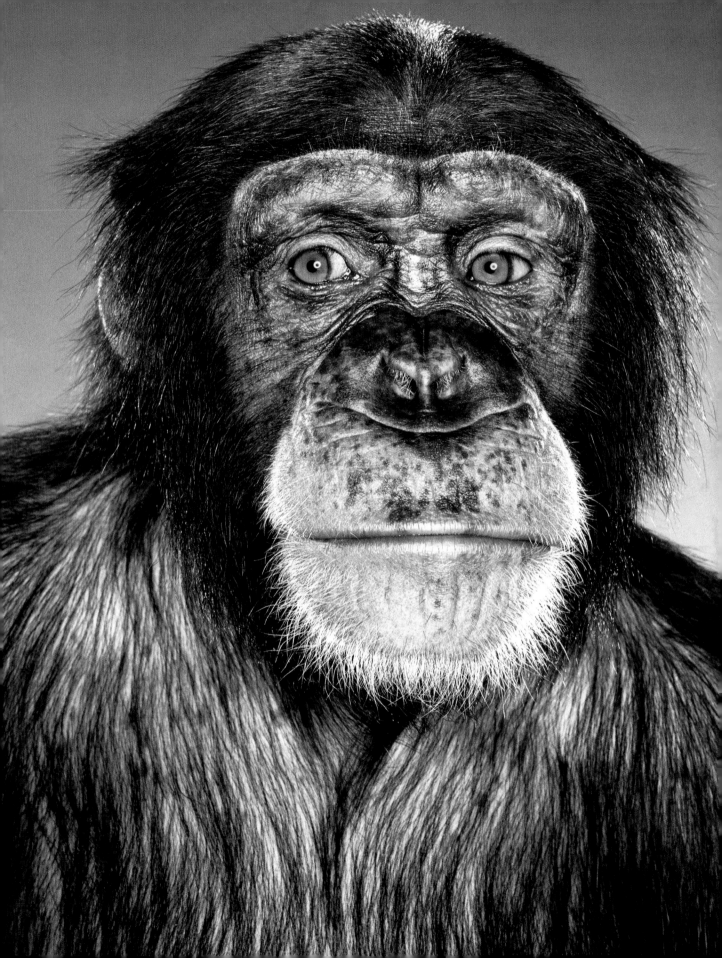

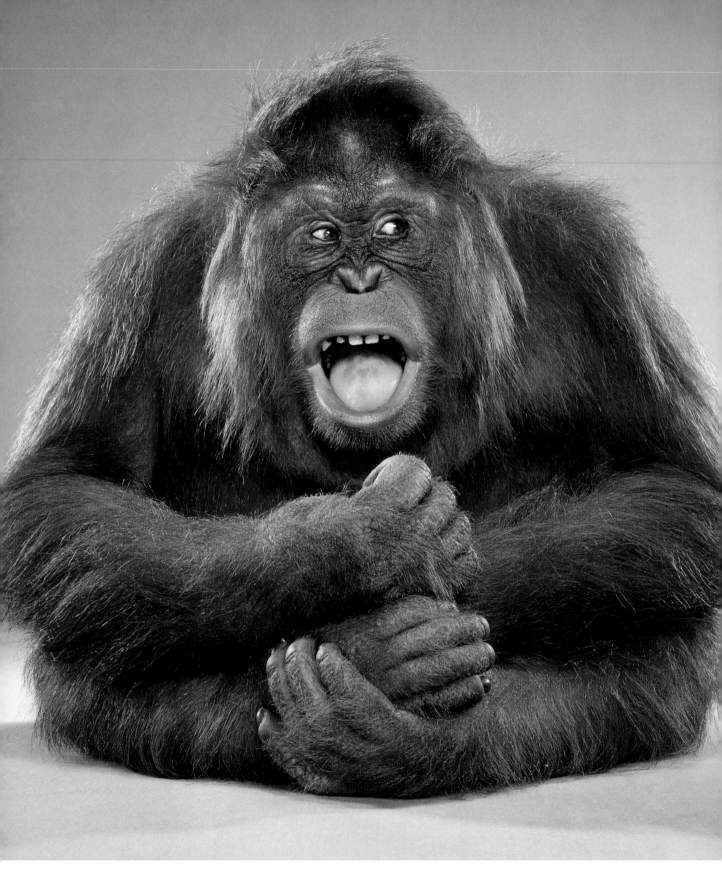

Contrarian

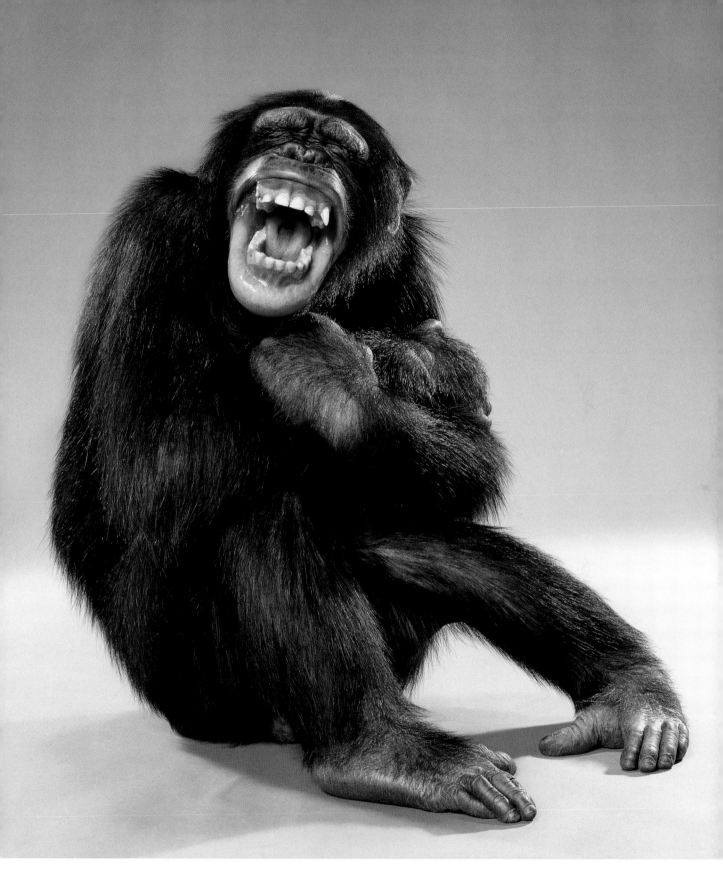

Sick

Offput

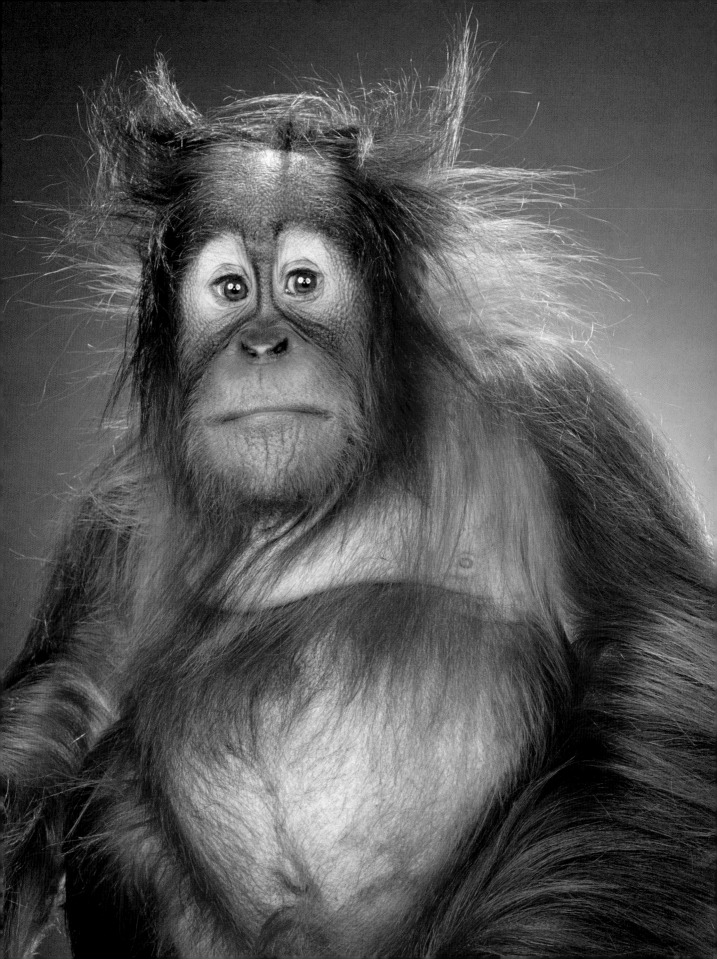

Rocky Portrait

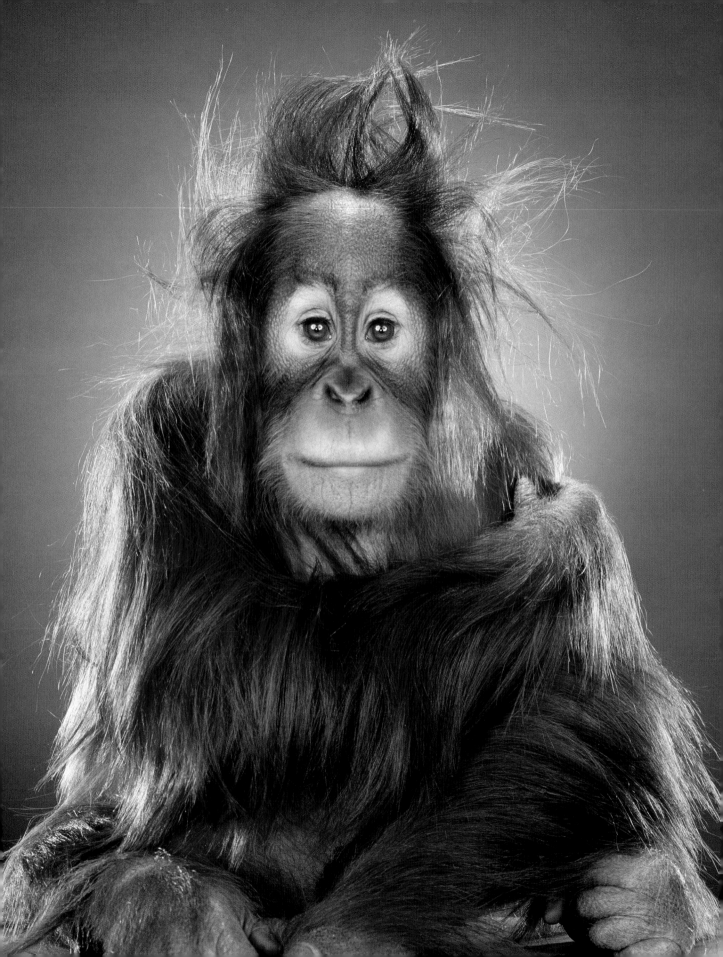

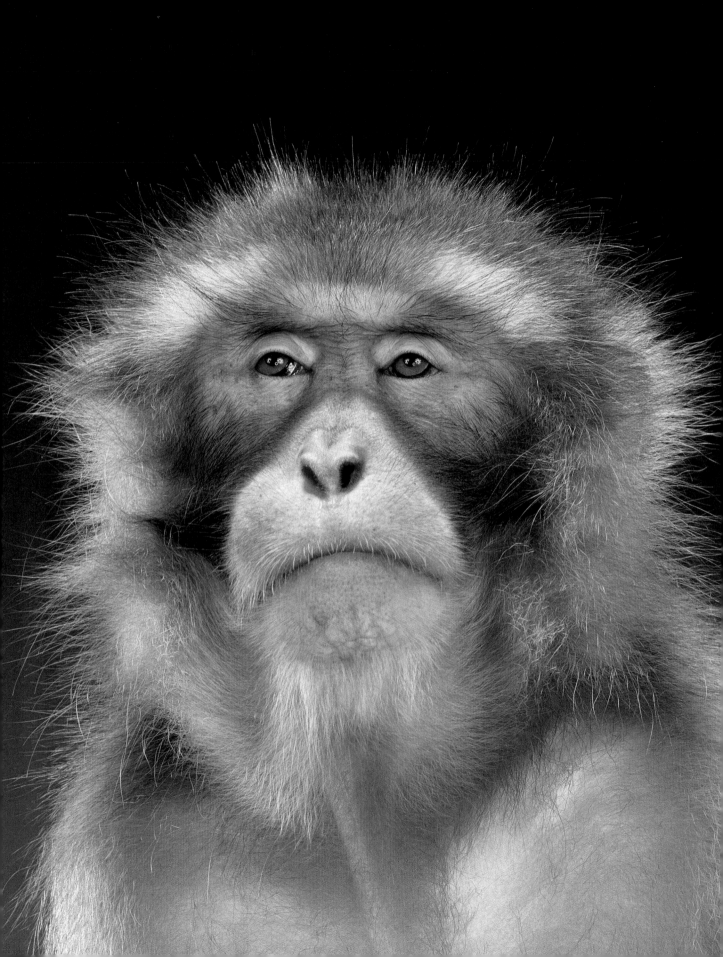

Monkeys are superior to men in this:
when a monkey looks into a mirror, he sees a monkey.

MALCOLM DE CHAZAL

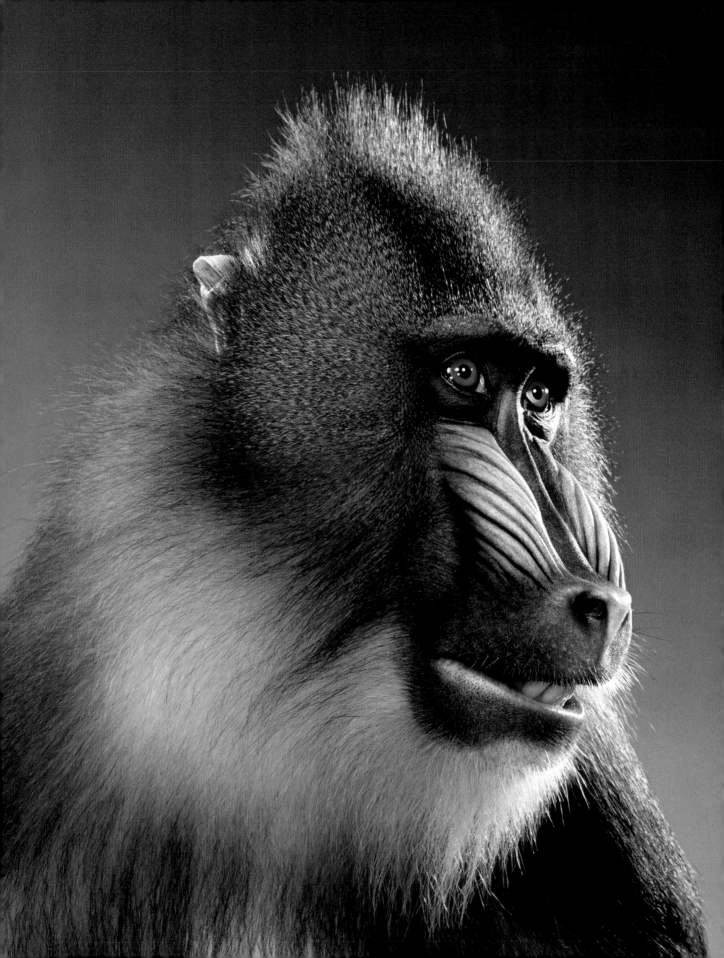

Kongo Portrait

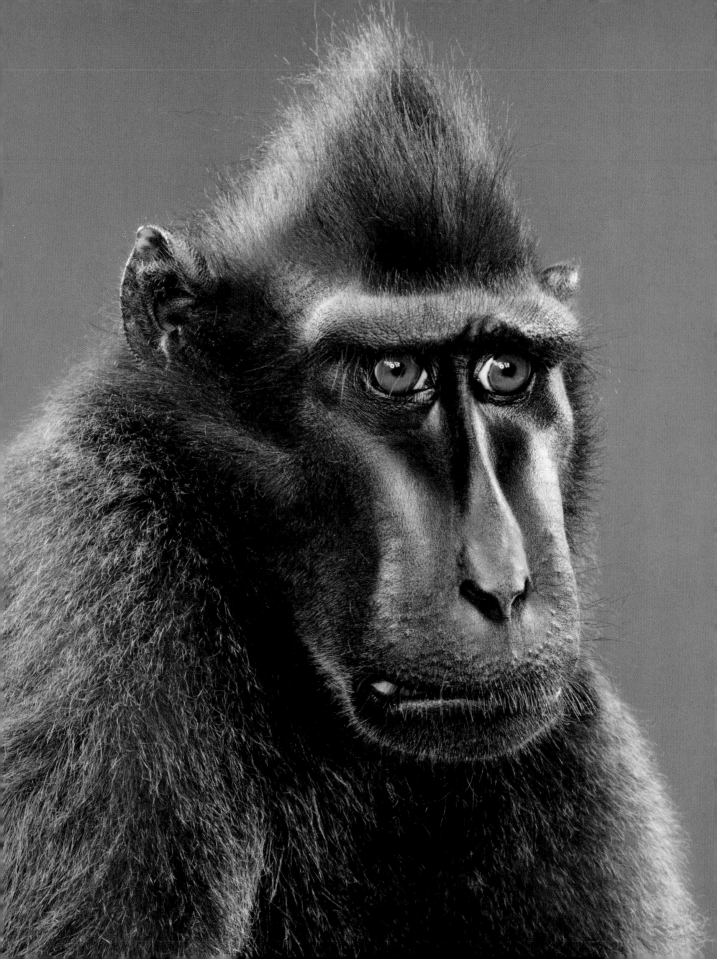

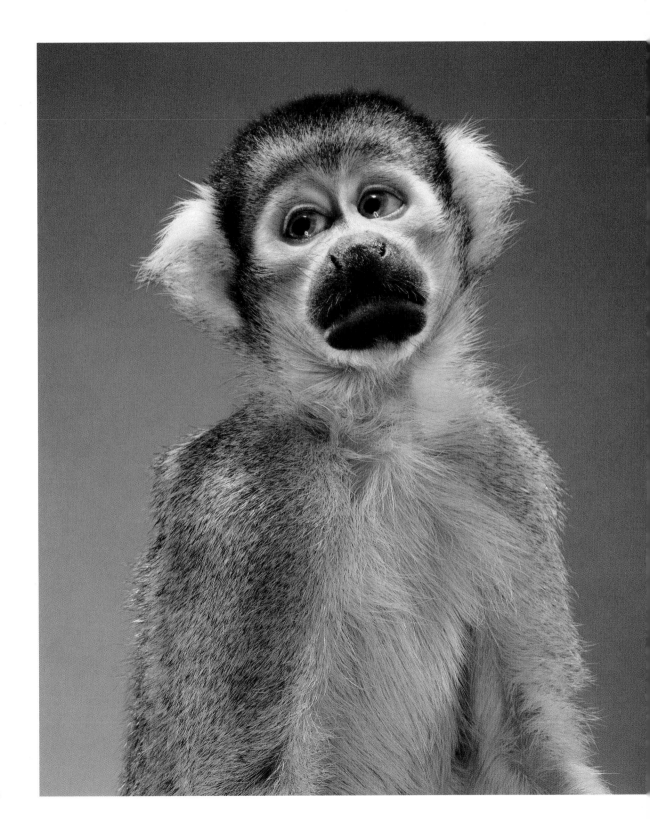

Anxious

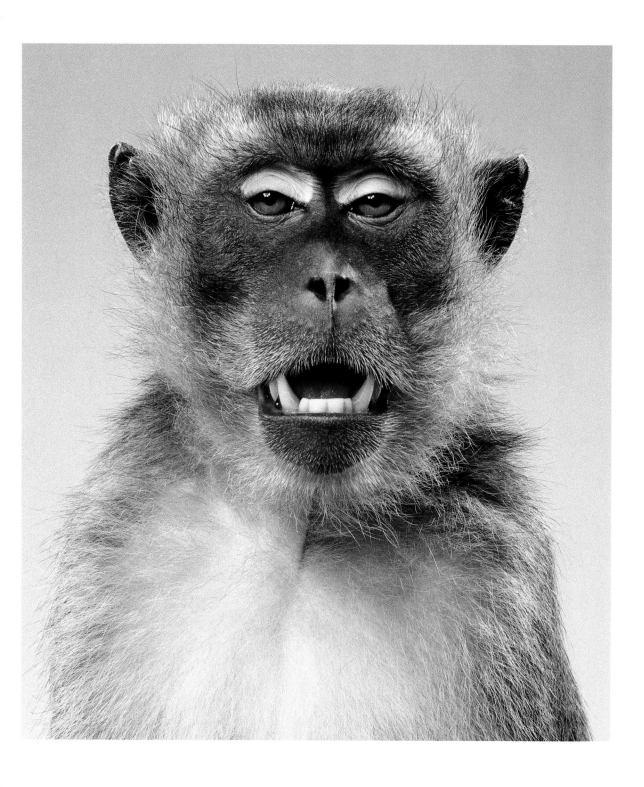

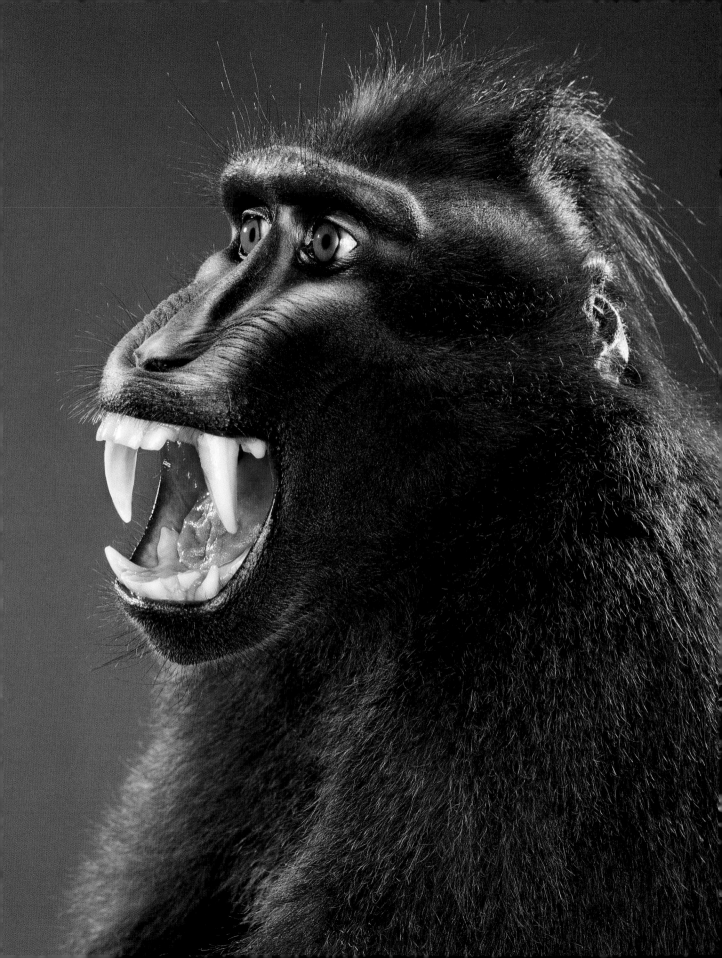

Still

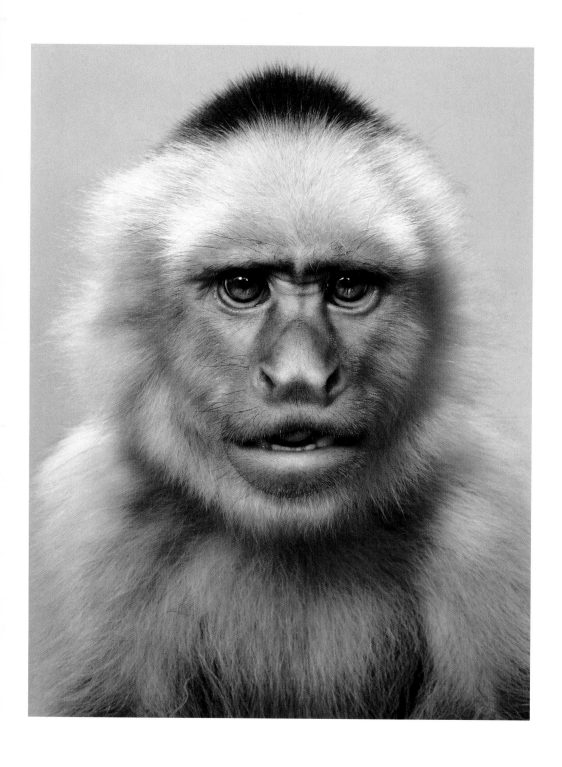

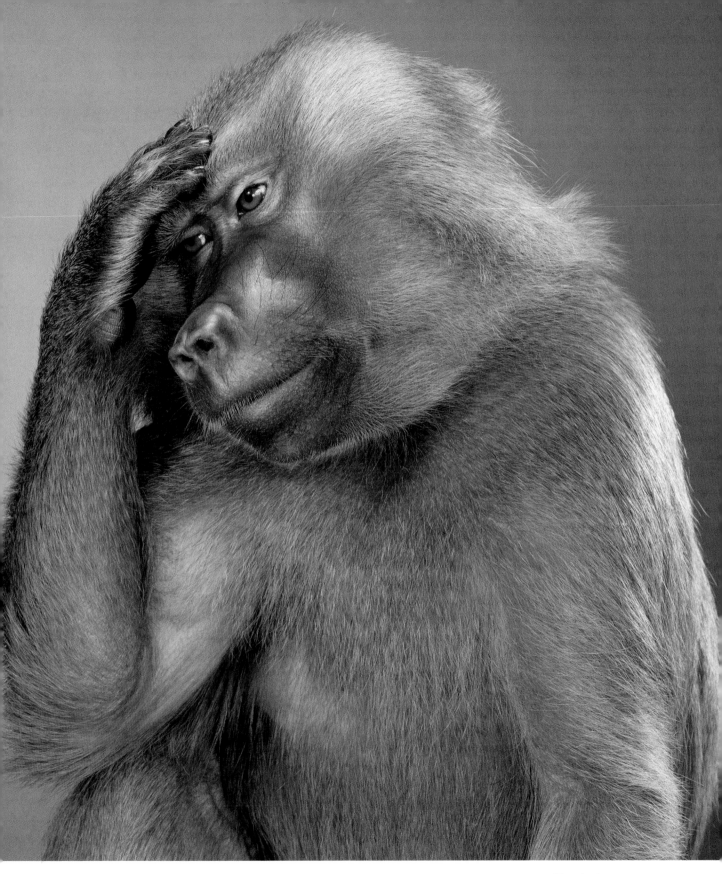

Headache

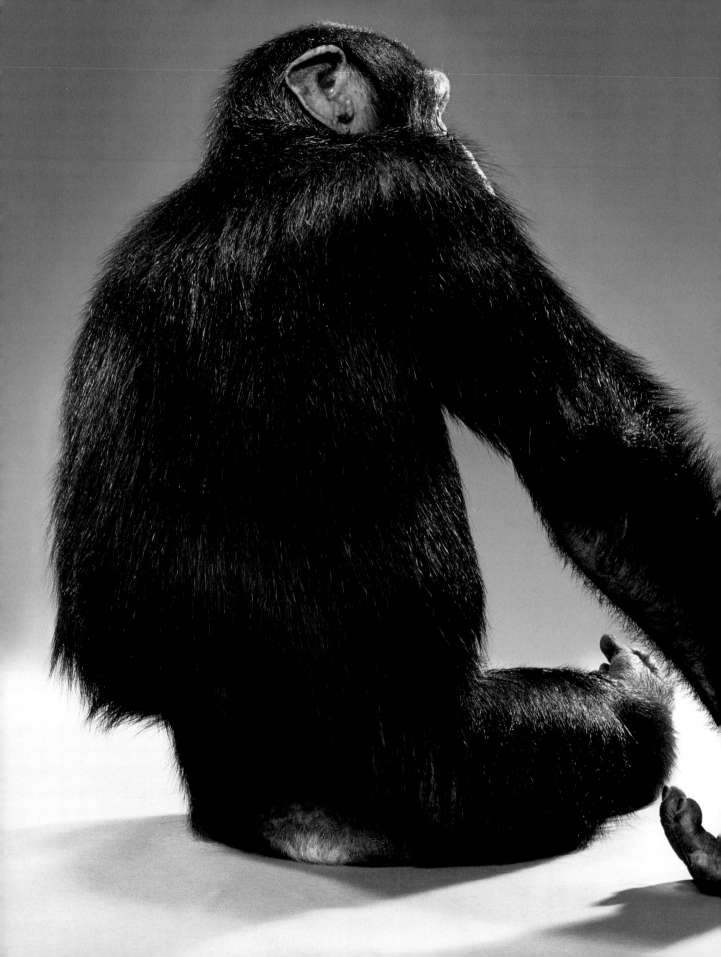

His life among these fierce apes had been happy.
EDGAR RICE BURROUGHS

Triangle

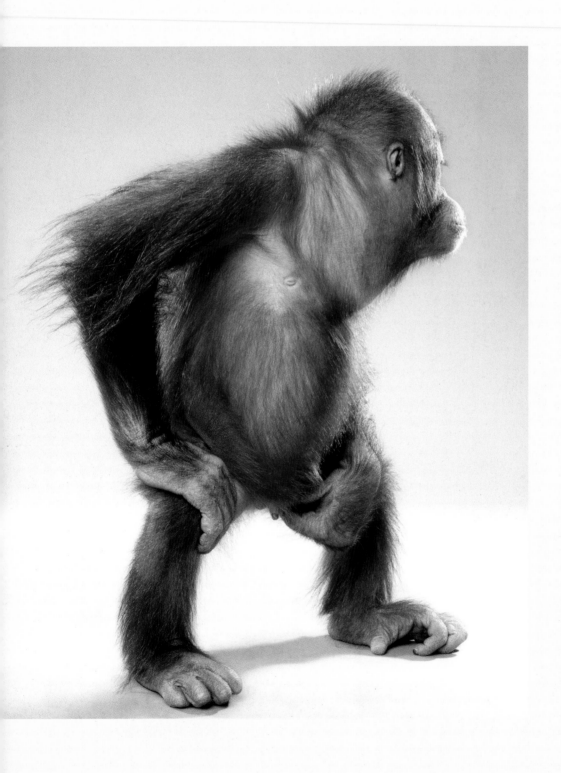

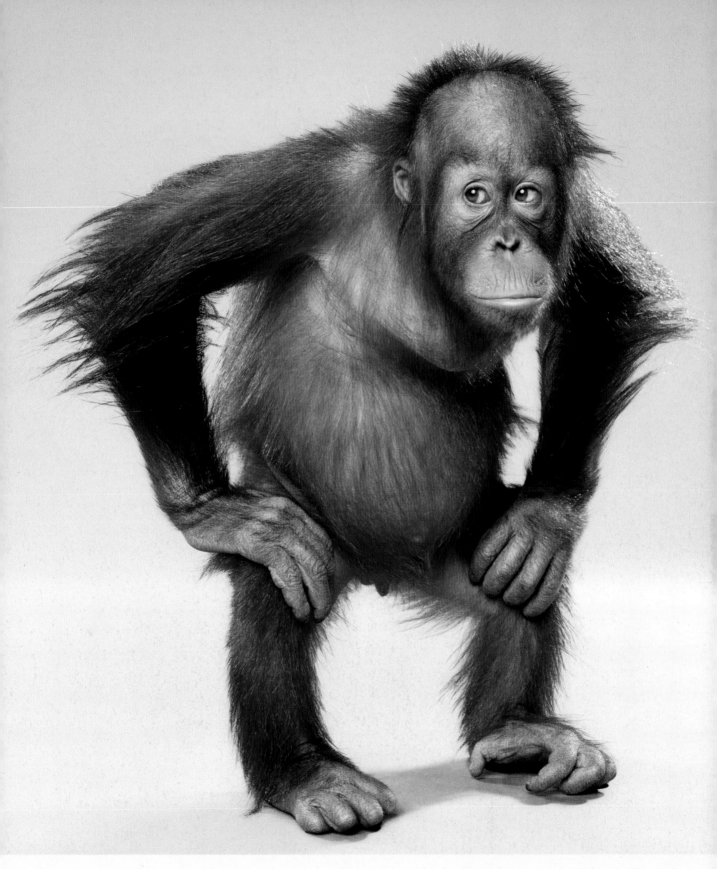

Following pages, left to right: The Cuddler, Money

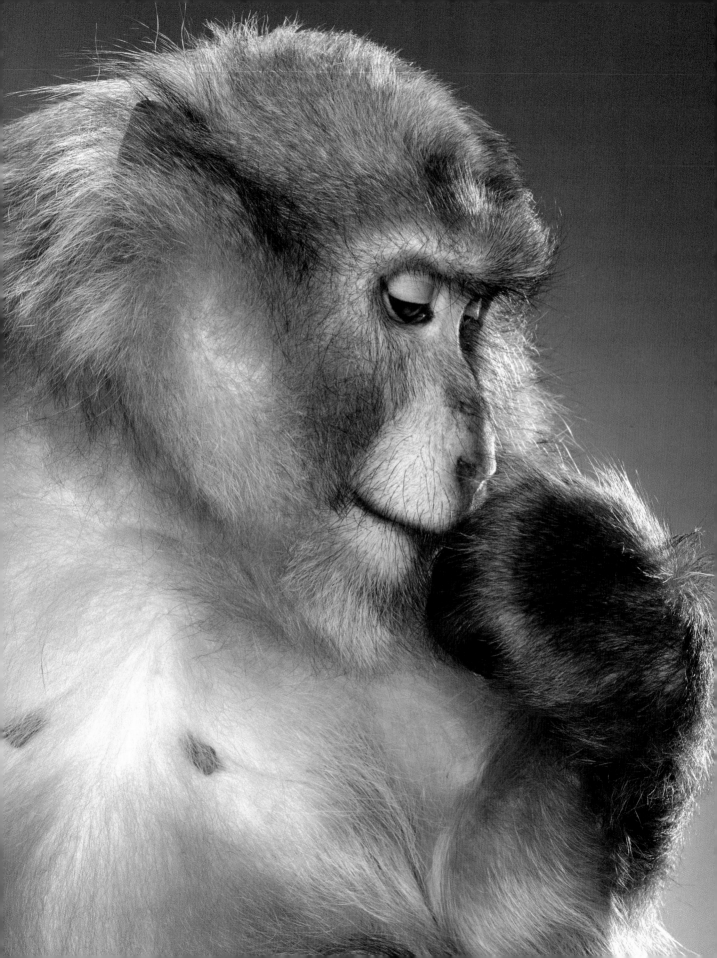

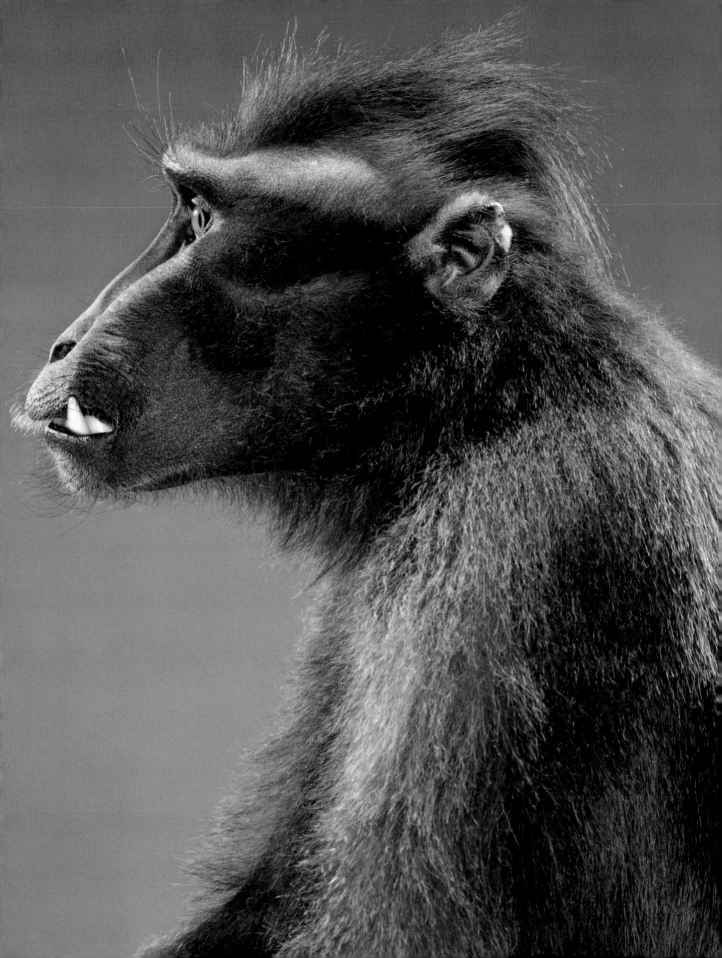

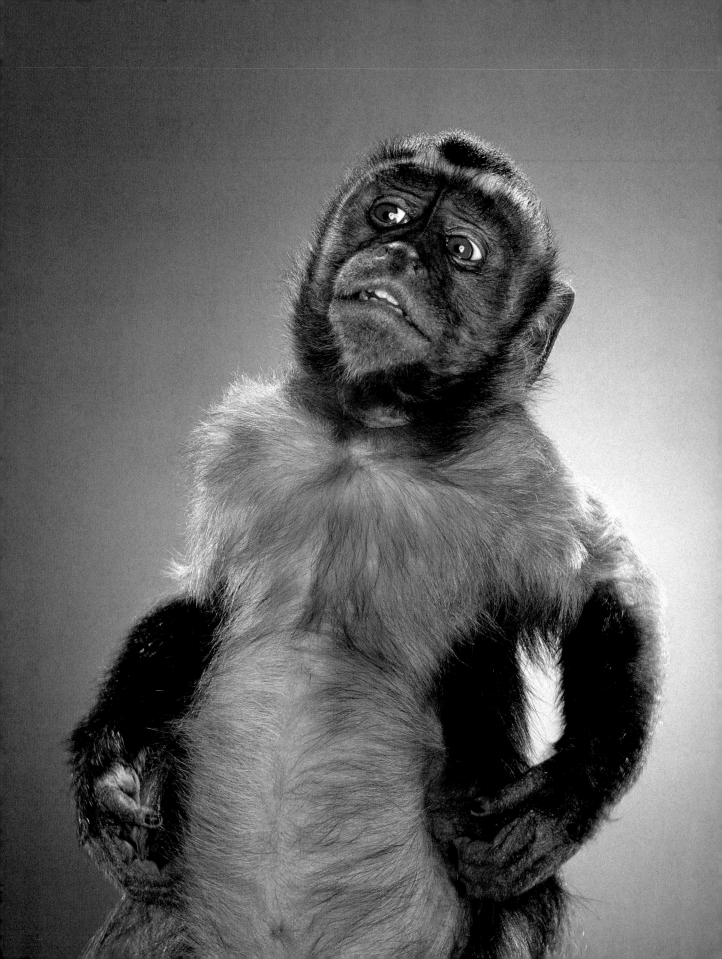

The monkey wears an expression of seriousness which would do credit to any college student, but the monkey is serious because he itches.

ROBERT MAYNARD HUTCHINS

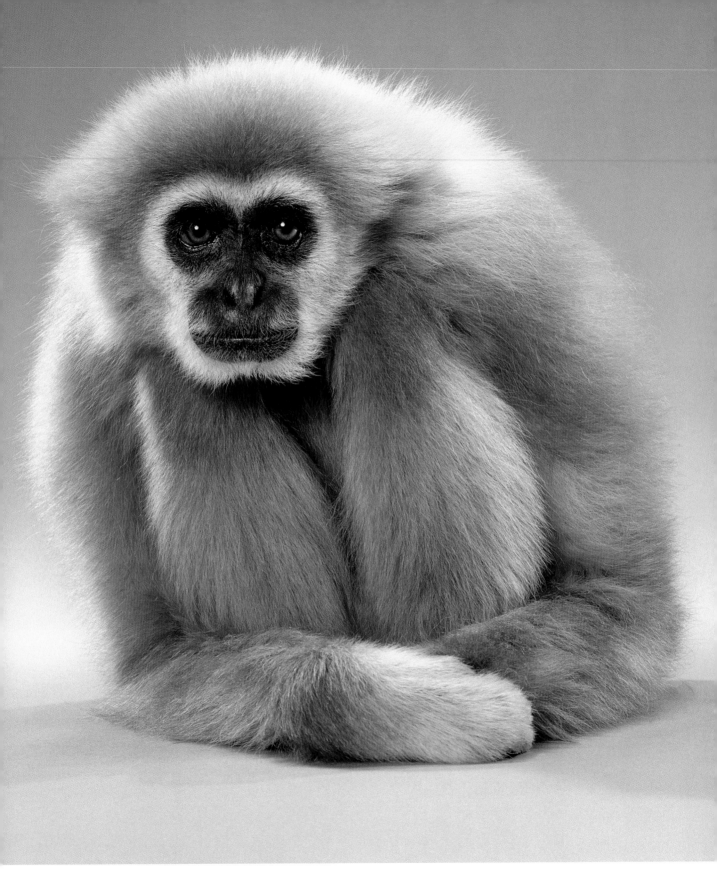

Gibbon Lean

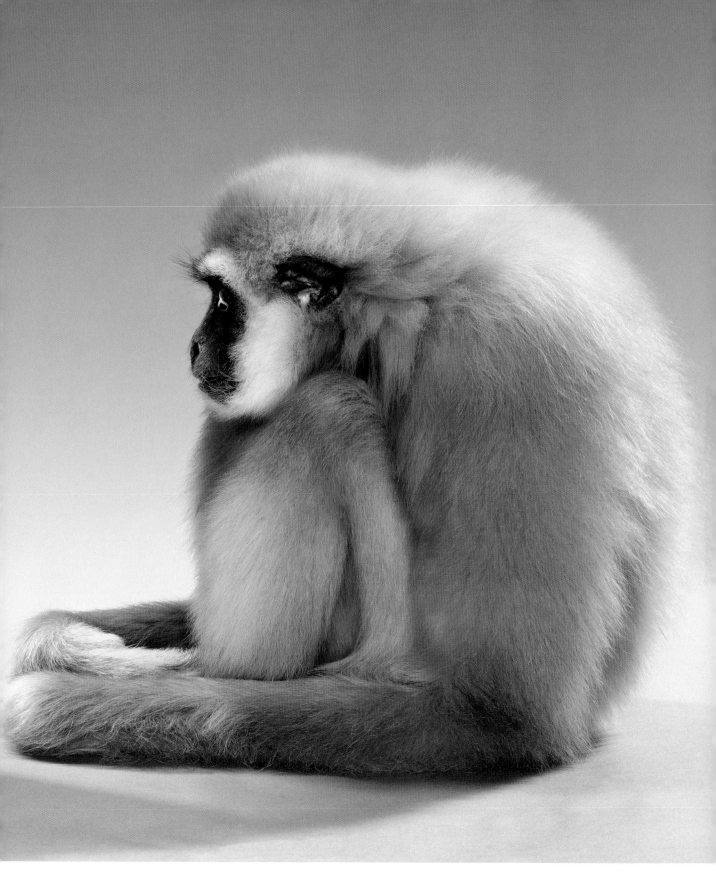

Gibbon Profile

Chatty Katie

Following pages, left to right: Farklempt Mandrill, Guilty

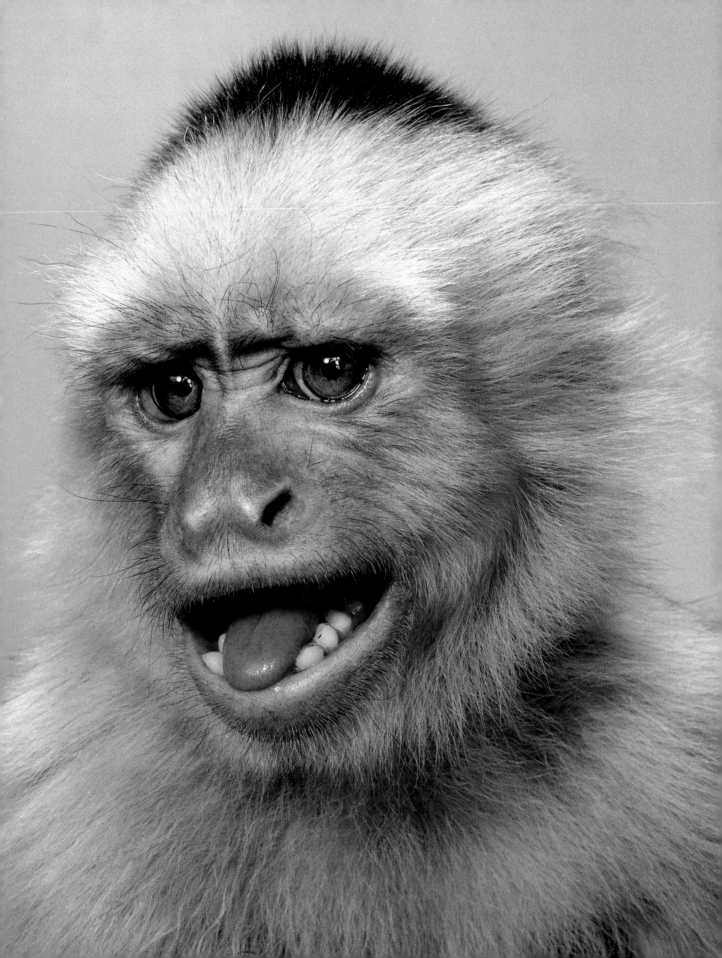

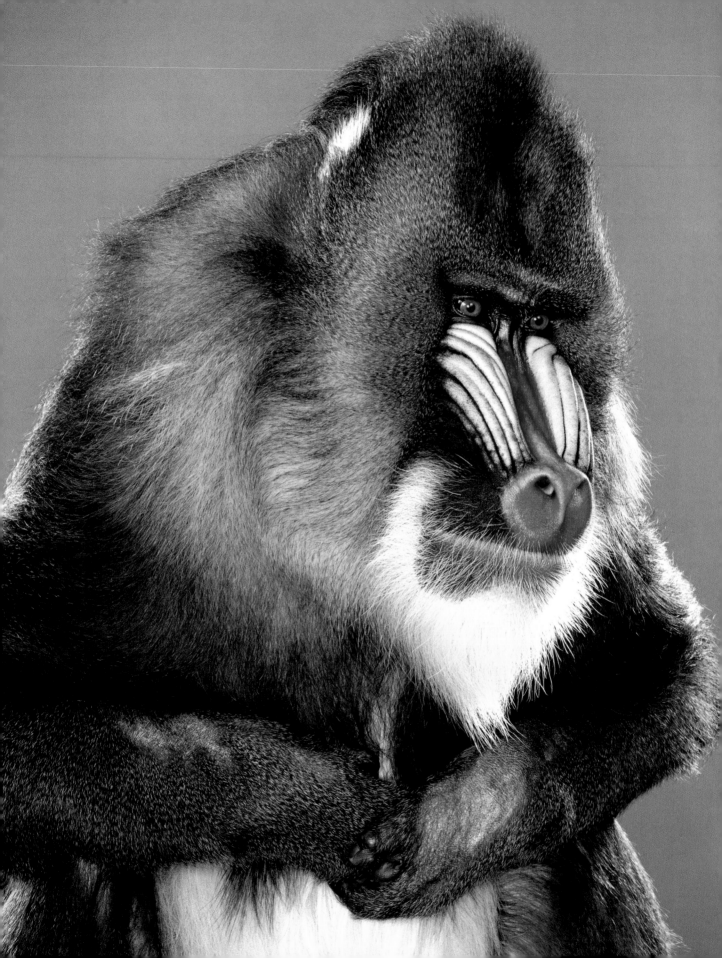

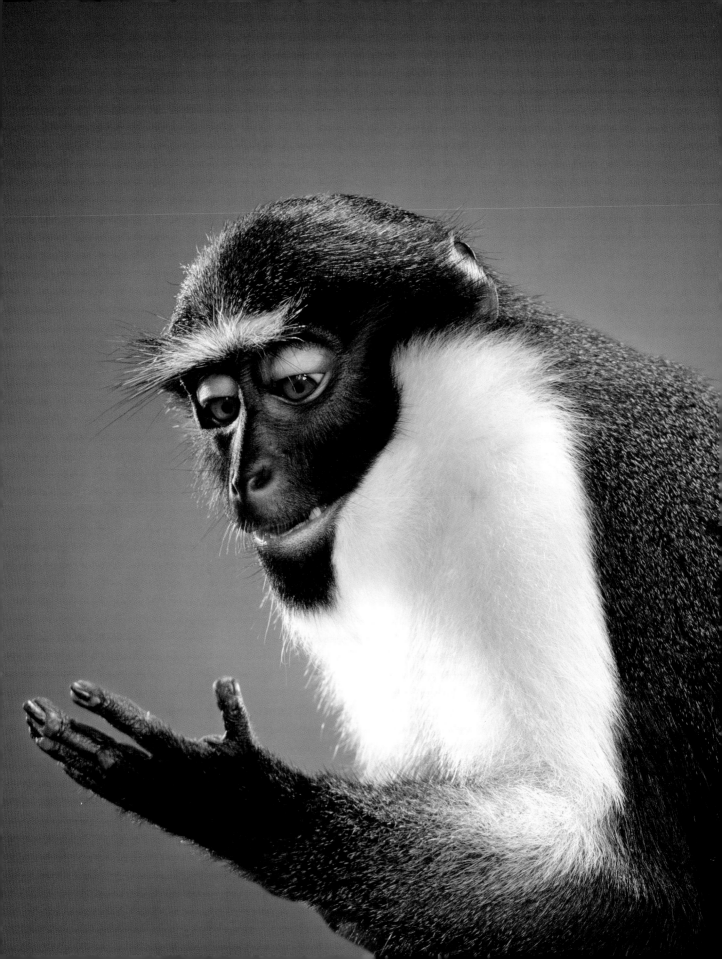

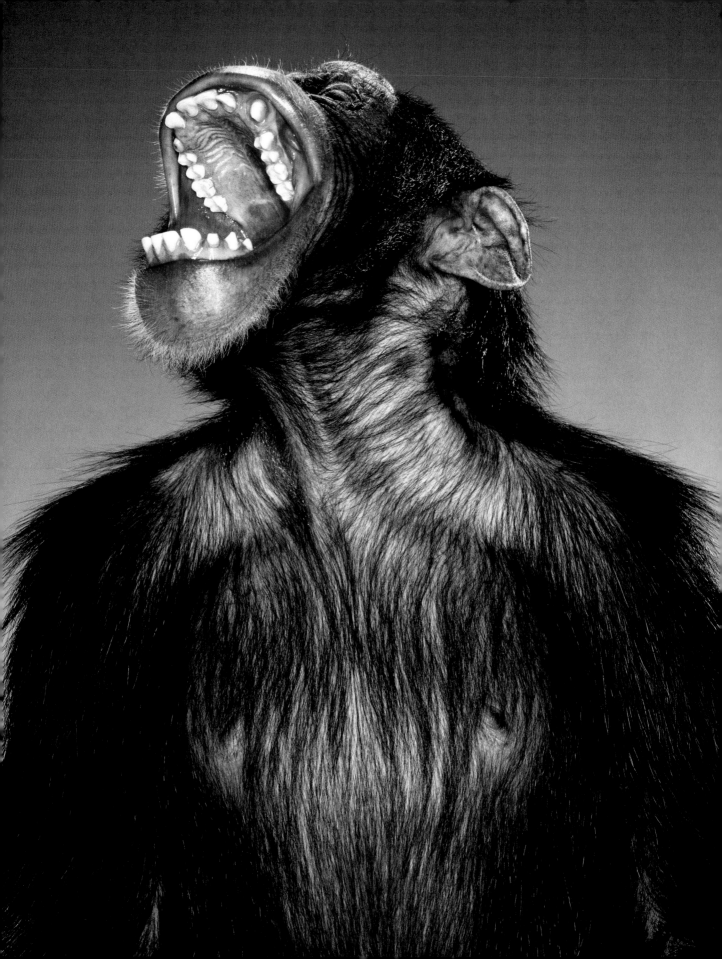

Kenuzy Scream

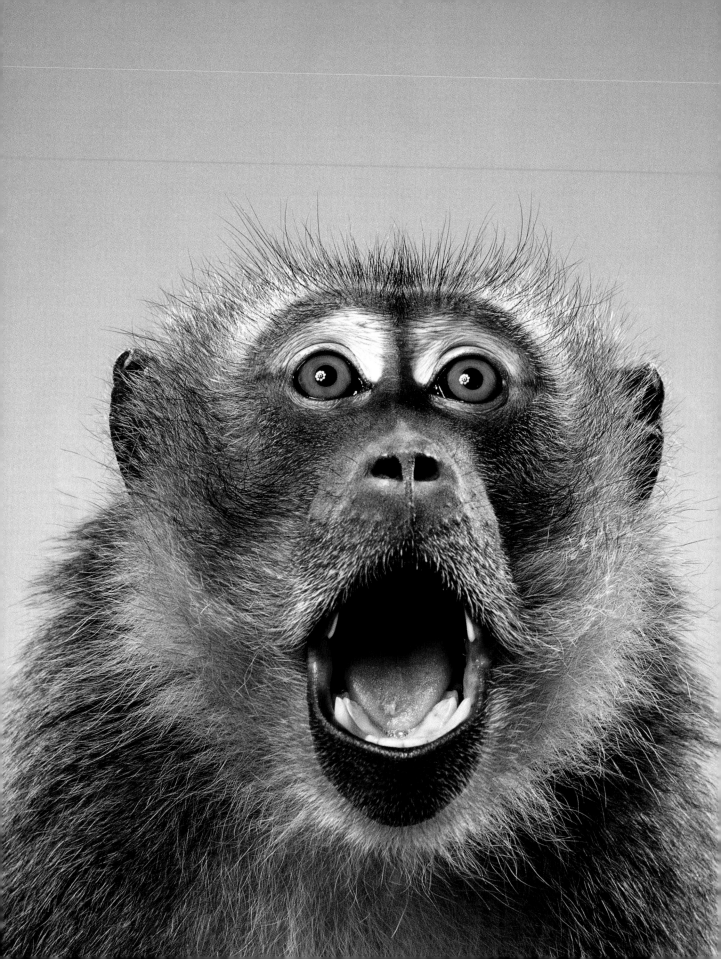

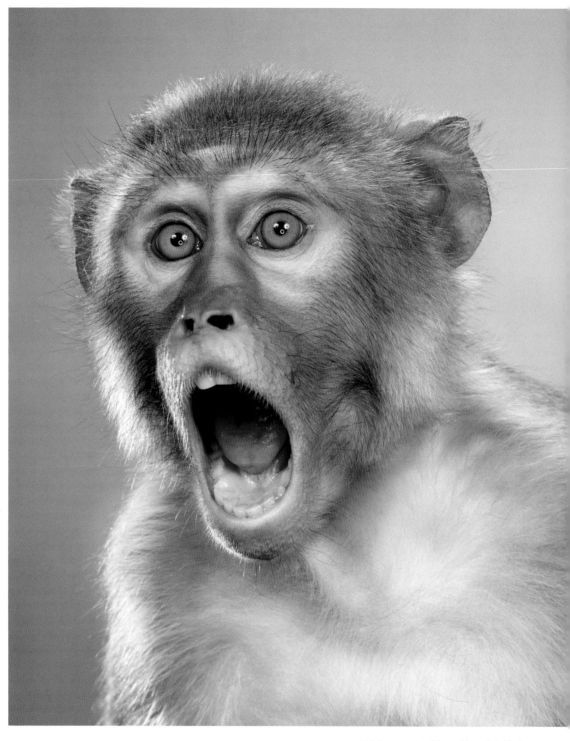

Welcome to Your Fascist Future

Little Screamer

Punk

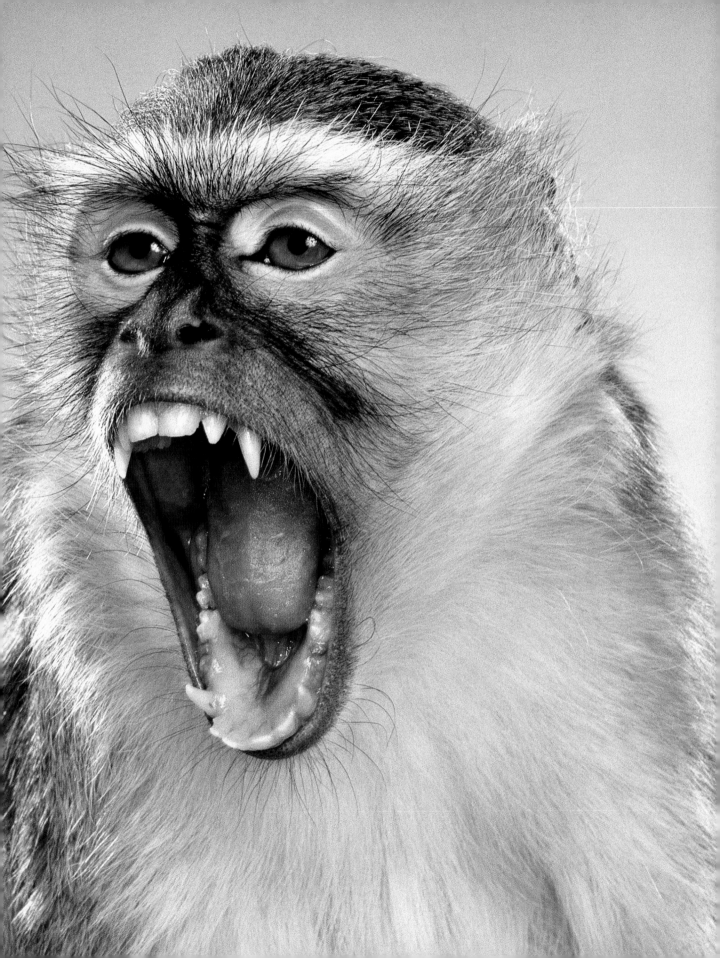

Pontificus

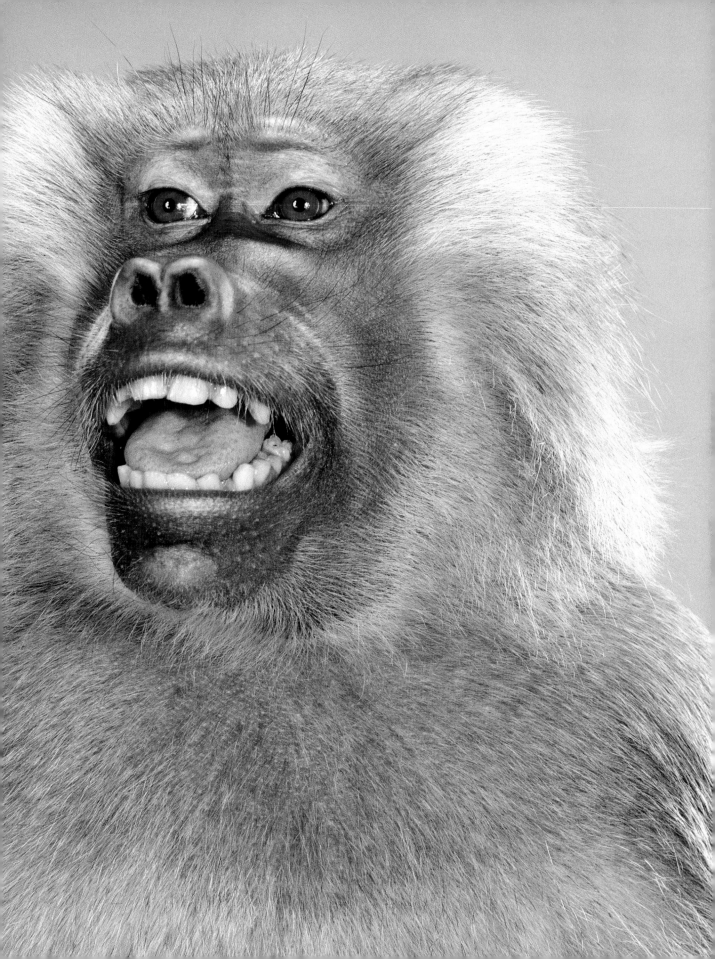

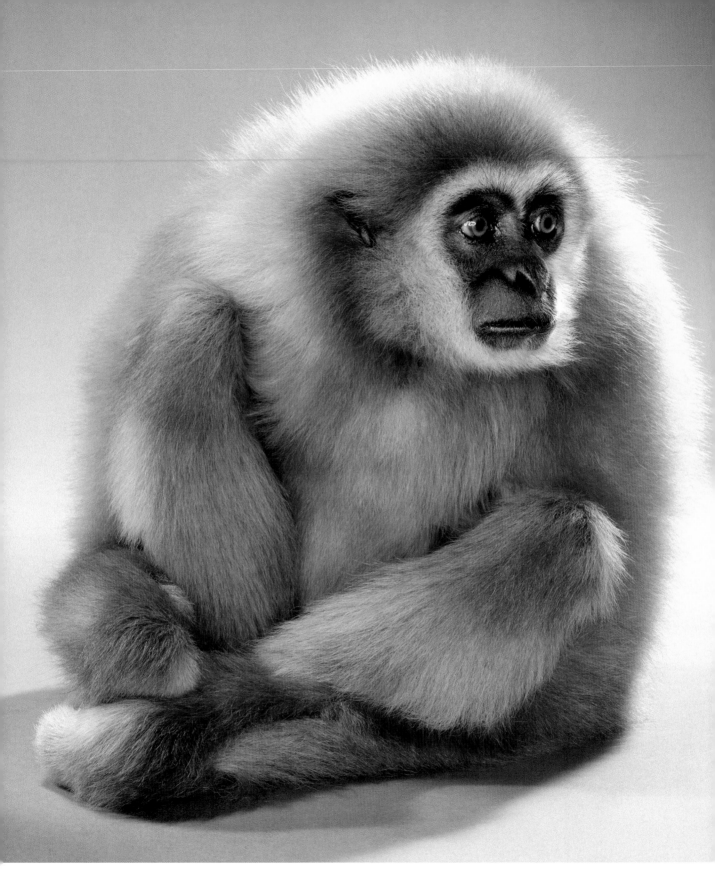

Curl

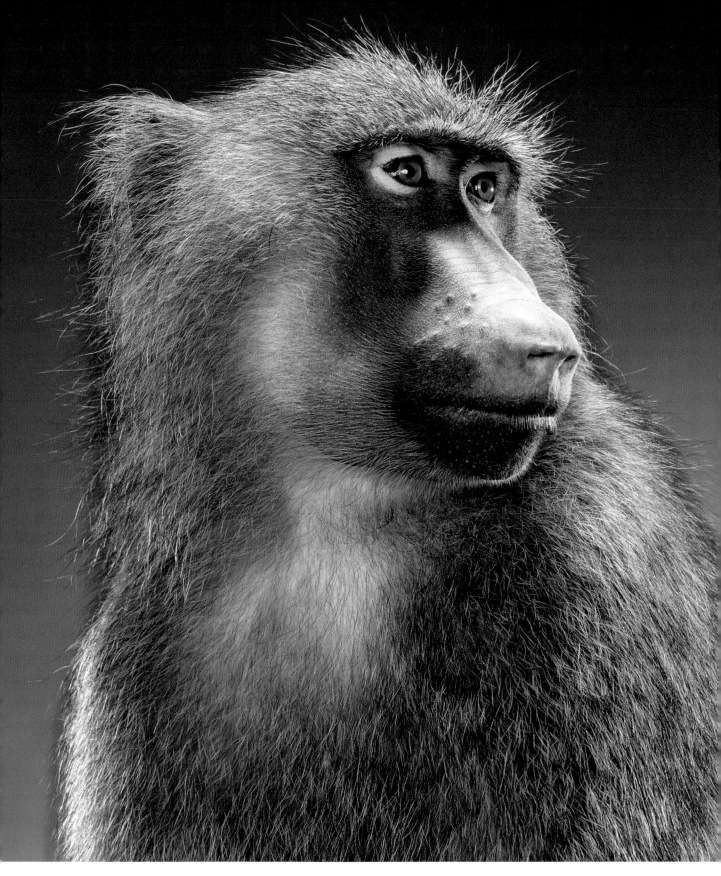

Mala Portrait

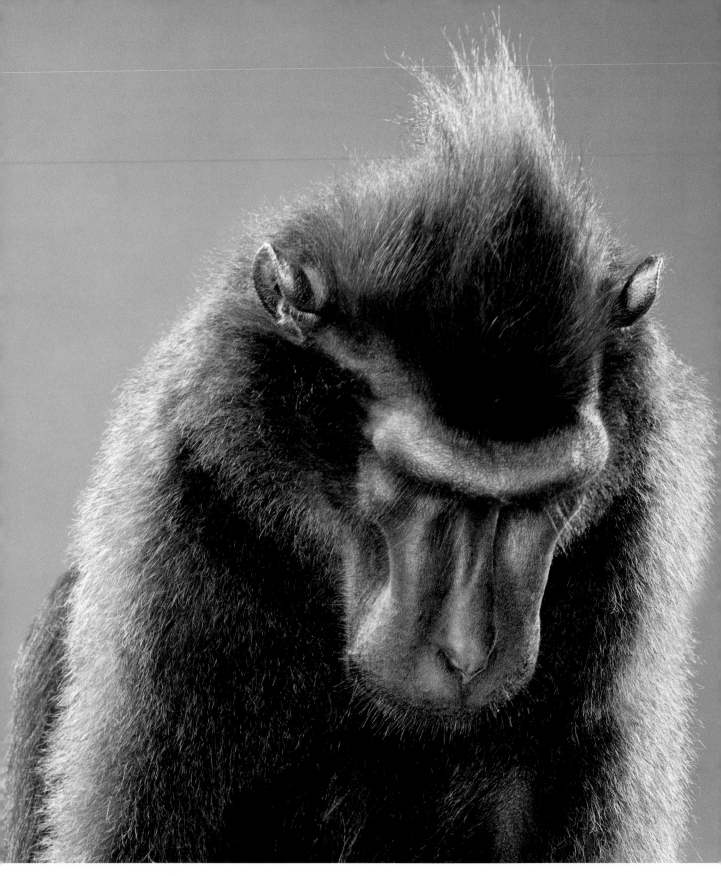

Downward

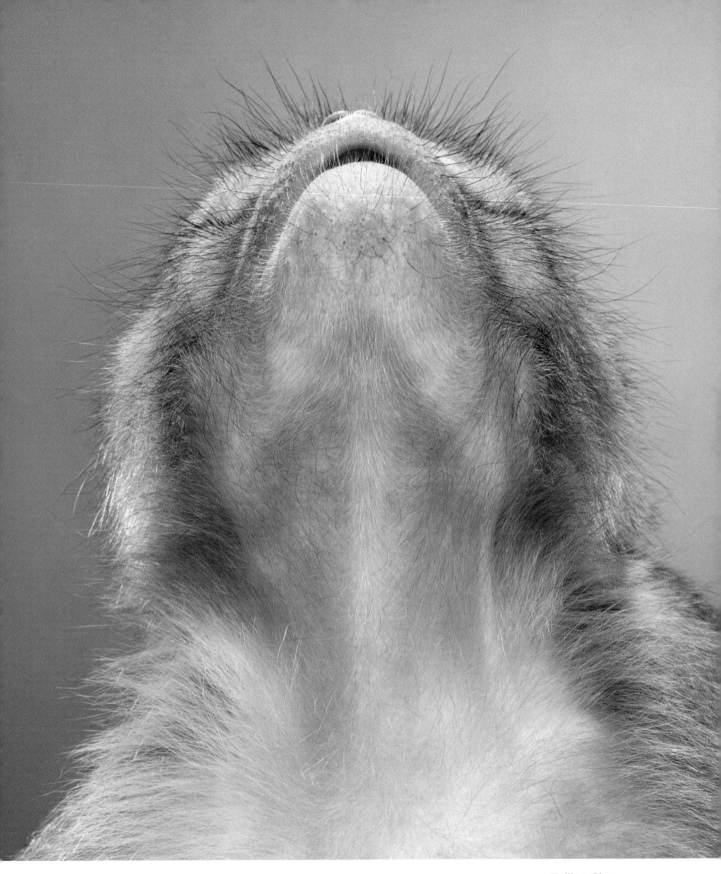

Falling Sky

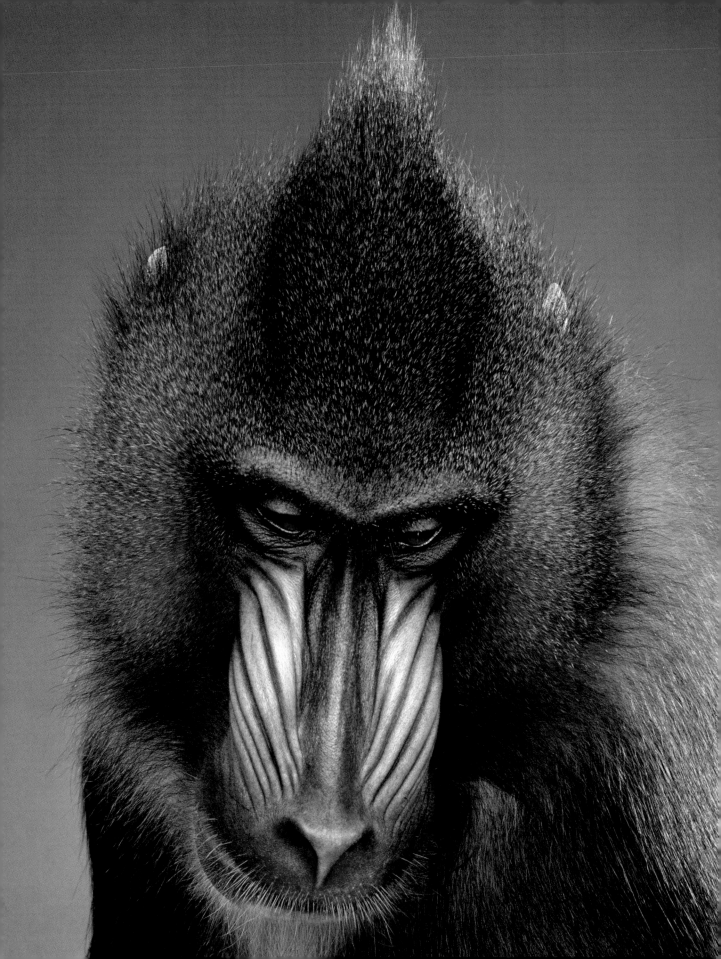

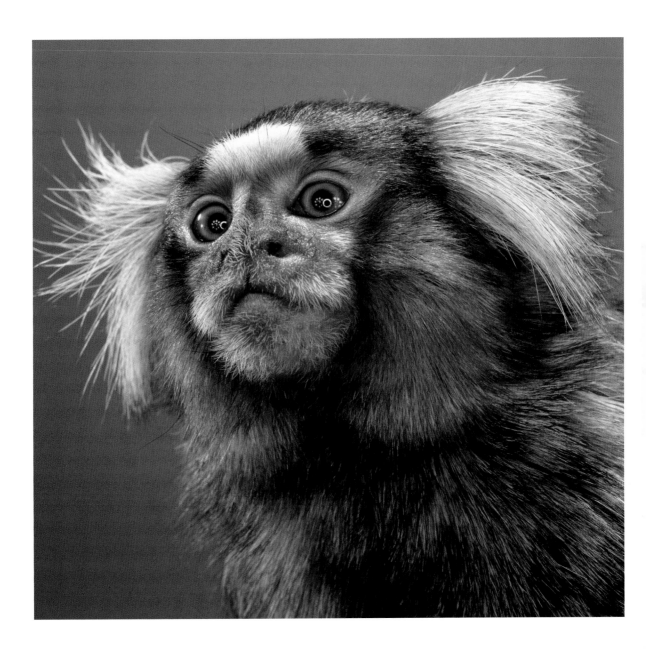

Downward Two

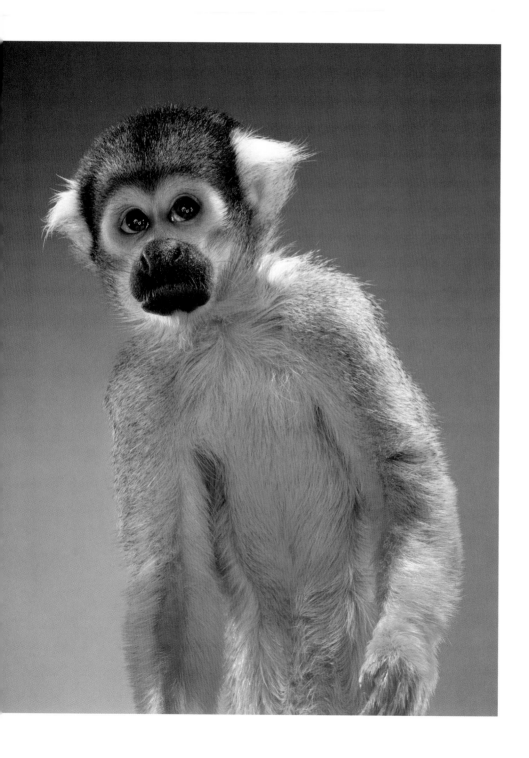

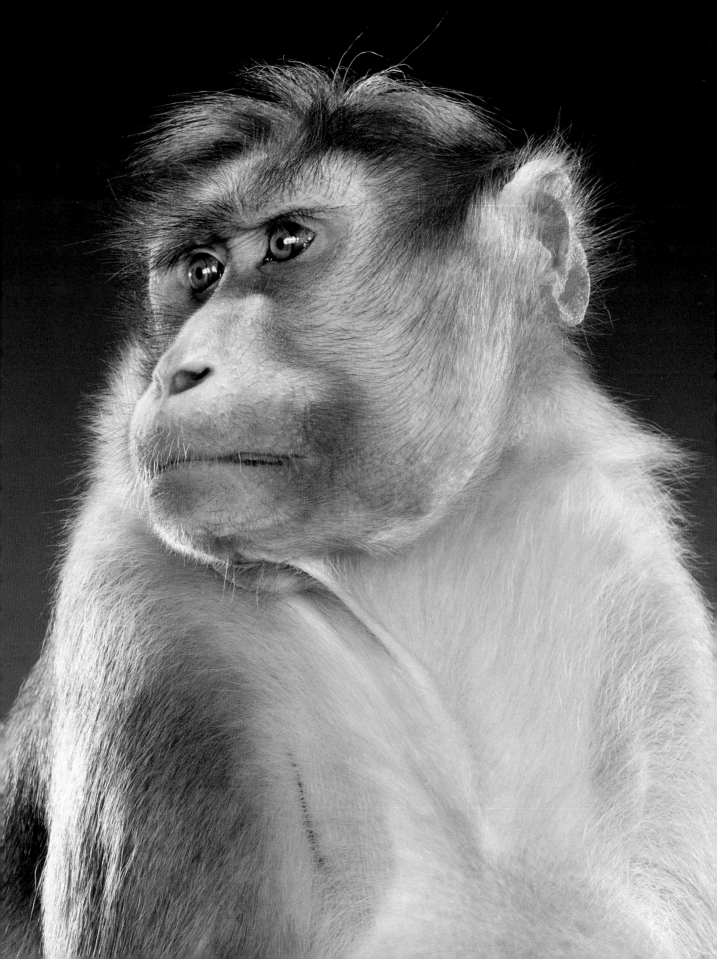

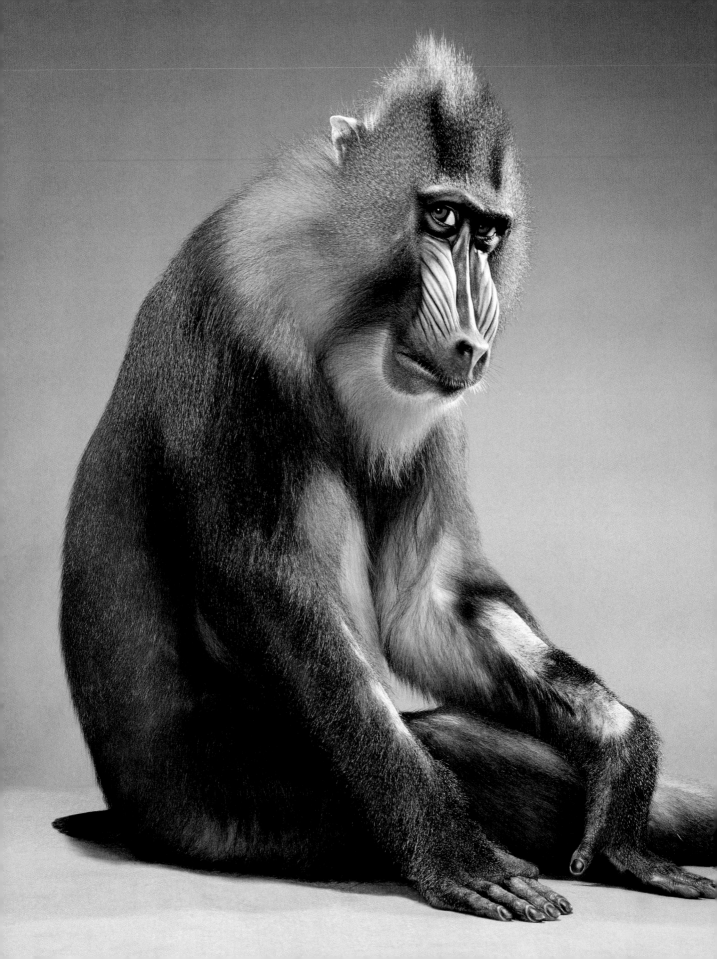

Whenever you observe an animal closely,
you feel as if a human being sitting inside were making fun of you.
ELIAS CANETTI

Oy Veh

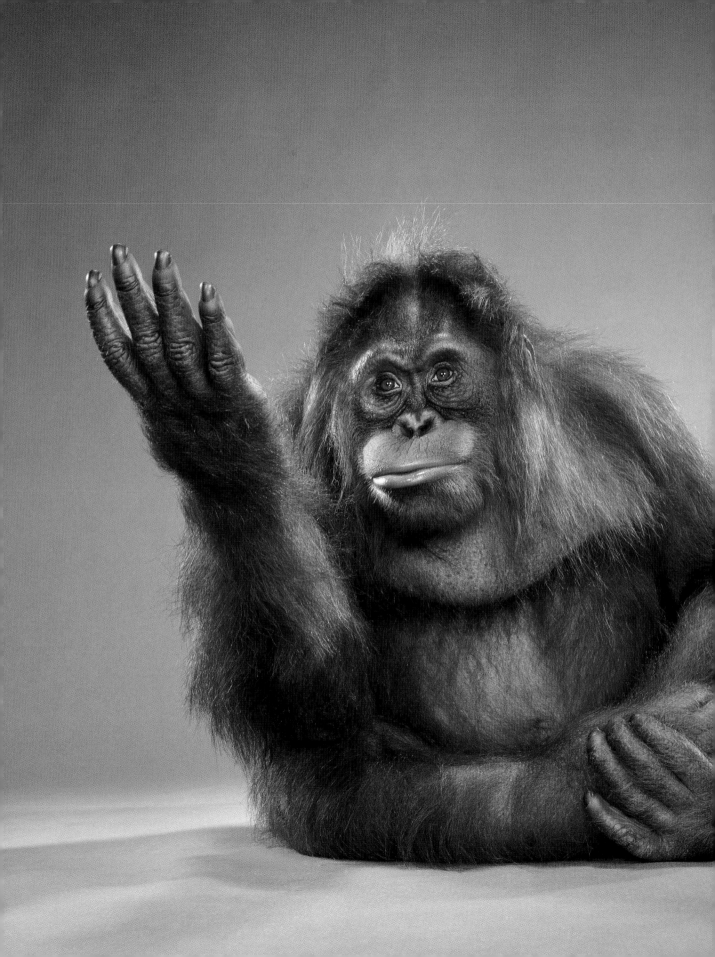

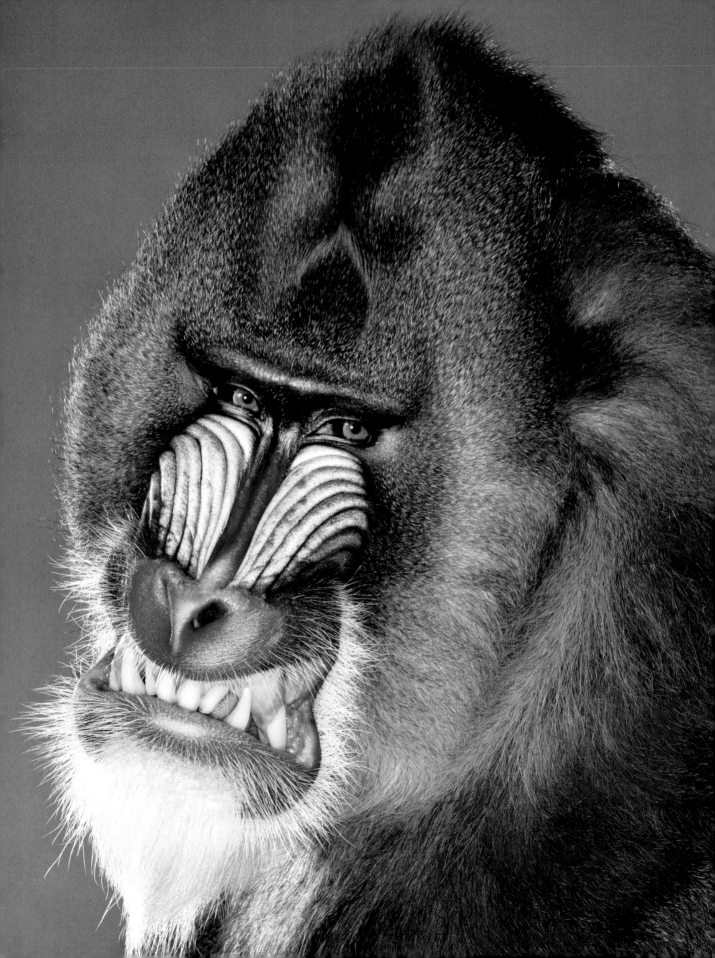

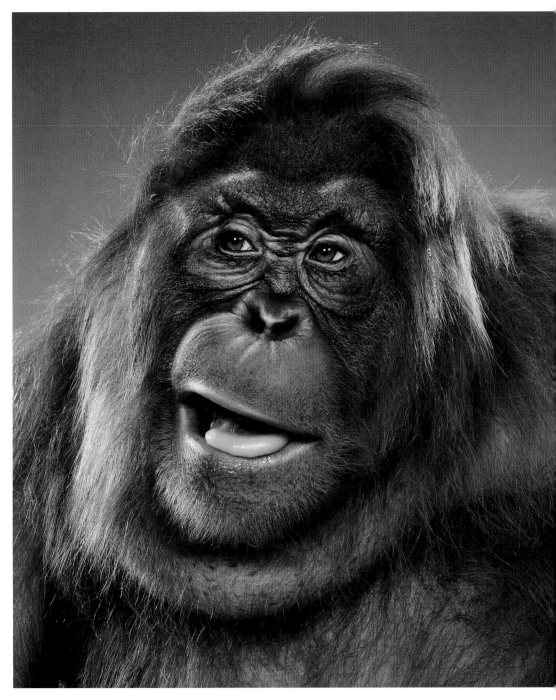

Jake Talking

Grrr!

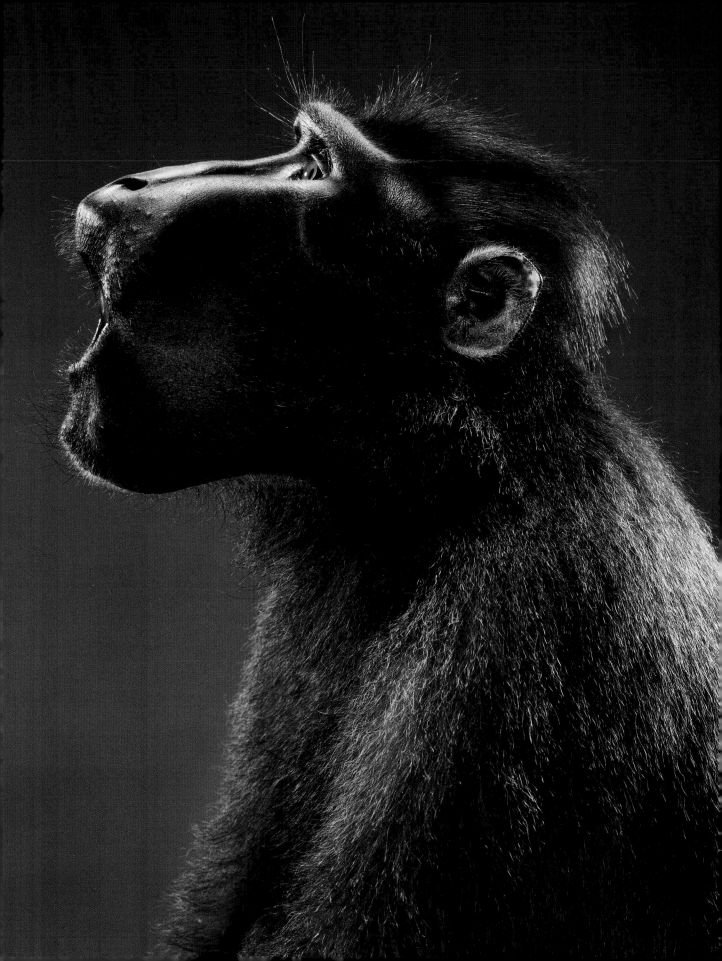

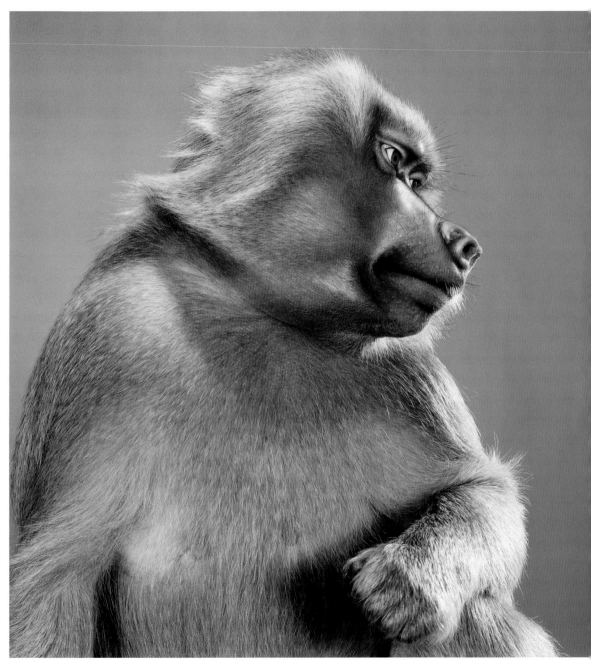

I'm Considering Rhinoplasty

"O" Face

Virtually nothing is known about the prehistory of chimpanzees,
but whatever they were, we were.

BILL BRYSON

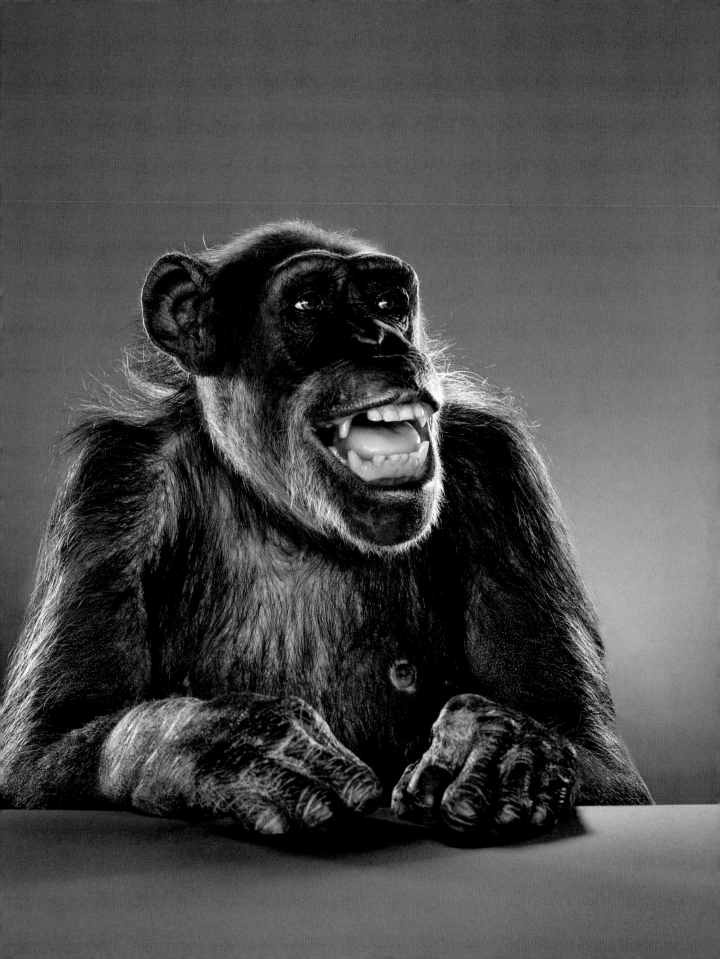

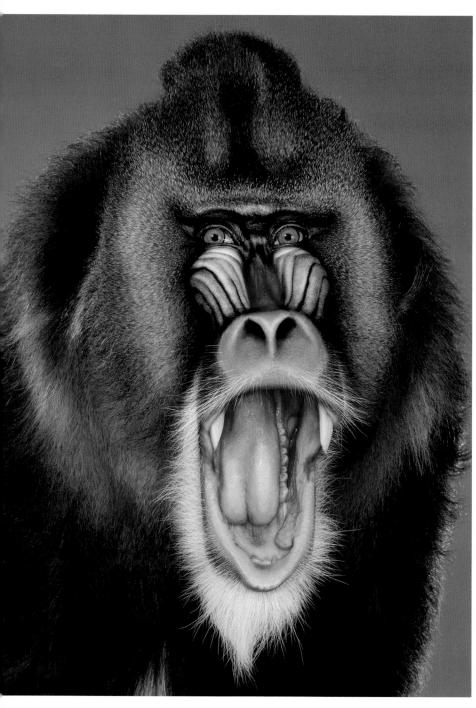

Mask

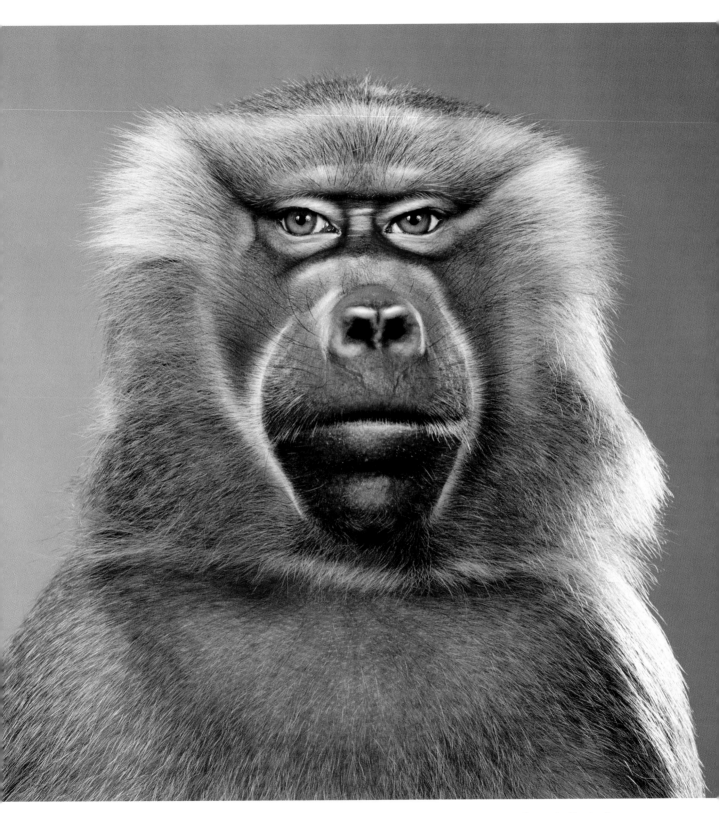

Georgia Portrait

Barfly

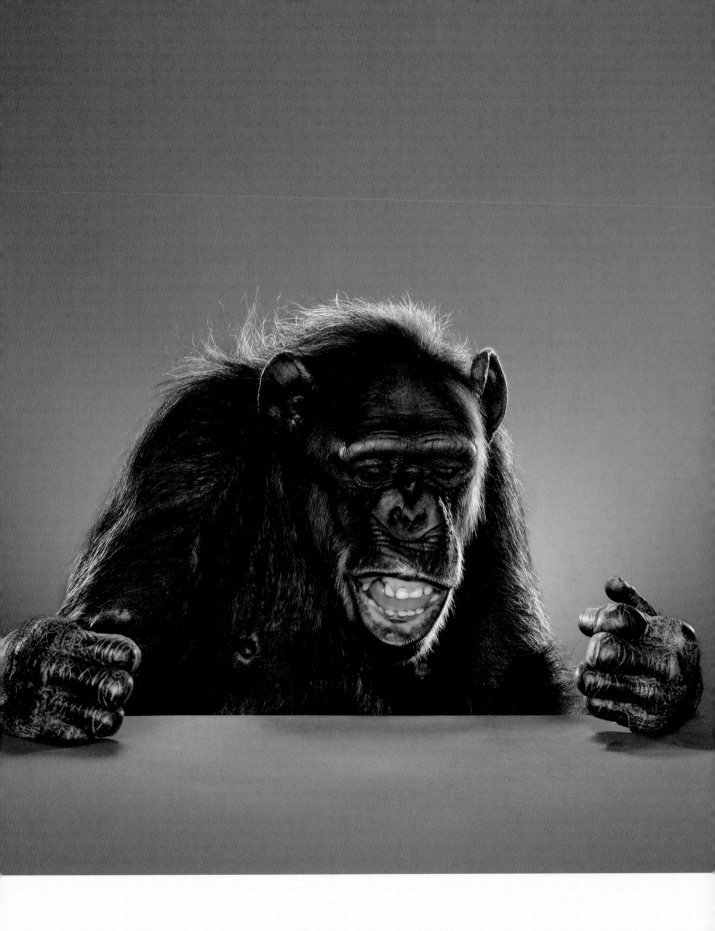

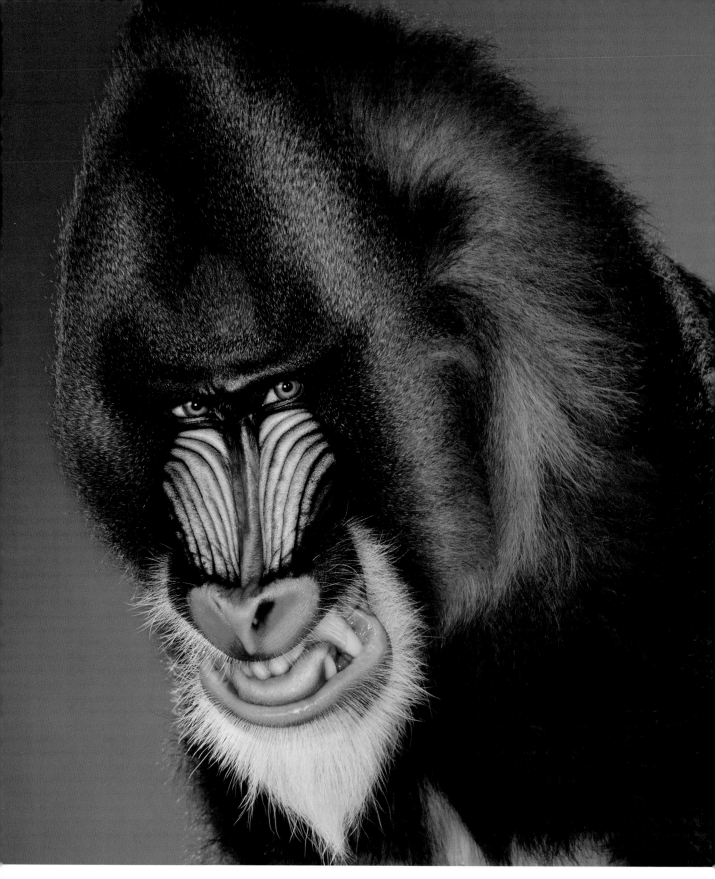

Thhh

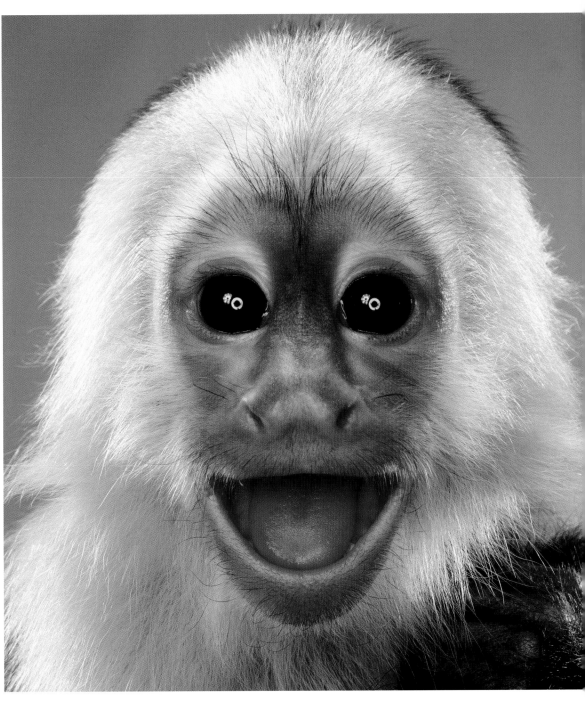

Baby Monkey

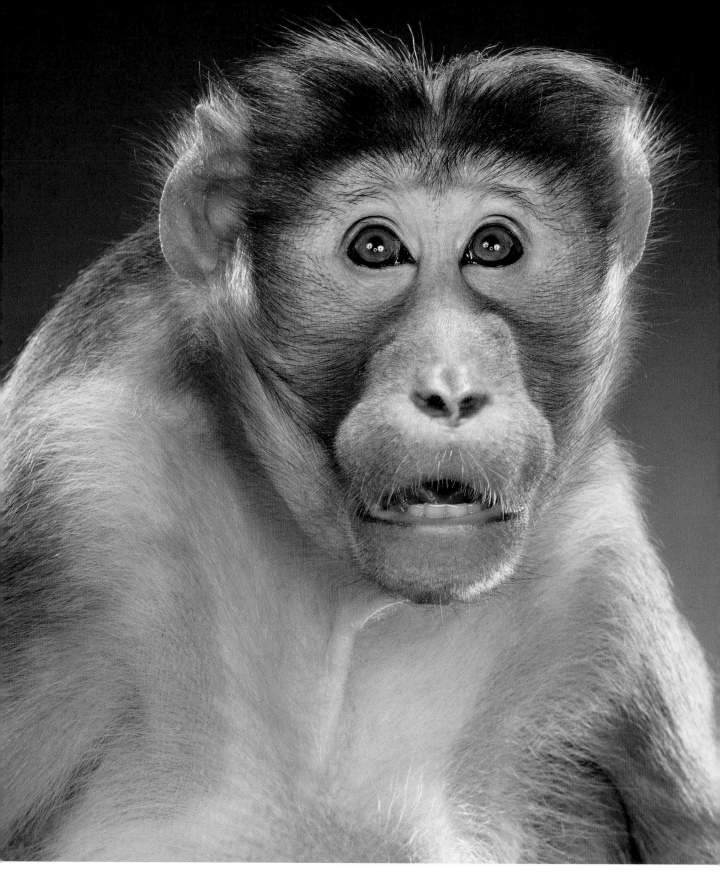

Shemp

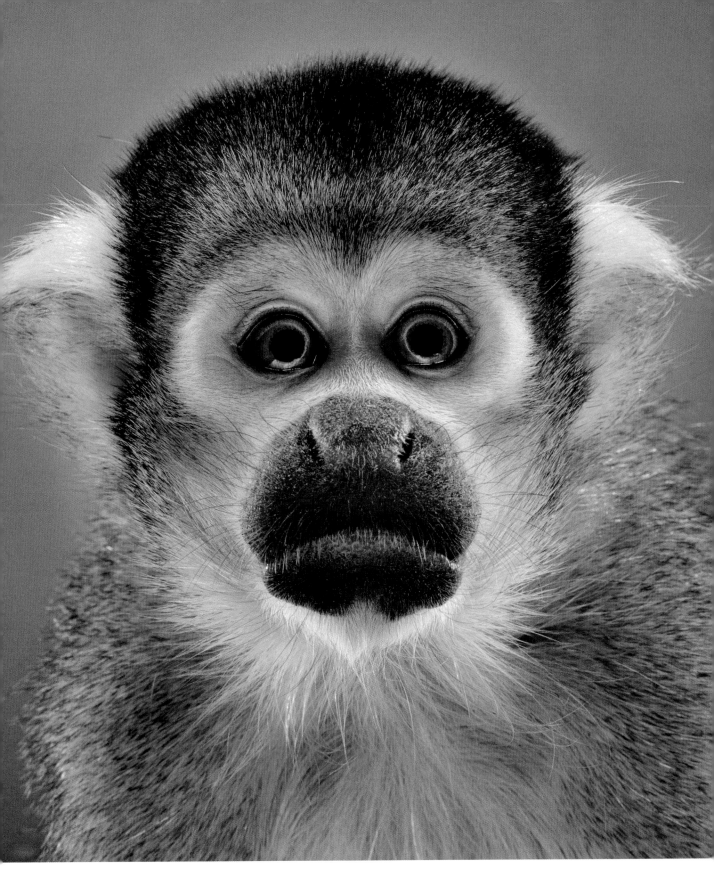

Zombie

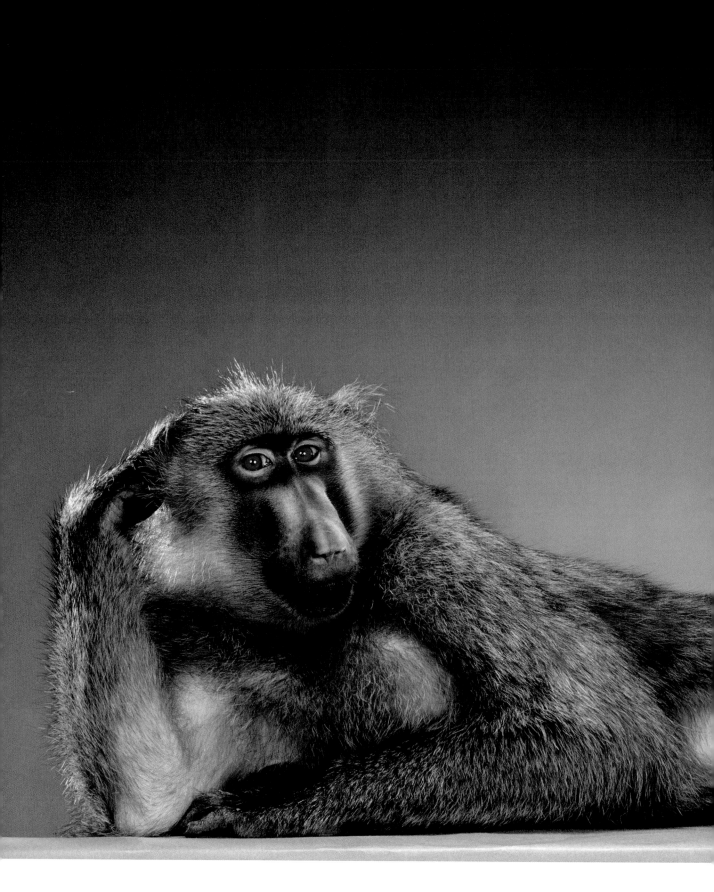

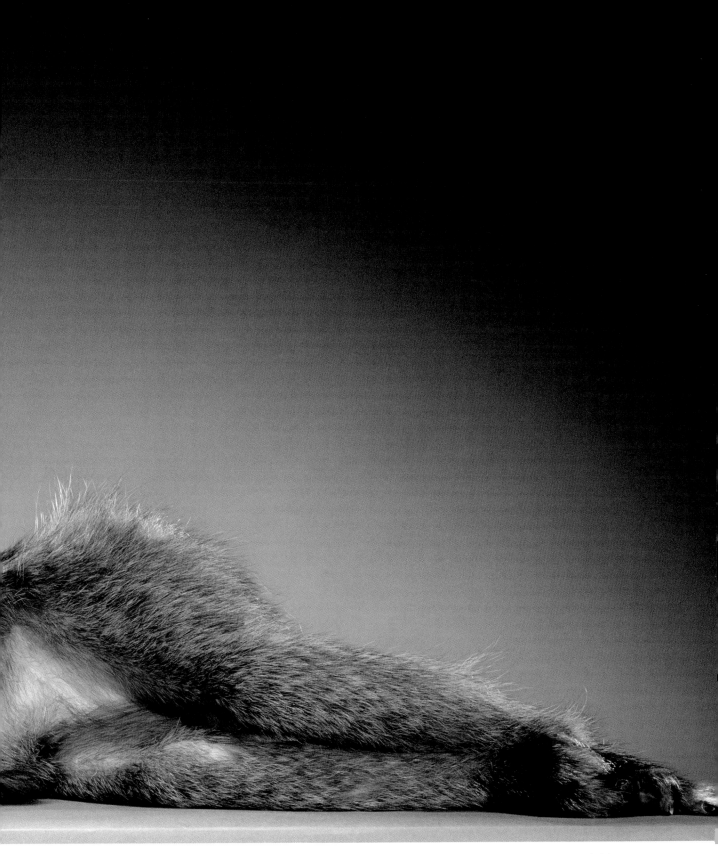

Mala Centerfold

The art of being wise is the art of knowing what to overlook.
WILLIAM JAMES

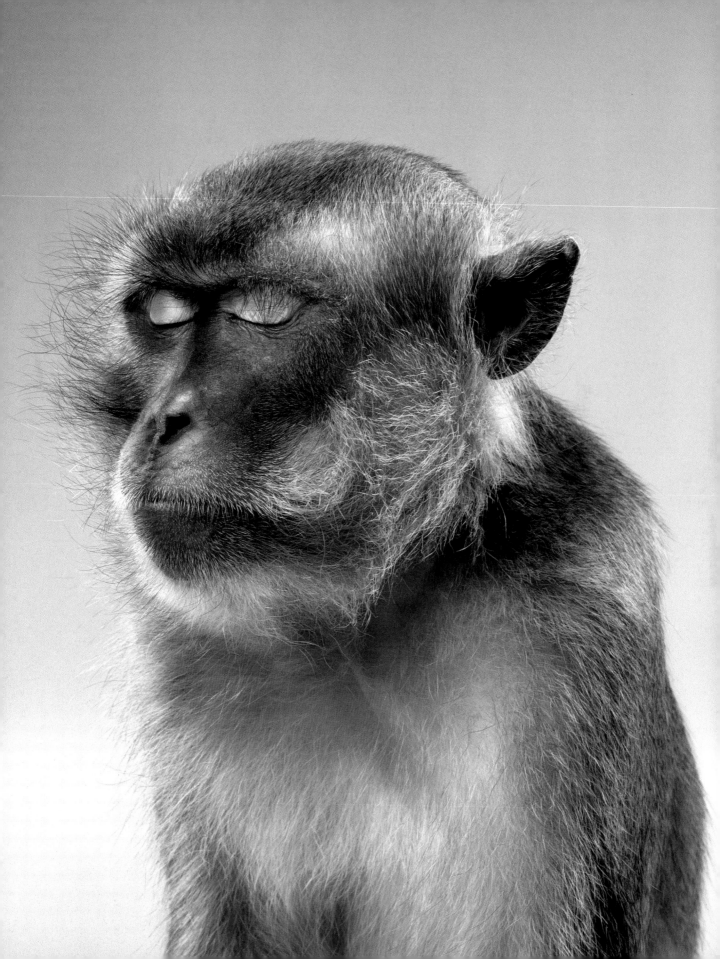

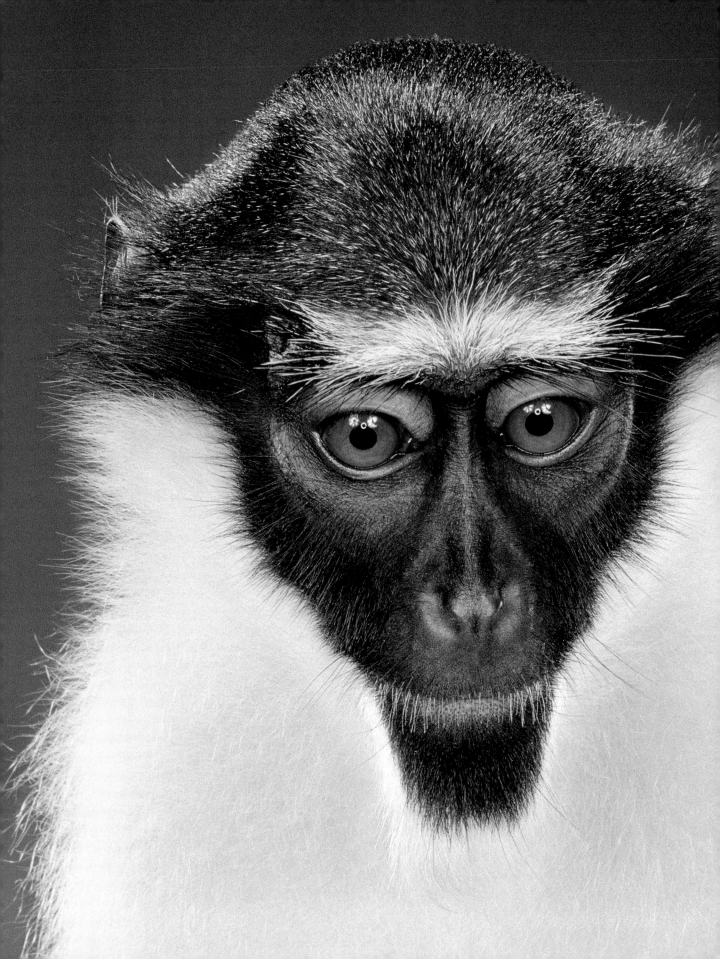

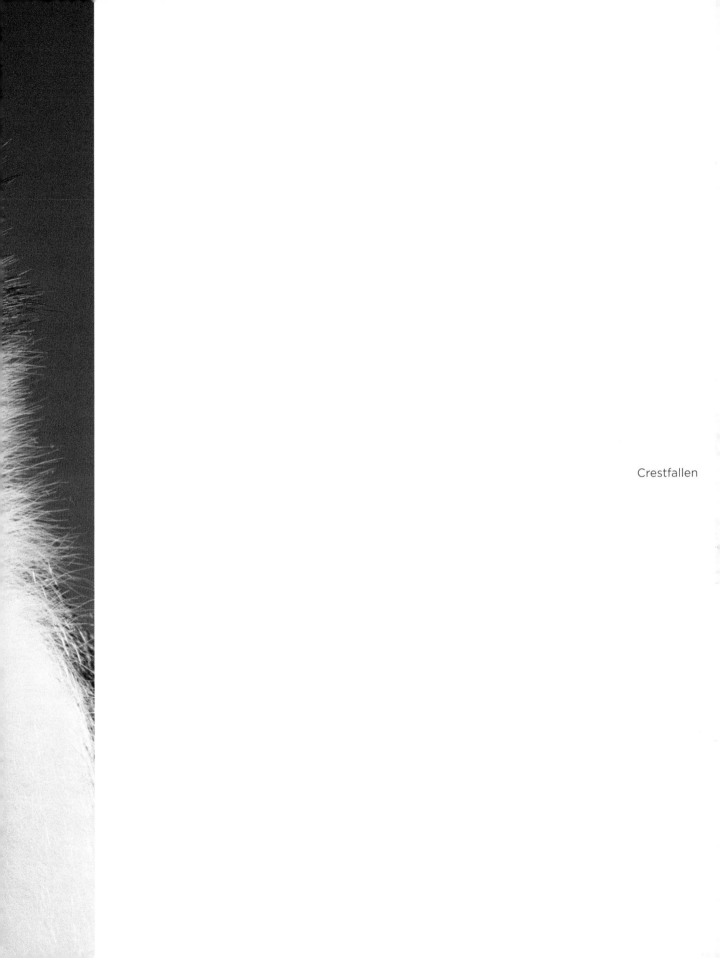

Crestfallen

Persecuted

Following: The Marmoset

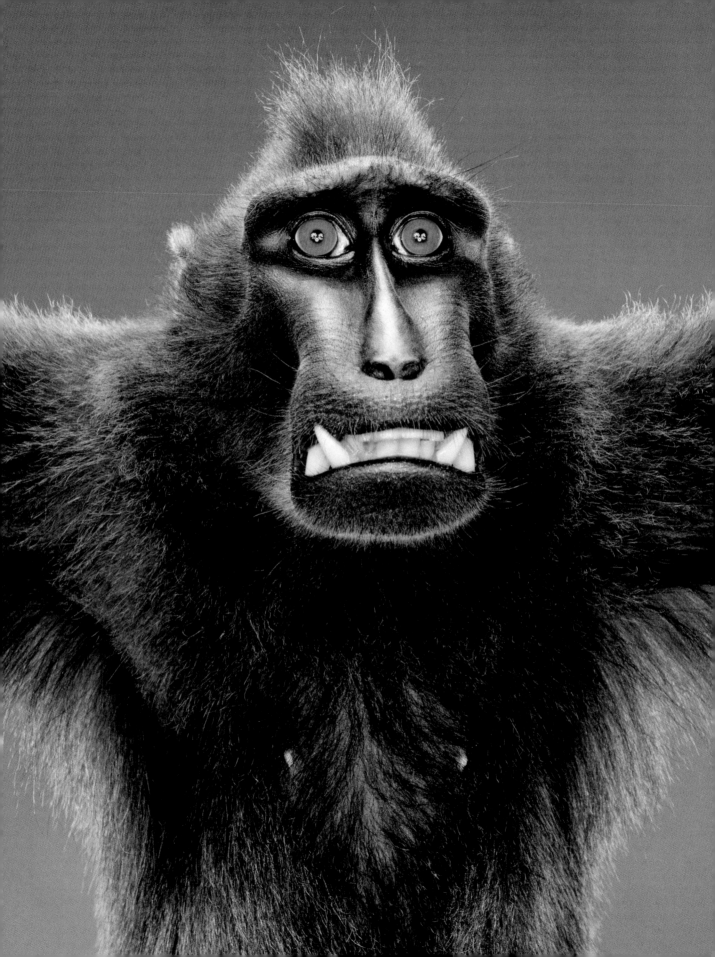

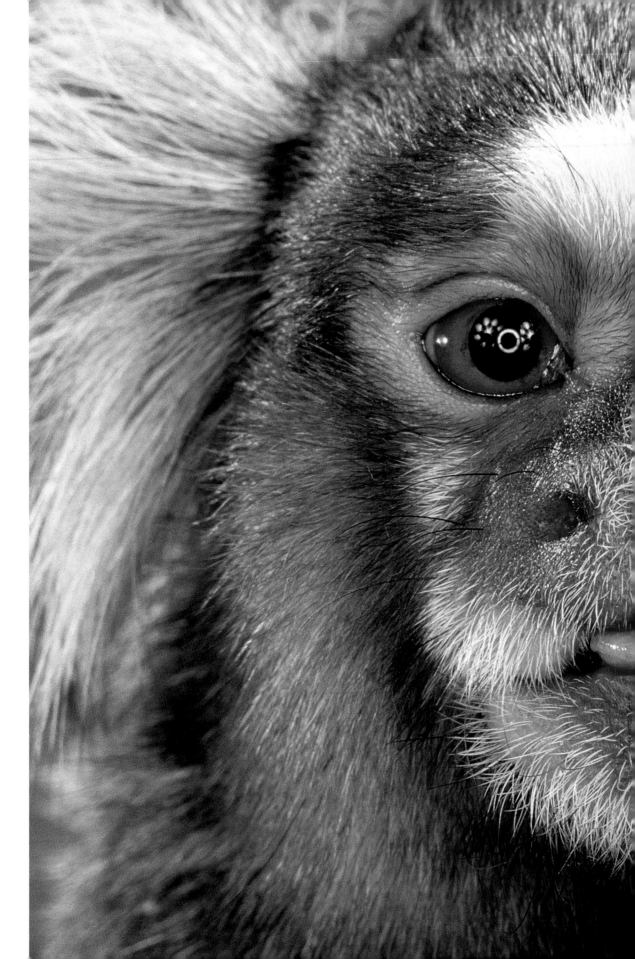

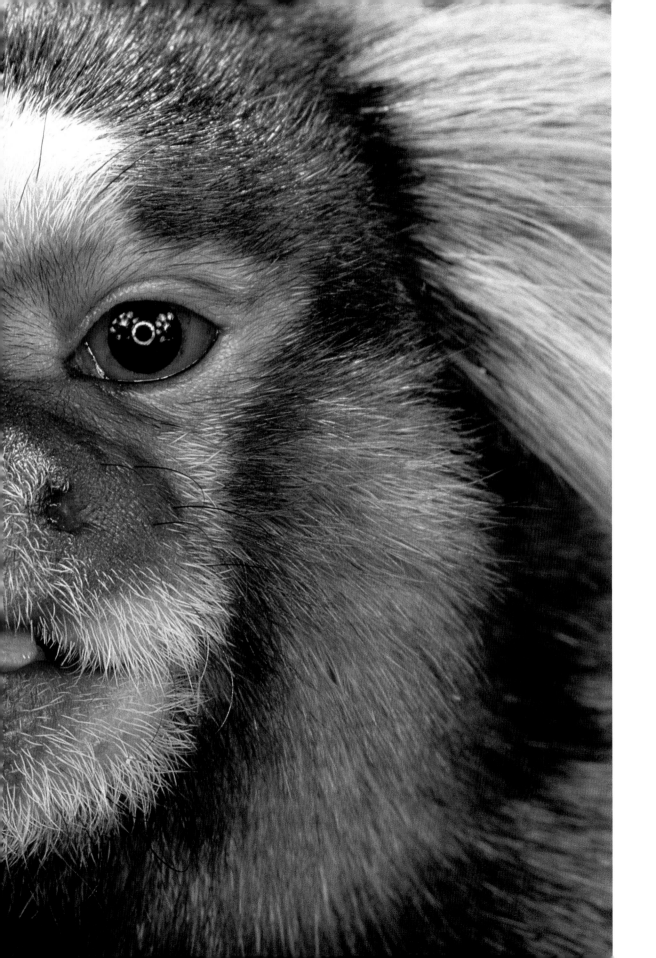

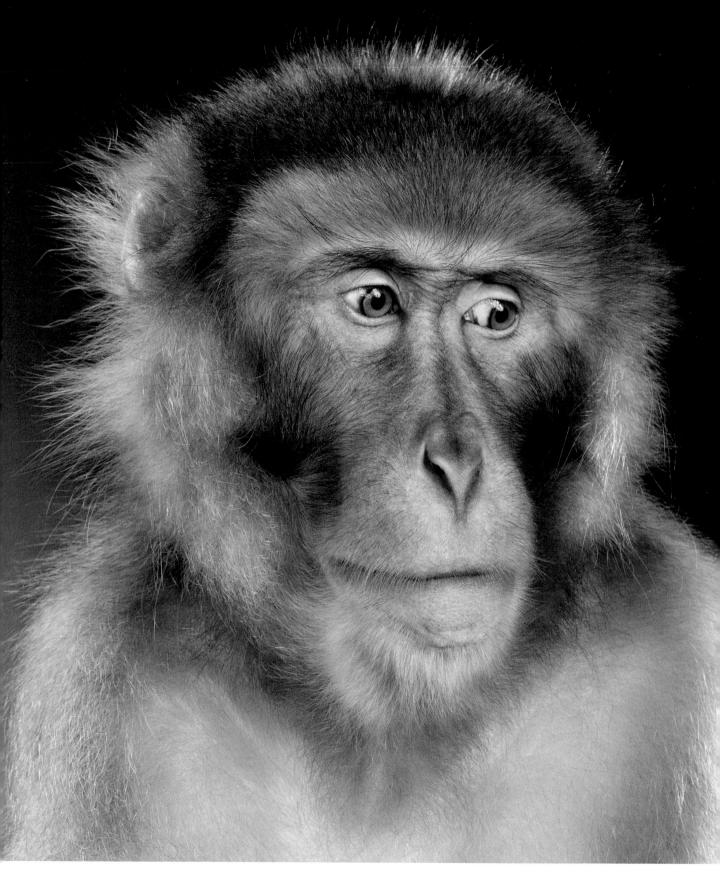

Distant

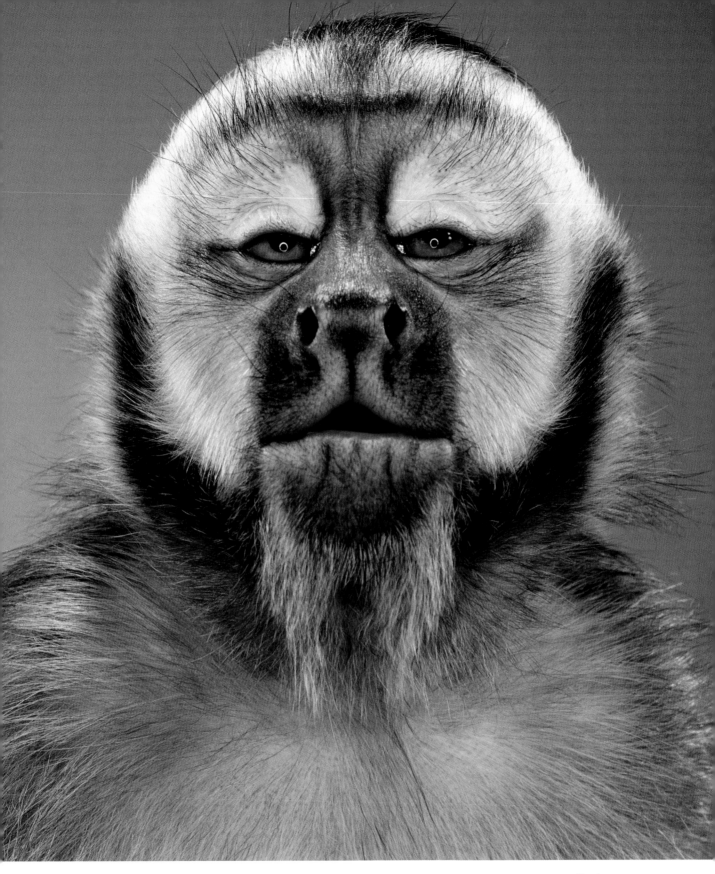

Dude

In the eye of his mother, a monkey is a gazelle.
SYRIAN PROVERB

Following pages, left to right: *Ooh!*, Porcine

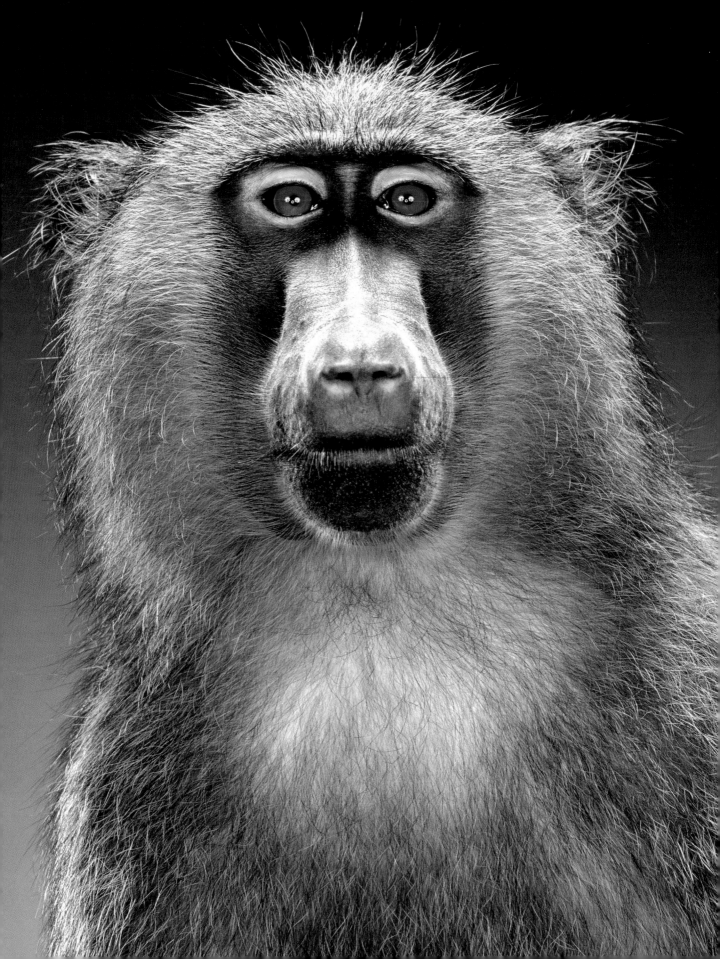

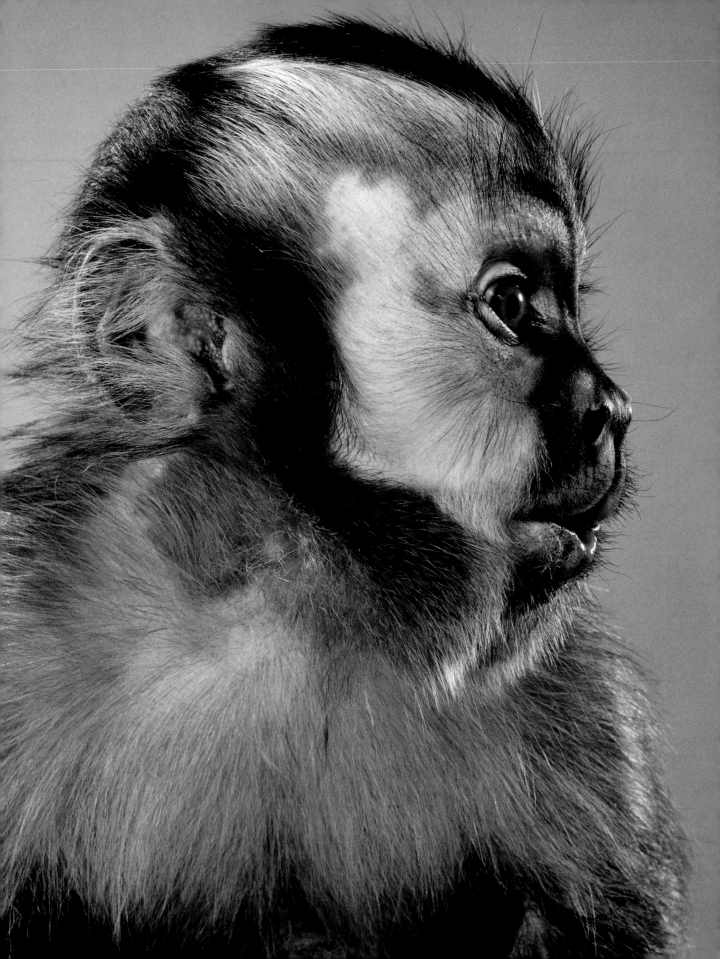

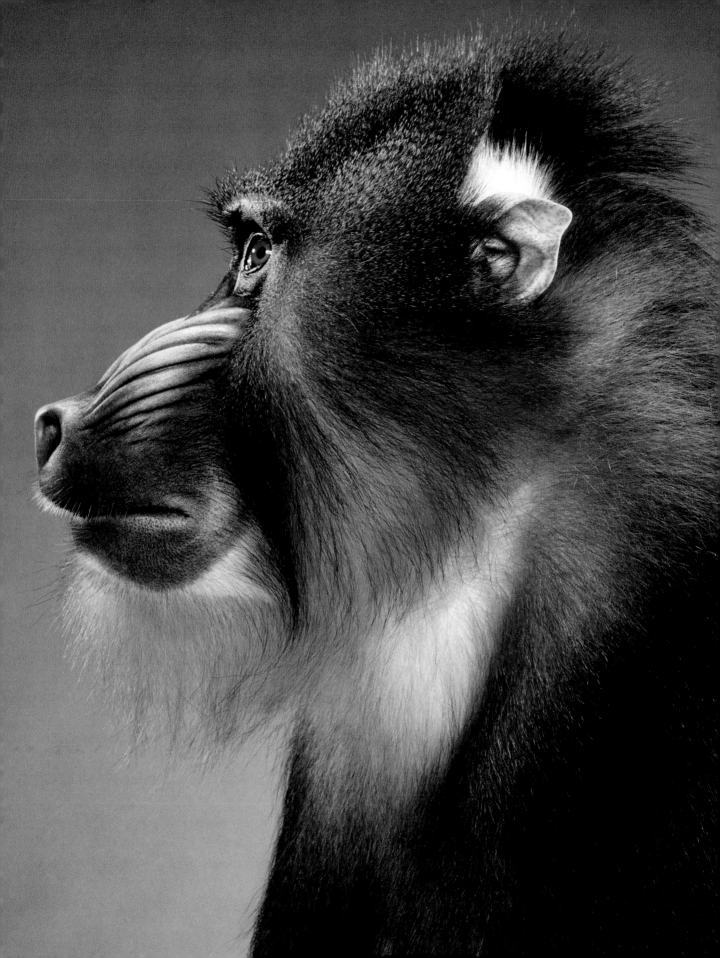

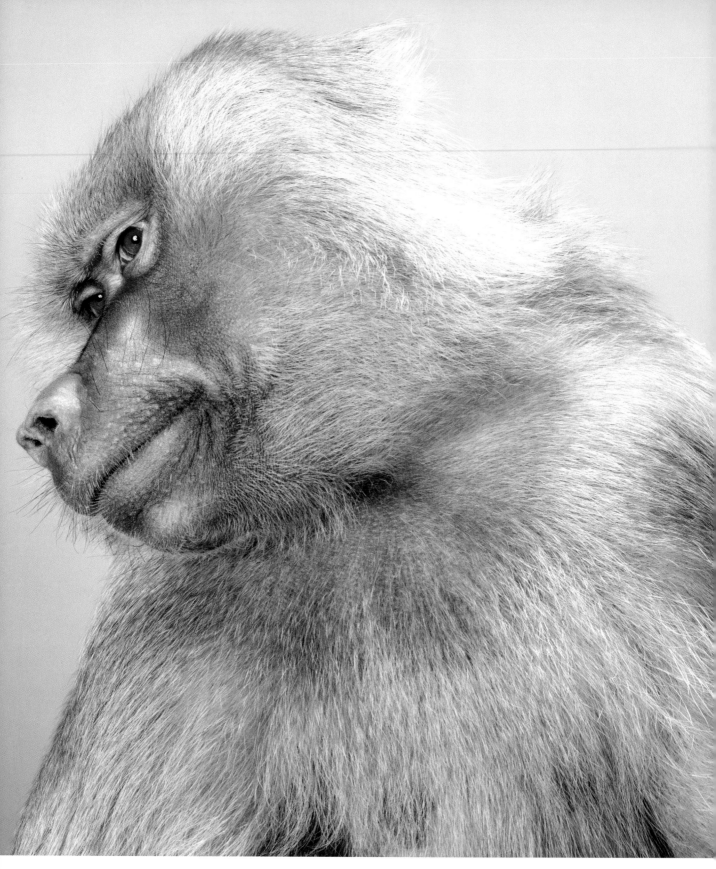

A Little to the Left

Aah!

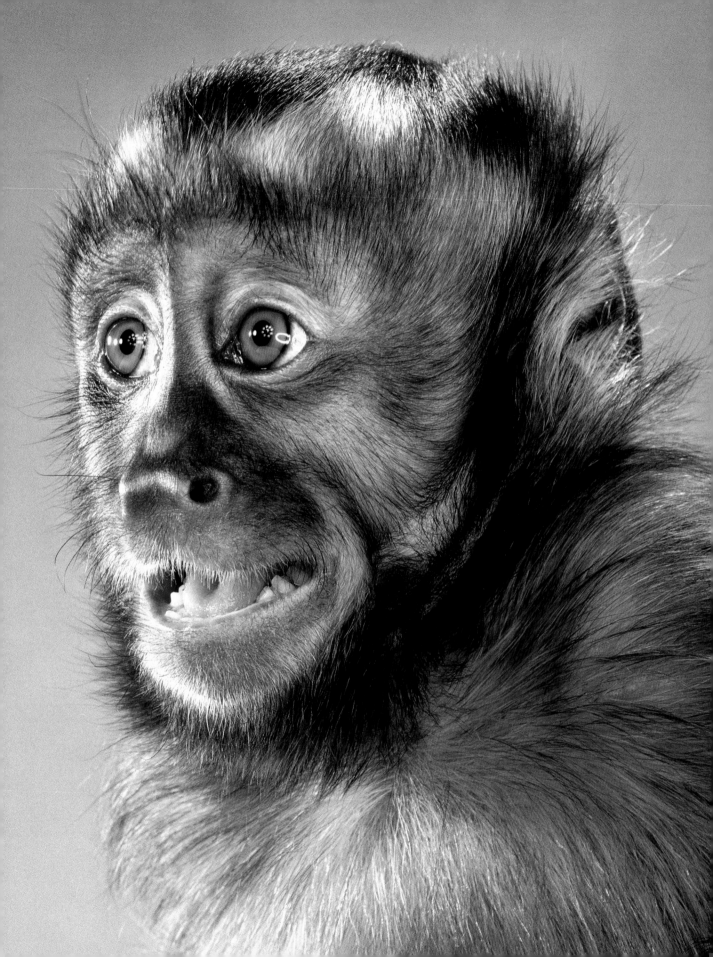

Scoldy

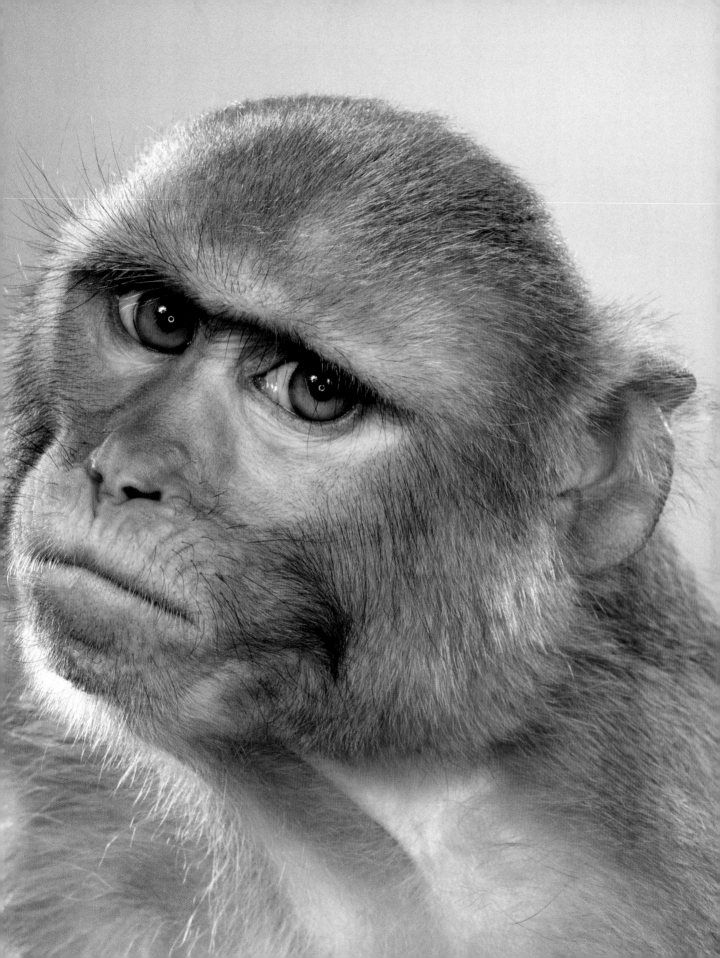

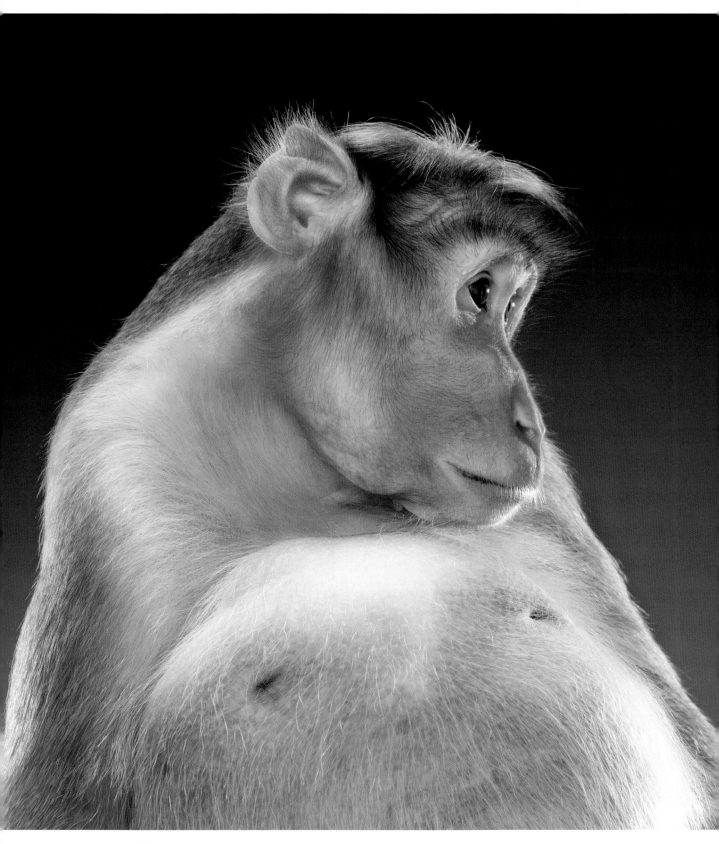

Fat Shemp

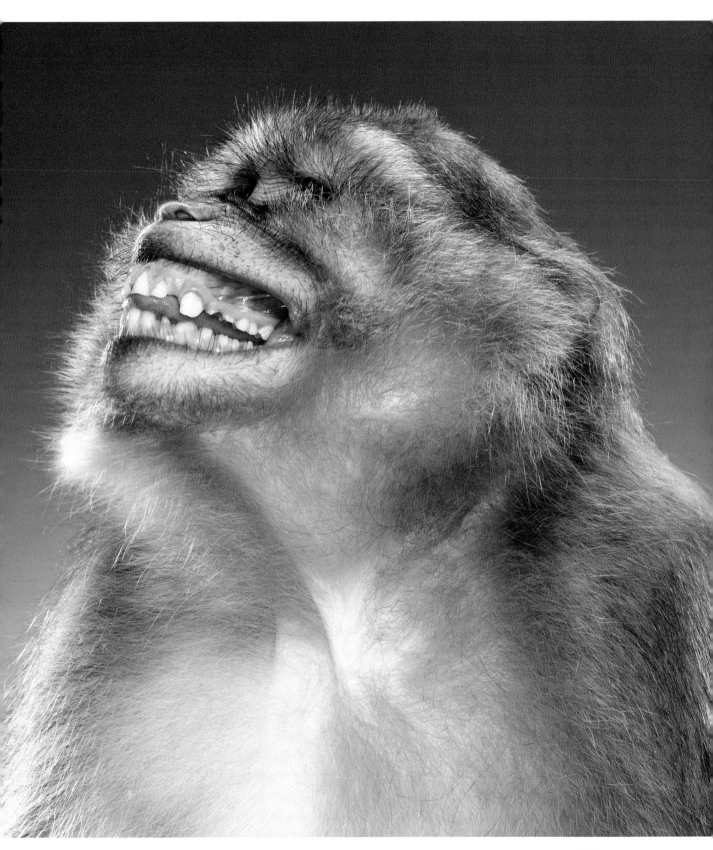

Ugly

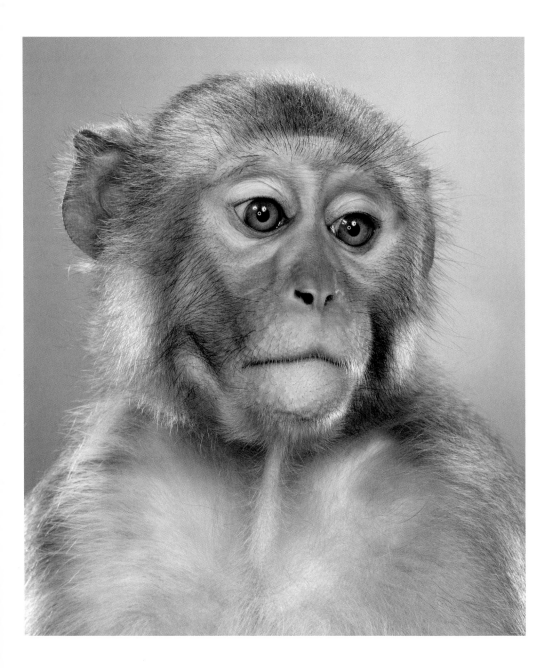

Following pages, left to right: Delirious, Wilding

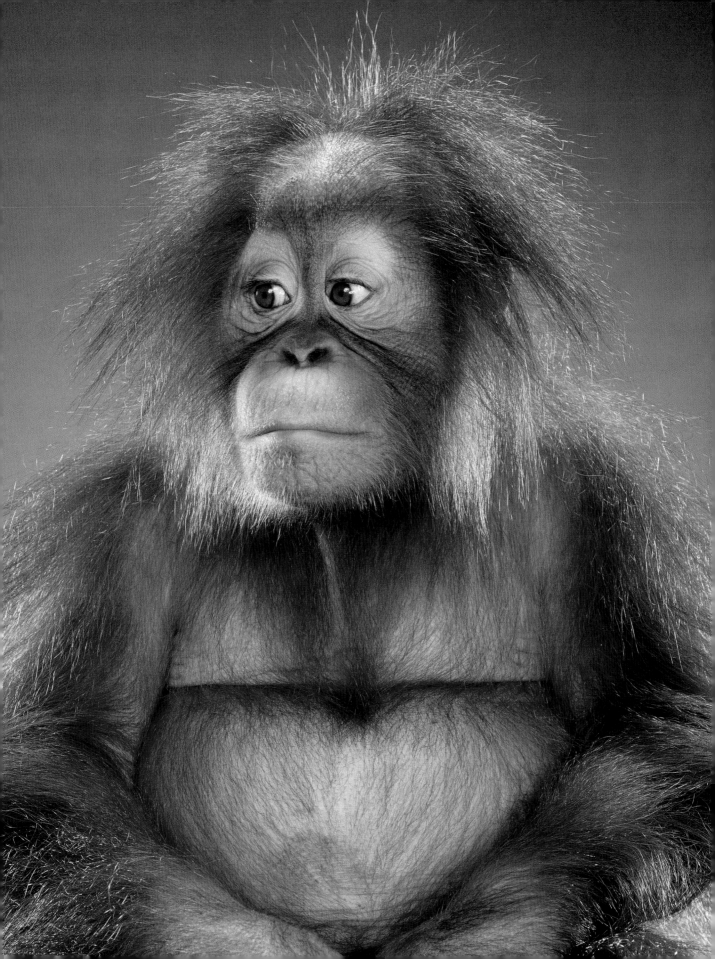

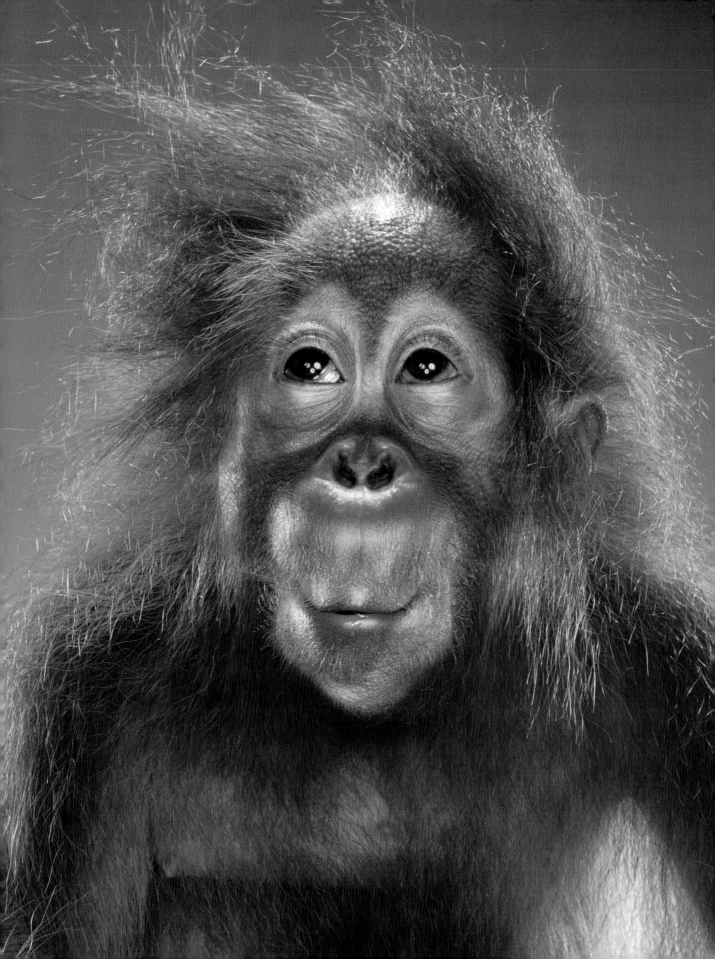

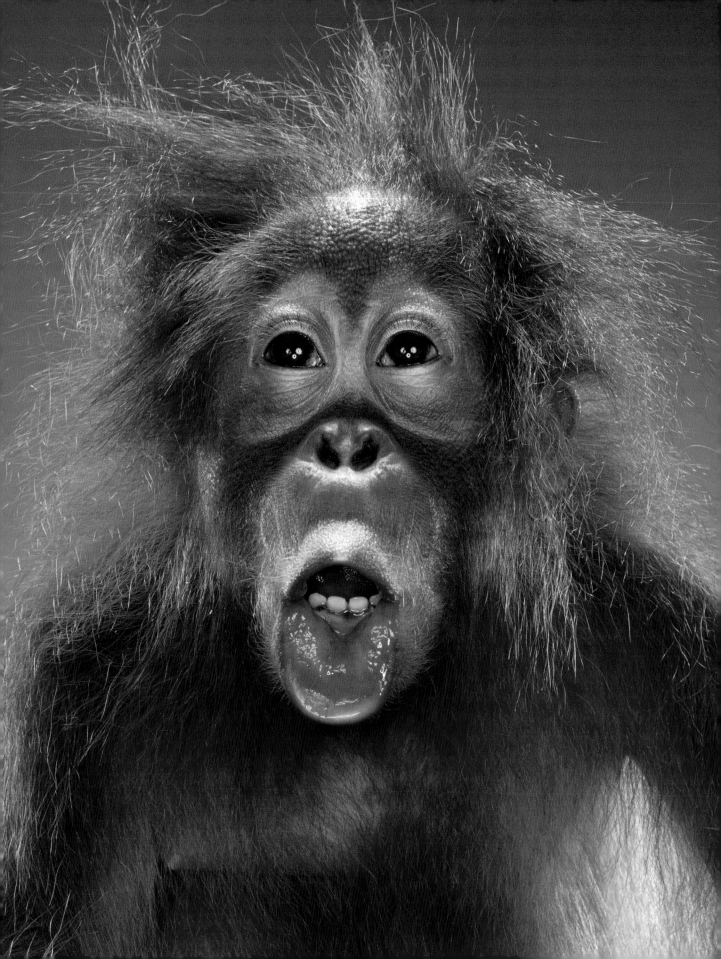

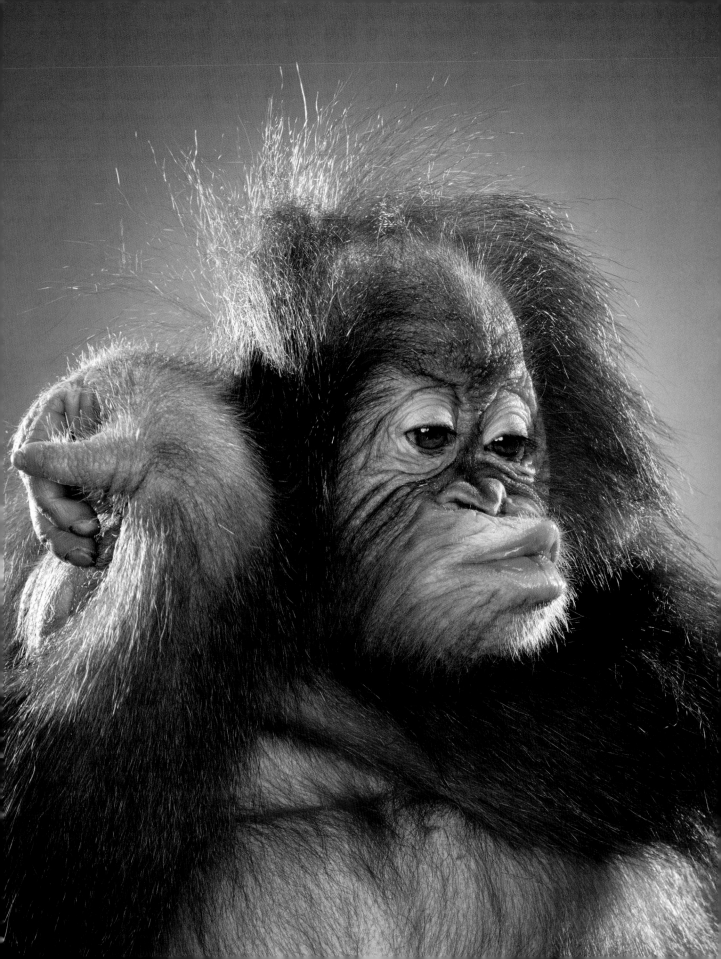

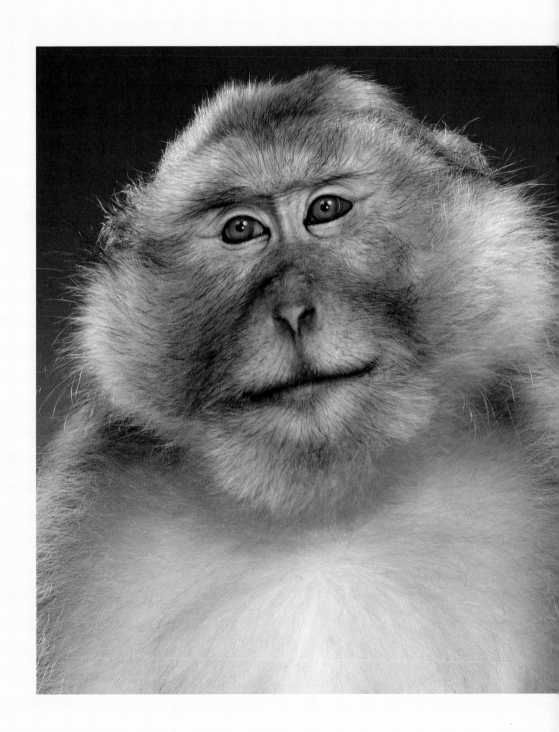

The Conundrum

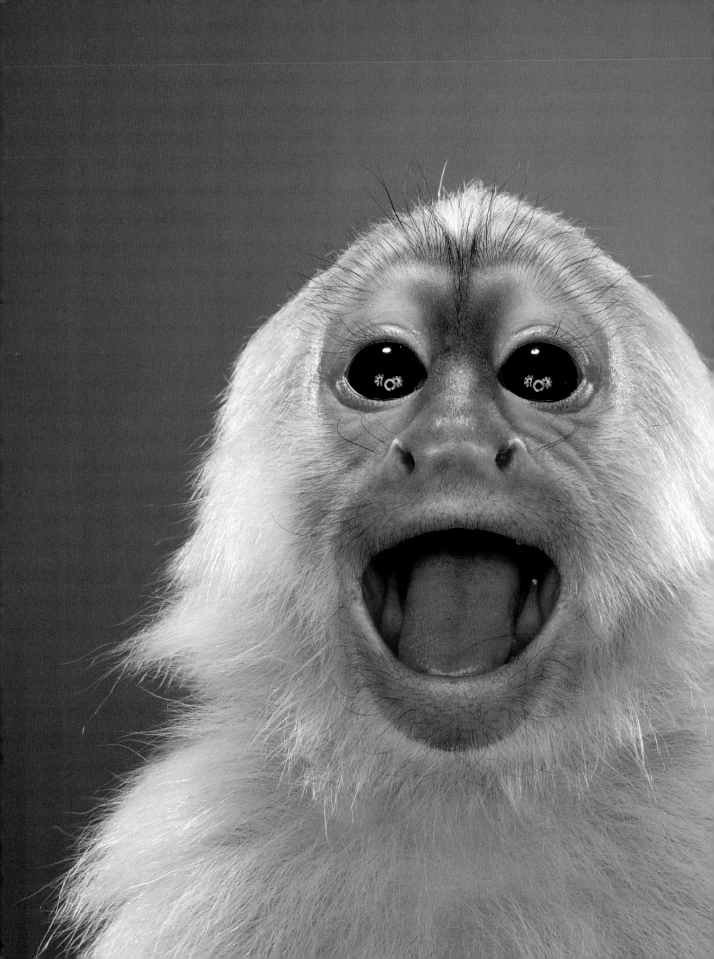

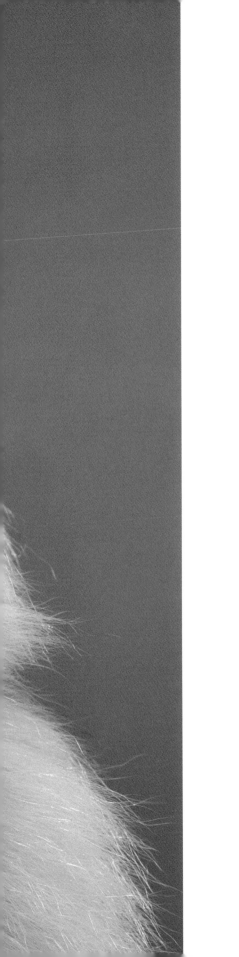

The Hatchling

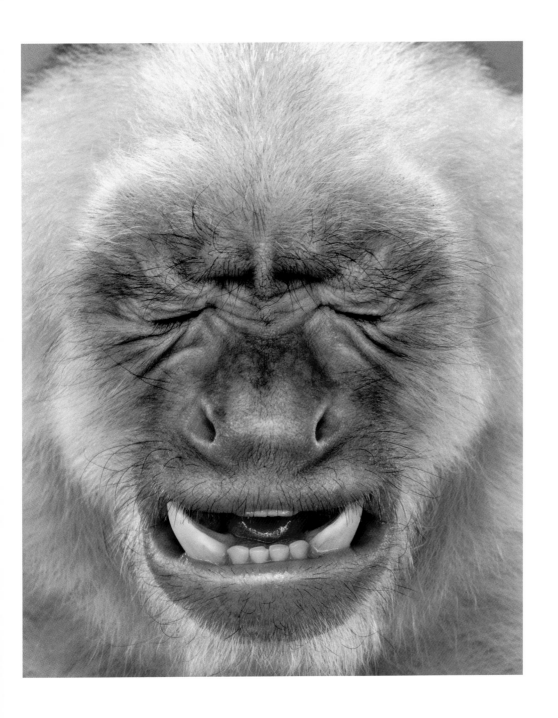

Wince

Worried

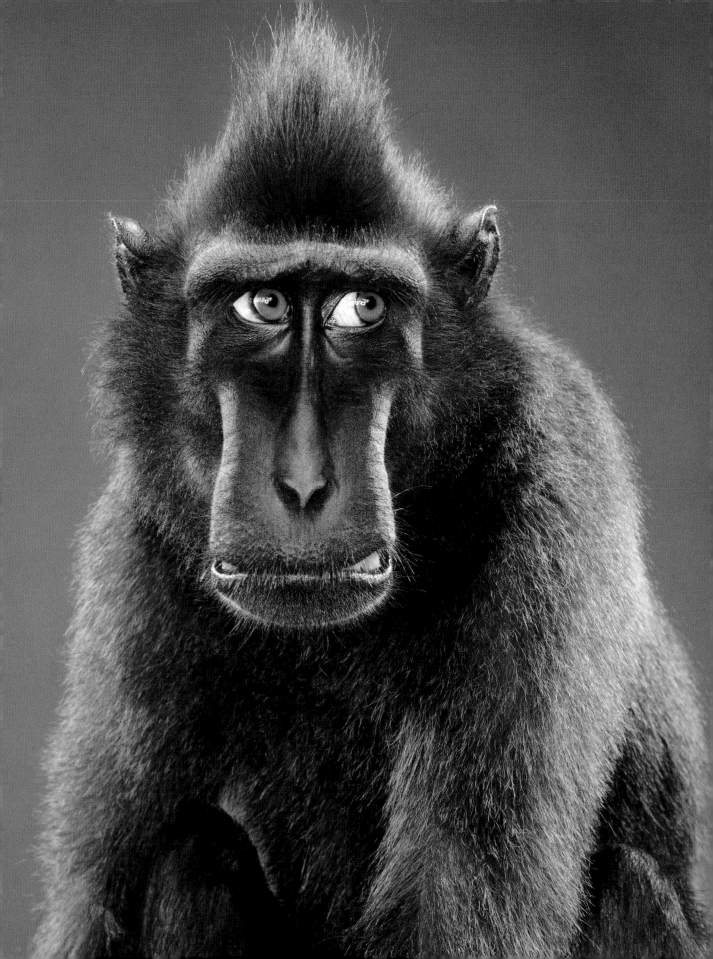

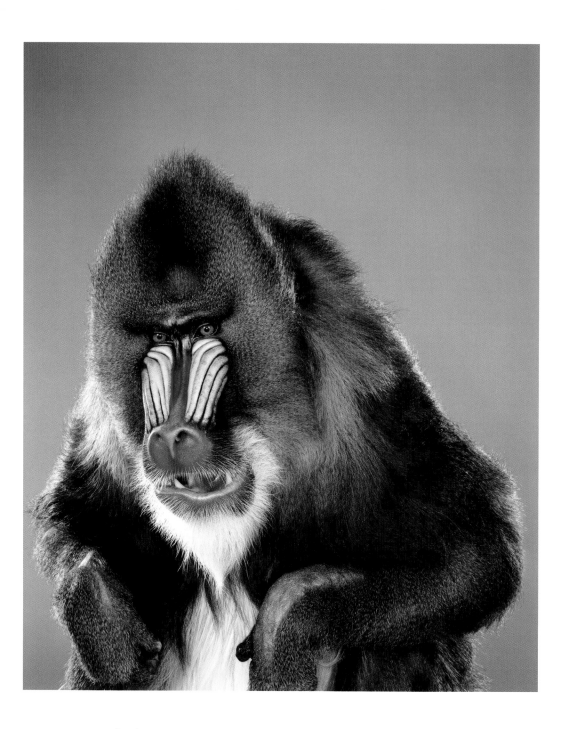

Uh-oh

Haughty

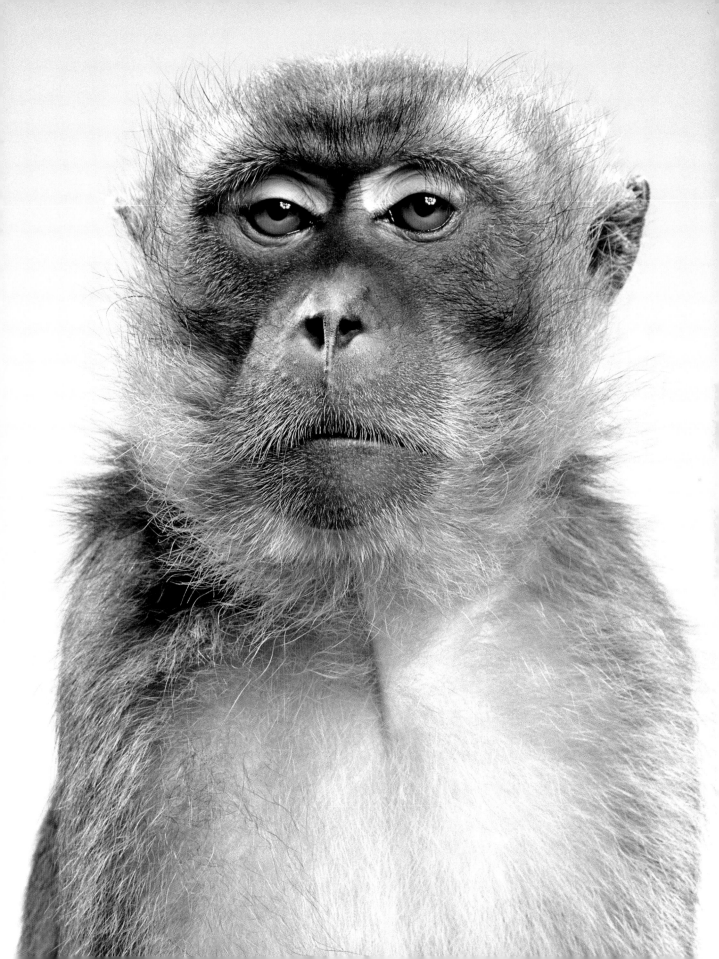

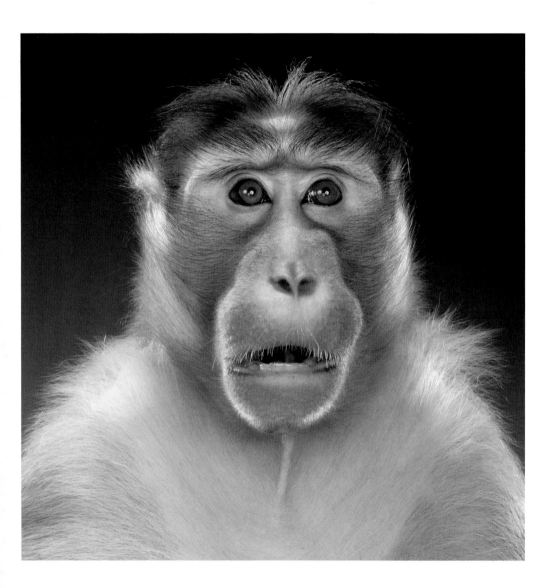

Awestruck

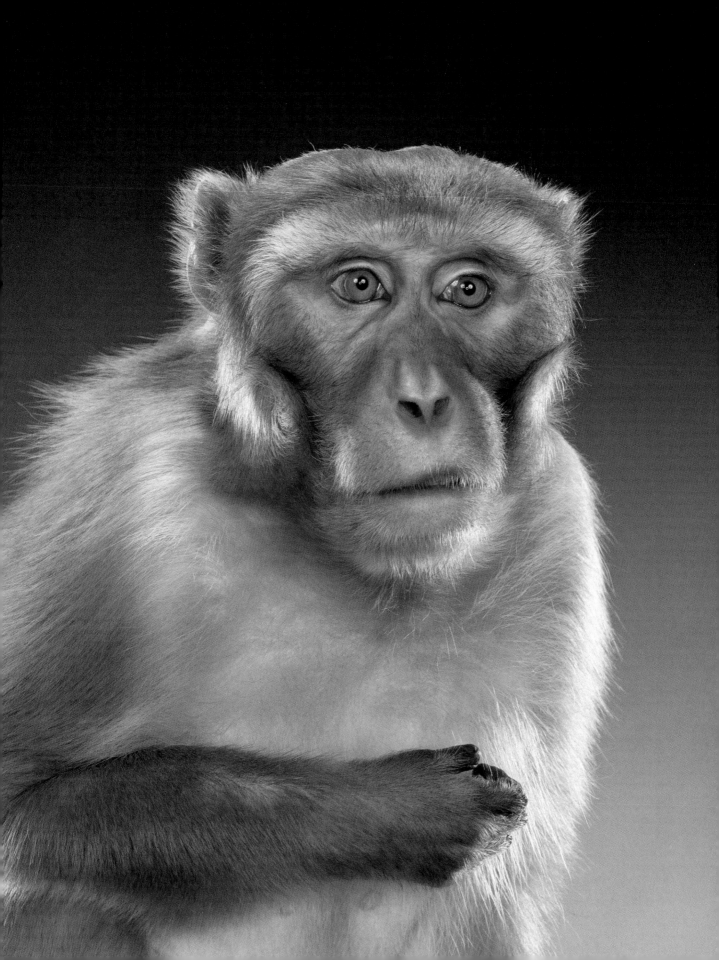

In the time of chimpanzees I was a monkey.

BECK

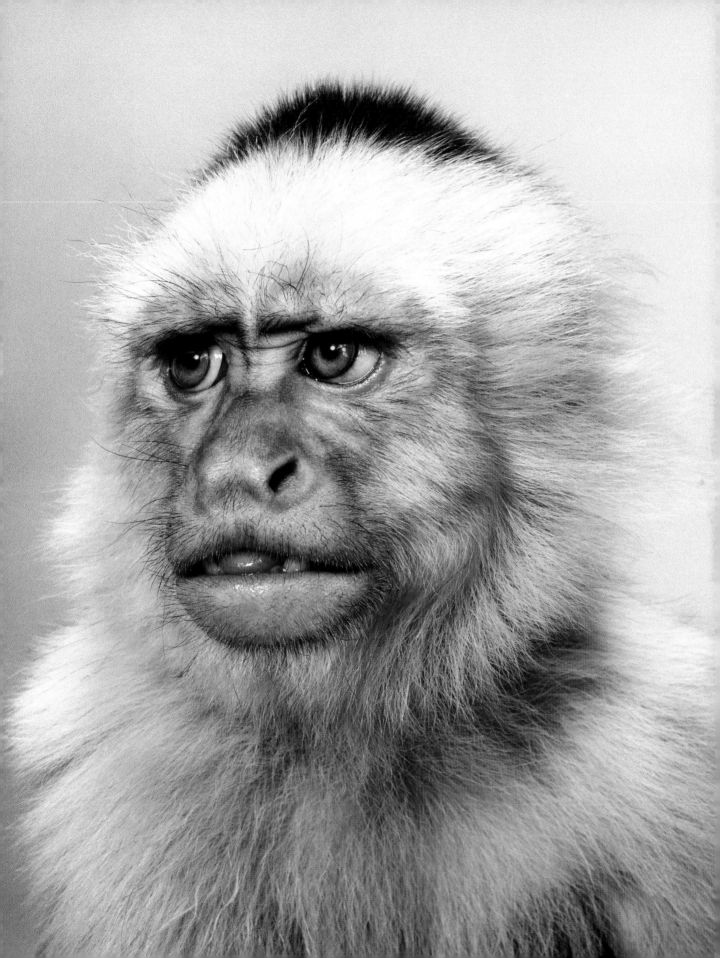

Ball of Fire

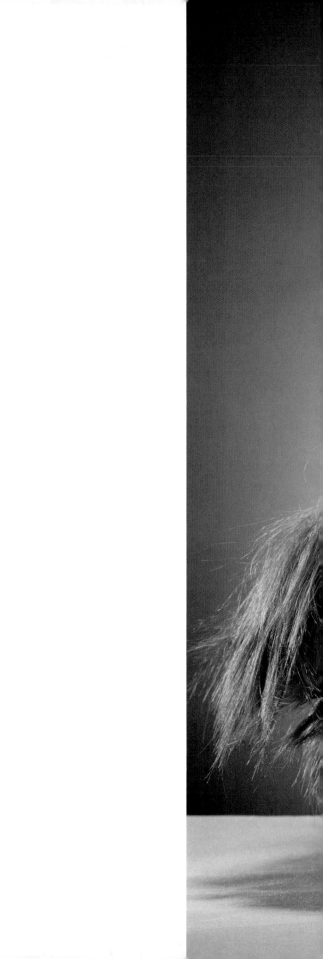

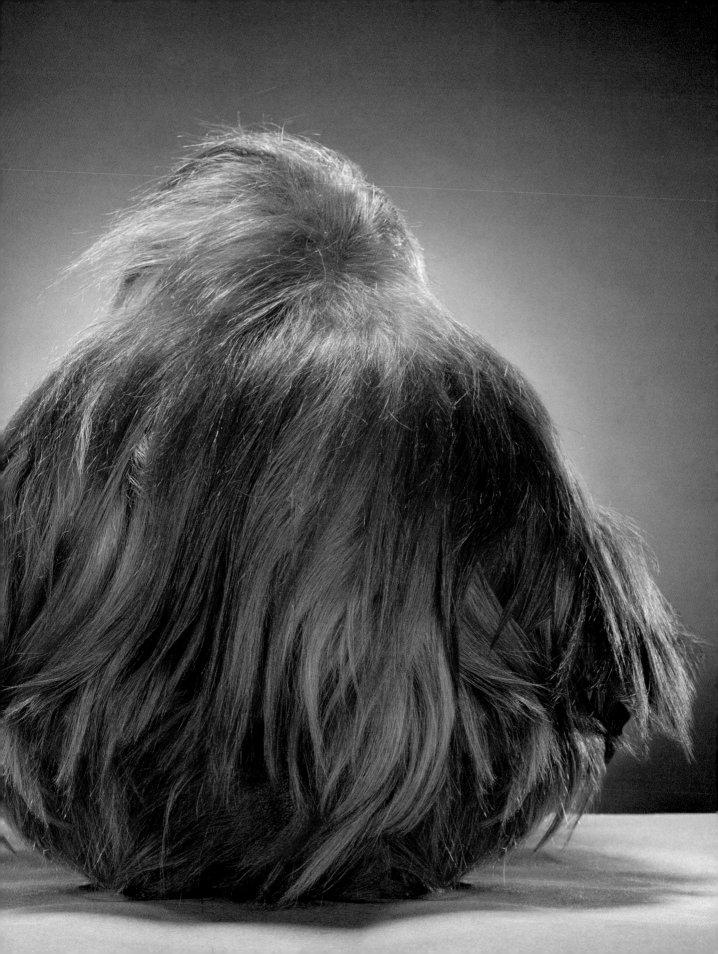

WHO'S **WHO**

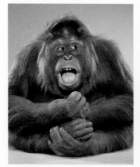

JAKE
Orangutan

Residence
Miami

Credits
King of the Jungle

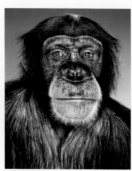

KENUZY
Chimpanzee

Residence
Los Angeles

Credits
The Animal
The Chimp Channel
Jack in the Box commercial
MCI commercial
PG Tips tea commercial
Sunny Delight commercial
Toyota Prius commercial

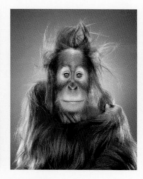

ROCKY
Orangutan

Residence
Los Angeles

Credits
Maxim magazine

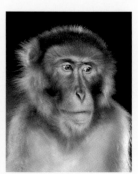

CHUBAKA
Japanese Snow Macaque

Residence
Miami

Credits
Ace Ventura: Pet Detective
The Jungle Book
The Road to Wellville
Carriers

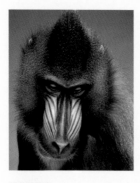

KONGO
Mandrill

Residence
Miami

Credits
Schweppes commercial

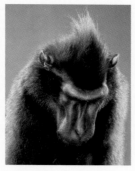

JOSH
Celebese Macaque

Residence
Upstate New York

Credits
Jack Hanna's Animal Adventures
Late Night with Conan O'Brien
The Maury Povitch Show
Black and Decker commerical

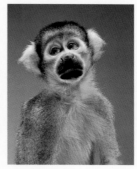

BAMBOO
Squirrel Monkey

Residence
Los Angeles

Credits
The Tonight Show with Jay Leno
Burger King commercial
Xerox commercial
Student films

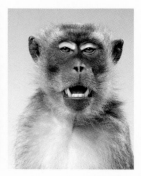

MOE
Java Macaque

Residence
Los Angeles

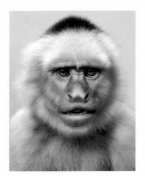

KATIE
Capuchin

Residence
Los Angeles

Credits
Bruce Almighty
King Cobra
Friends
Excedrin commercial
Pepsi commercial

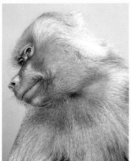

GEORGIA
Hamadryas Baboon

Residence
Monterey, CA

Credits
Born Free
The Lion King
Many national commercials

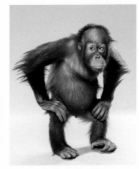

BAMBAM
Orangutan

Residence
Los Angeles

Credits
The Bold and the Beautiful
Passions
Rynkeby Juice

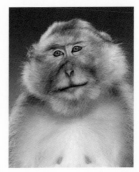

SALLY
Macaque

Residence
Westown, New York

Credits
Rescue Me
The Sally Jesse Raphael Show
Black & Decker commerical
Daisy Fuentes photo shoot
Martha Stewart Kids

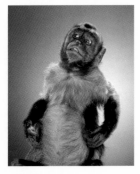

DAX
Black Capped Capuchin

Residence
New York

Credits
The Howard Stern Show
The View
Greeting cards
Private parties

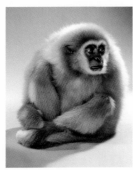

GABE
Gibbon

Residence
Los Angeles

Credits
The Jungle Book

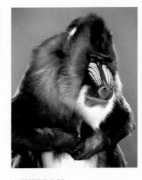

AZUMAH
Mandrill

Residence
San Francisco

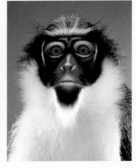

LOLA
Diana Monkey

Residence
Miami

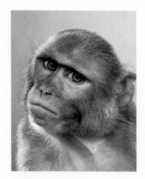

ASIA
Rhesus Macaque

Residence
Los Angeles

Credits
Medical Investigations

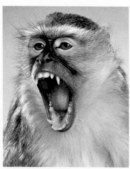

OBI
Vervet Monkey

Residence
Staten Island, NY

Credits
Chapelle's Show
Late Night with Conan O'Brien
Late Show with David Letterman
Corporate events for
   Tommy Hilfiger and Diana Ross
Various print ads
Vanity Fair

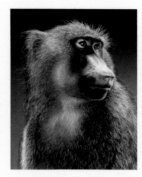

MALA
Yellow Baboon

Residence
Miami

Credits
The Tonight Show with Jay Leno

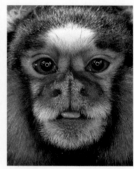

MONA
Marmoset

Residence
Monterey, CA

Credits
Works in Education department
   at Wild Things Animal
   Rentals, Inc.

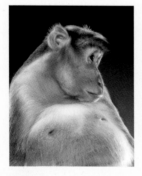

ZACK
Bonnet Macaque

Residence
Miami

Credits
The Simple Life

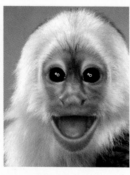

CHITTA
White-Faced Capuchin

Residence
Miami

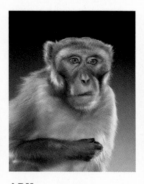

ABU
Golden Rhesus Macaque

Residence
Miami

Credits
Ace Ventura: Pet Detective
The Jungle Book
The Road to Wellville
Carriers

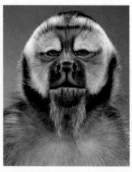

FOREST
Tufted Capuchin

Residence
Los Angeles

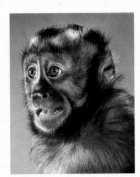

ABBEY
Weeper Capuchin

Residence
Los Angeles

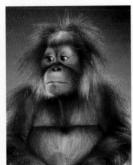

SURYA
Orangutan

Residence
Miami

Credits
Vogue

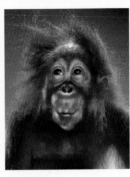

PUMPKIN
Orangutan

Residence
Miami

Credits
The Simple Life

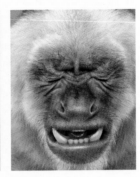

RIPLEY
White-Fronted Capuchin

Residence
Los Angeles

Credits
Gordo's Road Show
"Moldy World"
Morning Fog
Nickelodeon
Honda commercial
McDonald's commercial

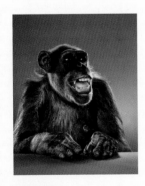

CHEETA
Chimpanzee

Residence
Palm Springs, CA

Credits
Twelve *Tarzan* films
Doctor Doolittle (1967)

AFTERWORD

Haven't We Met?

Stand in front of any magazine kiosk. The number of faces that look at you and tacitly invite you to look back — didn't our parents teach us that it's impolite not to look people directly in the eye? — is spellbinding. Sure, there's an occasional plasma TV, garden trellis, or hybrid car vying for your attention, but the vast majority of rack real estate is given over to faces. Why is this? From a vulgar, purely economic perspective that calculates a magazine's cover and content solely as a means to wrest the greatest added value from processed trees, portraits are ideal. They demand our attention and may possibly inspire a purchase. But even when we understand this marketing mechanism, the question still remains: Why do we love looking at images of other people?

Jill Greenberg creates portraits that seize our attention. Chances are that a magazine at the kiosk features one of her portraits on the cover. Over the past fifteen years, Greenberg has made memorable images of many of the world's most recognizable celebrities, in addition to creating a recognizable filter of vision itself. An early adopter of digital effects, Greenberg has developed a world that is somehow more intense, more razor sharp — let's say suprareal — than the one in which we typically reside. But not by much. At times, I suspect the appearance of the world is catching up with Greenberg's filter. Our smart, electric surfaces are expanding in all dimensions and glow from within, like light passing through a prism. Gravity is increasingly ignored as we lift our faces, our bodies, and our architecture. Everything is now malleable, with manipulations possible atom by atom, gene by gene, and pixel by pixel. It is not some vision of *the future,* as in the futurism of early sci-fi, but the nanosecond near-now, where science fiction as a genre is becoming moot because actual technologies are ever more rapidly entering our day-to-day world as science fact. Greenberg is able to presciently reveal this stage, this sense of what we are becoming.

In this book, Greenberg has created a series of monkey portraits and asks us to consider, in another way, where we are coming from. We look into the monkeys' expressions, their faces — their peculiar physiognomies — and somehow see ourselves. It is at once frightening and disorienting and exhilarating and awesome.

One of the few lucid theories proposed by French psychoanalyst Jacques Lacan is the mirror stage. Recognizing that the early development of baby monkeys far exceeds that of human babies in terms of motor coordination and physical wit, Lacan suggests that we are all born too early: our senses are senseless; our organs are unorganized; our joints are disjointed. Utterly dependent on our caregivers, we are chaotic and fragmented. But between six months and eighteen months of age, the human baby jumps ahead of the monkey and experiences a "startling spectacle" before her mirror image. Whereas the baby monkey quickly tires of the mirror providing a seemingly empty, meaningless image, the human baby engages playfully with her image. For the first time, she perceives a sense of "I" — an ideal image of unity, stature, and stability — that one day she can imagine obtaining and mastering. But Lacan insists that in this dramatic formative stage there is a fundamental misrecognition. For it is through a fantasy image, an image that is not one with us, that we come to understand ourselves. We misperceive the gap between our "I" and our reflection and so become alienated from our ideal.

Bleak stuff, if you worry too much over it; but Lacan, and many of his followers, have used this insight to try to understand our almost insatiable desire to both search for and re-create this formative unity and primordial completeness in images and fictions. Photographs of people, especially, provide the most powerful representations to address this desire.

I live on the island of Manhattan with at least 1.5 million others and occasionally feel like I have some as-yet-unnamed psychological disorder. I've asked around, and other people seem to share the same symptoms. It's the phenomenon of walking down the street or entering a restaurant or sitting on a stoop and glancing at people's faces and believing that you have met everyone before — literally *everyone*. If the glance is reciprocated, you're stuck, like a mainframe compiling data, searching your memory bank for context or the occasion of the meeting. But the thing is, most of the time, when the search is complete, you're confident that you have never met the person before in your life. Or somewhat confident. I have come to the provisional conclusion — an actual medical condition notwithstanding — that we recognize strangers because the gene pool that we *Homo sapiens* swim in is only so deep. We recognize people because we have in fact met their relatives on countless occasions. Everyone is a remix of the same code. It is this uncanny feeling, a slip in perception and knowledge, that at once binds us to our fellow earth travelers, but also, I think, explains our fascination with looking at portraits. We recognize, then misrecognize, then recognize ourselves, ad infinitum.

Moving back and forth from portraits of people to portraits of monkeys over the past couple of years, Greenberg has tapped into this eerie déjà vu and amplified it in startling ways. Together with apes and monkeys, we are in the Animalia kingdom, Chordata phylum, Vertebrata subphylum, Mammalia class, and — our club of about 235 species ends here — Primates order. Coined just over two hundred years ago, the word *primates* denotes *the first* and emphasizes the notion that we are superior to all other living creatures. Biologists have more recently acknowledged that this term is a taxonomical misnomer, but as an order, we share not-so-distant ancestors, evolutionarily speaking, and remarkable similarities. Remember those high school biology classes: primates all have limbs that move freely, flexible toes and fingers, big brains, and have all developed various complex social and linguistic skills. There is one last common trait that Greenberg, as a professional portrait photographer, has recognized and capitalized on: forward-looking eyes.

All primates have eyes set close together at the front of their faces, rather than on the side, and thus enjoy stereoscopic vision. A monkey's eyes are essentially our eyes. And our eyes, as the poets would have it, are seats of sentience, windows into our souls. We look into each other's eyes to find trust and love, to interpret what we are each thinking and feeling, to try to find empathy or sympathy or identification. Eyes bind us together. Would we love our pets as much if they didn't give us those looks? Daniel Dennett, the philosopher, artificial intelligence researcher, and dog lover, insists we must acknowledge that we have been genetically modifying our dogs for millennia with an unconscious, but purposeful, selection. The dogs that give us those eyes, expressions that are most like ours, are the ones we keep in reproductive working order. Our best friends have been selectively bred to be our best friends and to look lovingly back at us with gratitude. On the natural side of selection, just think about the murderous eyes of the hyena at night in those nature documentaries, eyes inhuman and alien, reflecting the tungsten lights of the cameraman's Land Rover.

Yet we have done nothing to influence the looks, the expressions, the eyes of monkeys. They have witnessed the past six to eight million years on their own. What we have done, and the sheer number of infamous monkeys in literature and pop culture attests to this, is try to look through their eyes. What do they see? More often than not, they see opportunities to cause some trouble. To name but a few examples: Sun Wukung, from *Journey to the West,* and Zephir, from *Babar the Elephant,* are respectable literary troublemakers; Curious George and Mr. Teeny, Krusty's costar on *The Simpsons,* are never far from mischief; Marcel, Ross's pet capuchin on *Friends,* and Klaus, Dieter's irresistibly touchable monkey on *Saturday Night Live,* never fail to provide material for ribald punch lines. The monkey is the rascal, the rogue, the miscreant; he is the devil whose antics remind us just how fragile the networks of social conditioning are that keep us under control, that keep us on the proper side of "civilization." As children first learning these things, we can't help but "monkey around"; we get wrapped up in "monkey business." *Tsk, tsk.* The monkey is the undisciplined beast that cackles and cavorts, throws its shit, and whacks off tirelessly. Indeed, I recently came across an experiment done by John Lily, the scientist portrayed by William Hurt's character in the film *Altered States.* In this experiment, Dr. Lily, then with the National Institute of Mental Health, attached electrodes to the part of a monkey's brain that causes erections and ejaculations, and provided the monkey with a switch. The monkey hit it every three minutes.

One could ask, at least with respect to the male gender, have we evolved all that much? But this, of course, is a stereotypical joke. What is not a joke is the unfortunate history of misunderstanding evolution, and in some ways we all still have a monkey on our backs. Throughout the latter half of the nineteenth century and into the twentieth, a new breed of pseudoscientist misappropriated the seminal work of Charles Darwin and produced great mounds of monkey shit. Nominally known as social Darwinists, they tried to find justifications for their already existing racism and sexism and false superiority by positing morphological links between the criminal, the colored, the slow of mind, the female, and the lesser primates. They measured brain mass and shape, facial features, and body types to find direct correspondence between the aforementioned groups and monkeys and apes, and when their results were inconsistent or flat-out wrong, they felt justified in altering their findings because they knew their theories to be true. Advances in the study of genetics have unequivocally proved the qualitative and quantitative falsehood of all social Darwinist theories. *Homo sapiens* are a separate species, genetically distinct, and categorically different from other primates. But every now and again we can catch a whiff of the monkey shit still in the air. It was the reason that sportscaster Howard Cosell was forced to resign after exclaiming, "Look at that little monkey run!" when commenting on a play by Washington Redskins receiver Alvin Garrett, an African American. In his defense, Cosell maintained that he started calling everyone "little monkeys" after spending time playing with his grandchild, who he had given this silly, sentimental nickname. But the malfeasance of social Darwinism, the institutional racism, sexism, and social hierarchies that it tried to scientifically establish still lingered strong enough twenty years ago to make Cosell's words inexcusable.

Now, any thinking person — who doesn't literally believe that the earth was created twenty thousand years ago and that the first human couple (recall the guy conspicuously missing a rib) walked the earth around six thousand years ago, and a little later all of the earth's good animals were saved on a very, very large ark — understands that through evolution we humans as a species have no substantive genetic differences from each other, and further, differ less from monkeys or apes than we had ever imagined.

Greenberg's psychologically charged monkey portraits insist that we consider the similarities. *Look at that little monkey looking back at us!* She mischievously shows us another type of mirror stage, where we confront an ancient and distorted reflection, another startling spectacle, and try to make sense of who or what we are seeing. By anthropomorphizing — or giving human qualities to — her monkeys, we can't help but identify with their gaze, and be reminded of people we know, expressions that we have seen before. Are they judging us? Laughing at us? Showing us that a couple of extra chromosomes just don't make that much difference when all is said and done?

Greenberg also shows us the indescribable beauty of monkeys. We might wonder when it will be possible to borrow some of their genes to get brilliant stripes of yellow or red in our own hair. Or perhaps, exotic patterns of luxurious facial fur will become de rigueur. But it is in their foreignness, the uncanniness of their facial structures, that their natural beauty is revealed, in a way, to be more truthful than our own. Artists have often depicted animals in their work. One thinks of the austere portraits of prize horses and hunting dogs that were often commissioned to underscore the pride of possession; or more recently, William Wegman's brilliant dog portraits, literally showing us dogs acting like humans. But I can think of no other animal portraits created with the subtle, yet breathtaking filter Greenberg provides. It is a place toggling back and forth between the primitive past — our evolution — and the very near future — our incipient genetic age.

Look forward, look backward, look again at your reflection: you just might recognize something that was staring at you all this time. *Haven't we met?*

Paul Myoda

ACKNOWLEDGMENTS

I would like to thank all of the animal agencies and trainers who made these sittings possible: Serengeti Ranch, All Tame Animals, Steve Martin's Working Wildlife, Bob Dunn's Animal Service, Benay's Bird and Animal Source, Wild Things A.R., Inc., and Dawn Animal Agency.

I would also like to thank my friend Carah von Funk, who introduced me to Simon Green, who found that Betty Wong and Michael Sand at Bulfinch were interested in making this book with me. Thanks to Gary Tooth at Empire Design Studio. And special thanks to my husband, Robert Green, who supported and encouraged me to do this series.

GOURMET BOUQUET

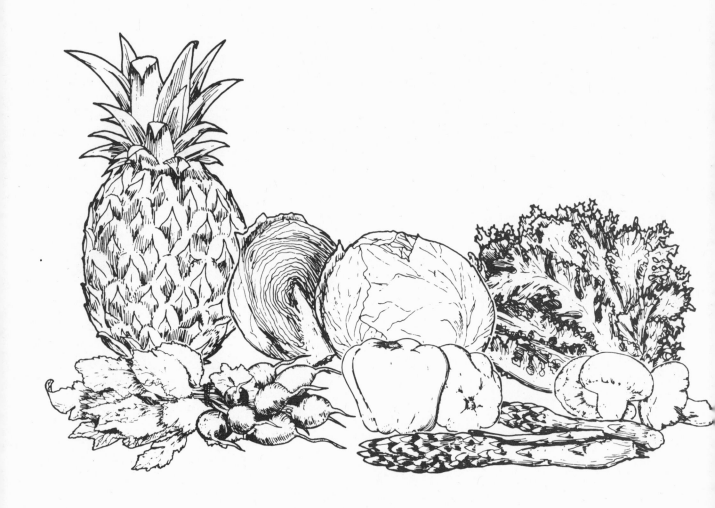

GOURMET BOUQUET

Julia Weinberg

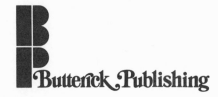
Butterick Publishing

Library of Congress Catalog Card Number: 77-608283
International Standard Book Number: 0-88421-042-1
Copyright © 1978 by Butterick Publishing
708 Third Avenue, New York, New York 10017
A Division of American Can Company

Hardcover
First Printing, January 1978
Second Printing, August 1978
Third Printing, February 1979
Softcover
First Printing, February 1979
Printed in U.S.A.

TO ALL THE SPECIAL FLOWERS
ON THEIR WAY TO BLOOMING

Acknowledgements

Some of us have green thumbs, some have white thumbs, but very few among us have people thumbs. These are the perpetual gardeners who nurture and encourage others, who cultivate the sleeping talent within us all. I am fortunate to have met several such gardeners; however, one in particular led me to discover my own creative potential, which until then I had denied. This special gardener was Barbara Hauptman, who found time to encourage and support my creative efforts until I was able to recognize them and admit their existence.

I met this angelic tornado several years ago when our medical (and other) backgrounds literally collided in the X-ray room of the doctor for whom I was working. We immediately became friends and discovered we had many things in common. As the years went on we became closer, not only in friendship but also in business. We shared an interest in foods and medicine as well as a certain philosophy. Barbara is a nurse with exceptional warmth. She is also a caterer with a unique philosophy of hosting which combines creativity with wit. It was Barbara who first suggested the idea of putting vegetables on a stick. Little did I know that this suggestion was to become the vehicle for an important part of my personal education as well as for the discovery of my own creative potential.

One can be a gardener and a flower at the same time. Perhaps the terms are even interchangeable, since the one who encourages the creation of a thing of beauty is as much responsible for its existence as the artist. When we are gardeners we are flowers as well, for helping one to find his or her true creativity and the freedom to develop it is surely the highest expression of growth and loving. Barbara, the world needs more gardeners like you.

I am grateful also to the following people:

Kitty–The beautiful nightingale whose special talent spreads joy and warmth to all who are near. Her support will never be forgotten.

Richard–Who so inspired and encouraged me through humor and shared with me a positive approach toward everything.

Mamusha–My mother who initiated my interest in foods and entertaining.

Fran, Sam, Saul, Jay, and Richie–My sister, brother-in-law, and nephews whose family unity and support warms me.

Father Schallert–Who with gentleness taught me how to see.

Elaine and Lynn–My extended family who shared with me their loving philosophy and creative flow.

Evelyn–My editor, whose voice from afar was all I knew. She conveyed enough reassurance and support to help me meet the deadline.

Special thanks to:

Andy Strauss–Whose humor made the many hours of photography pleasant.

Bob Klein–Literary consultant who kept me on schedule.

Dave Destler–Who completed the drawings in marathon time to meet the deadline.

Dick Dodge–Advisor and sounding board.

Alan Burks–Who remembered the Gourmet Bouquet and assisted in its publication.

Bill Edwards, Erma Zeff, and the entire Westward Ho Market Staff–For their moral support and speedy service.

Also thanks to:

Mark Coppos–Who paid special attention to every detail.

Ruth Mckinney–Art consultant.

Hanns Albers, Art Director, *L. A. Times* "Home Magazine"–For his encouragement.

Bill Platt–Who was sensitive to what I meant to say and helped me express it.

Contents

PART ONE
BOUQUET BASICS
15–81

PART TWO
THE GOURMET GARDEN
83–155

Entering the Garden

You can enjoy the delights of gardening without planting, cultivating, or watering. Some people raise plants in terrariums; others grow spices on window sills. I bloom flowers in the refrigerator, and everything in my garden is edible! There are no seasonal planting charts—no perennials, no annuals—I can enjoy Gourmet Bouquets the year round, and you can, too. Think of it: each bouquet is a charming party novelty, a delectable floral arrangement, and, considering today's interest in plants, flowers, and gardening, a most timely conversation piece. With *Gourmet Bouquet* you can create over thirty varieties of edible flowers as well as other distinctive blooming delicacies. And this is just the beginning. With imagination there is no limit to what you can create. It's all at your fingertips. Your culinary craft will be satisfying—both artistically and nutritionally.

You don't have to be an artist, a floral designer, or a gardener in order to create a magnificent bouquet. All it takes is a sharp paring knife, fresh vegetables, and a desire to express yourself. Don't be discouraged if at first your flowers aren't perfect: remember these flowers are edible. If at first you don't succeed, eat your mistakes.

Someone once remarked to me, "All you need for one of these bouquets is plenty of time, money, and talent." I vigorously disagree. What the bouquet really takes is ingenuity, practicality, and a touch of thrift: the ingenuity to *make something* from what is on hand, practicality to make *use* of those goods, and a dash of thrift for inspiration.

And how time-consuming is the creation of the bouquet? I'd like to let you in on a little secret; I sometimes make all my plans on the spur of the moment. The bouquet need not be organized with the precision and logistics of a military maneuver. Although I recognize the need for a workable plan, I suggest a light, casual approach. Have fun with it. The bouquet is designed with enjoyment in mind. So relax.

The inviting feature of gourmet flower making is that you can fit preparation time into nooks and crannies of your schedule without noticing the time spent. The actual cutting of the vegetables requires the most time, although I sometimes think waiting at the grocery store check stand does. Some of the flowers require less cutting and carving than others; it depends on how elaborate they are. It is difficult to predict a reliable time frame for each flower or bouquet, but as you continue making your flowers, your repertoire and expertise will increase, and the flowers will take much less time.

I suggest that you begin your first bouquet with radish blossoms (see page 92) and fill in with condiments (see page 131). For a small to medium bouquet, I purchase about four radish bunches. They take about forty-five minutes to carve and between fifteen minutes to one half hour to bloom in ice water. Vegetable flowers can be cut the evening before and left in ice water in the refrigerator till skewering time. Once the flowers and other embellishments have been cut and skewered, it's only a matter of putting the filler foliage (see page 85) into your container (see page 47) and attractively arranging the final bouquet.

The ornateness of your bouquet does not depend on your budget—but on your imagination. There's no waste; everything from the roots of the vegetables to the stems can be used creatively. The bouquet can be comprised of leftovers: last night's dinner rolls, toasted and cleverly cut into cookie cutter shapes, then topped with a condiment; or a pot roast, thinly sliced and rolled into rosettes. Cooked carrots (if they are not too soft) can also be delightfully recycled. All these leftovers can be transformed into blooming hors d'oeuvres. The current price of vegetables in your area determines the price of the vegetable flowers for your bouquet. So shop for supermarket specials and seasonal delights; then improvise and harmonize.

Finally, to make the most of your walk through the garden, begin, if you will, by leafing through the book and taking special notice of the full color pictures. Then turn to Part One, Bouquet Basics. Here you will discover lots of preparation tips and special features such as coloring, containers, and gadgets. Then go on to Part Two, The Gourmet Garden where you'll find specific illustrated step-by-step instructions for fashioning flowers, condiments, and other bouquet embellishments.

It is my sincere wish that you find the walk through this garden stimulating to your creativity, your sense of beauty, and, last but not least, your appetite.

ENTERING THE GARDEN

Part One

BOUQUET BASICS

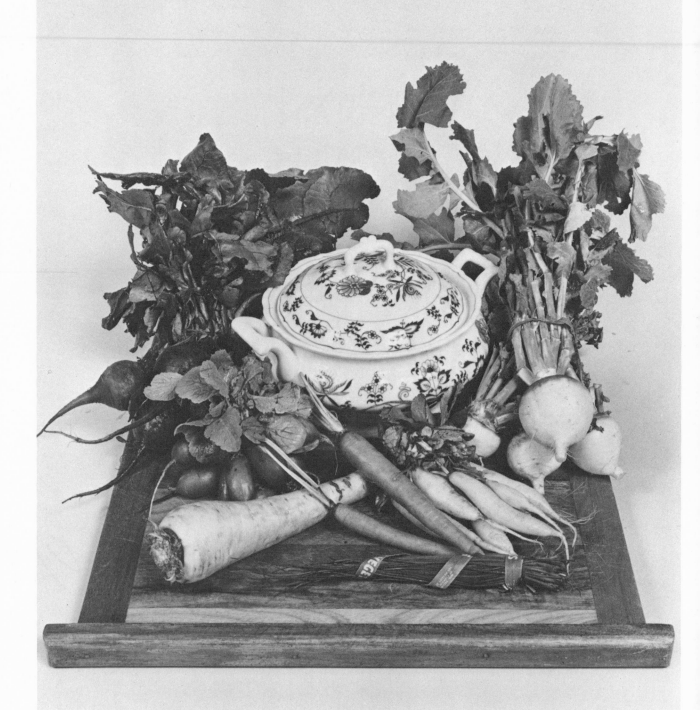

Putting It
All Together

An overview of bouquet making with hints on selecting, shaping, and serving your gourmet creation.

A Gourmet Bouquet is your creation. It can be elaborate and ornate or as simple and unpretentious as you like. You may give it as much or as little time as you care to. It can resemble a genuine floral arrangement or ascend into flights of fancy. Whatever you decide and whatever the result of your final creation, it will be a unique and appreciated center of attention because you created it. "But," you ask, "how do I put it all together?" Here are the steps to follow:

1. *Select* the flowers, foliage, stemmery, stickery, sniffery, and container you want to use. Begin with the bouquet plans (page 59) and scan The Gourmet Garden (page 83). List all the elements you plan to use.

2. *Shop* for the items needed.

3. *Slice, carve,* and *cut* the vegetables into flowers. Bloom the flowers in the refrigerator, if necessary.

4. *Skewer* everything that goes into the bouquet.

5. *Shape* the design of your bouquet by skewering in a pattern. See page 56 for suggestions.

6. *Serve* as a centerpiece, on a buffet table, as a unique salad, or as a meal in itself.

It's just as simple as that and, with a little more elaboration, I will walk you through, from purchasing to presentation.

Select

The first thing I do when planning my bouquet is to consider the occasion. How many people will there be? How many flowers or hors d'oeuvres will I need? (I usually figure on three vegetable flowers or hors d'oeuvres per person.) Where will the bouquet be placed, on a buffet table or on a dining table as a centerpiece for a dinner party? Will the bouquet bloom hors d'oeuvres or vegetable flowers or both? The answers to these questions will assure the most appropriate bouquet for the occasion.

The size and shape of the container are determined by the space available and by the theme of the occasion. This is where I begin. Then I select the filler foliage, the vegetable flowers, the condiments, and finally the stemmery, stickery, and sniffery, if any are to be used.

Shop

Before I do the shopping, I scan every cupboard and hidden spot in my refrigerator for anything I already have and can incorporate into the bouquet. Then I make a list (which I invariably don't stick to; this just makes me feel I'm being efficient). After making my purchases, I immediately tend to those vegetables that need crisping.

Slice

At this point, I start assembling all my gourmet gadgets and ice water. I pick the spot where I'm going to work—usually in the middle of the living room floor, where I sit cross legged with my back propped up against the couch. Though my style of preparation is casual, cleanliness is a major consideration when handling food, so I spread plenty of paper towels or sometimes tear open a brown paper shopping bag and place my cutting board on top. I place my vegetables on the cutting board beside a container of ice water waiting to receive each new blossom. Then I begin cutting, carving, scraping, and scooping. This is usually when friends or neighbors pop in and inquire, "Hey, what are you doing?"

The answer generally inspires curiosity, and compels the person (despite protests that he will get lost and sink amidst the pile of peels forever) to join in the carving. The great fun of the bouquet is not only in the product but in the preparation. All members of the household can join in and contribute their ingenuity. It's amazing how everyone gets absorbed! Then the laughter starts and the carving competition begins. Everyone's newly carved radish, turnip, or beet becomes an enchantingly original flower. No two seem to look alike. (I'm told there are thousands of species of flowers and hundreds of variations of these, so when I produce an unidentifiable, exotic-looking flower, I refer to this fact.) These carving gatherings often remind me of the old-fashioned taffy pulls; it seems that the preparation has turned into the social event and the bouquet is its by-product. Now if I could just figure out how to pull peels . . .

The technique involved in the carving of the flowers is one I call slivery slicing and mastering this technique is essential. This will make the difference between a stiff and unyielding lily and one that is pliable and graceful. Of utmost importance is a very sharp, smooth-edged knife. A serrated edge will not do for this procedure, as ruffles and ridges would appear in all the wrong places. The knife should be larger than a paring knife, but small enough to be handled with ease and dexterity. With a swift, clean motion, make the first slice diagonally into the vegetable. This will give you a good smooth starting surface. In order to make paper-thin slices, place the edge of the knife just under the surface and, with tiny back and forth motions, work the knife down to the bottom, pressing slightly against the vegetable. Don't expect the first slice to be perfect. At this stage, you're just limbering up your knife. It will probably take several attempts before you get it right. Don't get discouraged if you go through an entire turnip or daikon without producing a slice you can be proud of. Unless, of course, you are developing a case of vegetable elbow. At this point, it's time to take a break and make a salad with the rejects. What you are trying to achieve is a thin slice that is pliable enough for shaping and folding. This is particularly critical in making the Easter lily and yam rosette.

As each fabulous little creation is carved, plop it into ice water for proper blooming. (In the ice water the vegetables curl into shapes resembling real flowers.) After completing all the flowers you wish to make, place the ice water containing the flowers in the refrigerator. While your flowers are blooming, you can be coloring. Prepare the vegetable colors (if they are to be used) as described on pages 41 to 46. After these have been prepared, place them in the refrigerator to cool. Then prepare the container for the bouquet. If this part of the preparation brings you close to serving time, proceed to fill the container with filler foliage. Cover it with a cold moist paper towel or place it in the refrigerator, if you have room. If you are preparing a day in advance, leave the preparation of the container and filler foliage until just before you are ready to serve. Place the fully bloomed flowers in vegetable coloring until the desired color is achieved.

Skewer

While the flowers are coloring, skewer the stemmery, stickery, and sniffery. This should be done as close to serving time as possible. Store the remaining ingredients for refilling the bouquet. Since these are fantasy flowers, we need not adhere rigidly to the principles of floral design, and as these creations were made to be eaten, place them randomly with confidence and creative license.

Shape

You may wish to refer to Arranging Bouquets (page 56) and Chapter 4, Color Concoctions (page 41), for hints and suggestions, but do not feel bound by them. Floral arranging, an art in itself, requires some study and instruction beyond what I shall cover here, but don't let any lack of floral training inhibit your talent. Have a good time and try your hand with your own inventiveness.

Serve

Begin the evening with a bouquet of vegetable flowers. As the evening progresses, you may wish to transform the bouquet into blooming hors d'oeuvres. As some of the vegetables are eaten, gradually add the condiments, changing the theme, color, and shape. The flowers themselves, depending upon the vegetable from which they were fashioned, will remain fresh about one to two hours, or when glazed, till the following day (see below). However, I have found that most of the blossoms are eaten within the first half hour. So have plenty of refills ready in the refrigerator. Spray your bouquet with a fine mist of ice water just before serving. Dips served along with your bouquet are an appealing side dish. There is a wide variety of dips suitable for dipping anything. These incidentally are a favorite among recipe exchangers and neighborhood party arrangers, so a good recipe will not be difficult to find. Be sure to have enough dip available; it goes almost as fast as the vegetable flowers, since they are eaten together. The flavor of your dip can augment the theme of the bouquet. The dip can also be served in imaginative containers such as hollowed out melons, oranges, and tomatoes. See Containers and Bouquet Arrangements (page 47) for additional container suggestions.

Glazing

The idea of the Gourmet Bouquet is, of course, to display a beautiful centerpiece your guests can eat. However, if you expect that your vegetables won't be eaten within two or three hours, it is wise to glaze them; glazing insures against wilting and drooping. It not only keeps the vegetables fresh, but also polishes them with a bright lustre. The process of glazing can be done in several ways, using different additives. The glaze I use is an unflavored gelatin which acts as an edible sealer. For our purposes, I recommend an uncomplicated procedure that will preserve the flowers beautifully for the entire evening and usually the following morning.

Dissolve one package of unflavored gelatin in ¼ cup cold water. Heat this mixture, stirring constantly, until it is hot. Allow it to cool. Just when the gelatin starts to thicken, spoon it evenly over

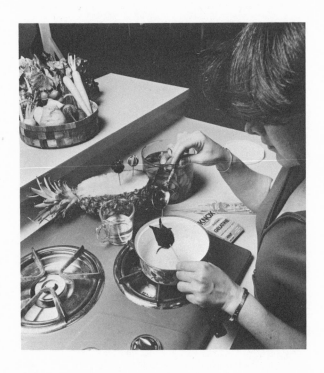

Stick the (still skewered) glazed flowers into a leftover pineapple or grapefruit shell and store in the refrigerator until serving time. This keeps the sides of all the flowers from bumping and sticking to each other until the glaze is hardened and sticking is no longer a hazard. Just before serving time, place the glazed flowers in the bouquet, being sure to announce to your guests that everything is edible.

Vegetable Vernacular

It occurs to me that since we are going to be working together, you should know the meanings of my vegetable vernacular. Since some of these terms are spontaneous creations, they won't be found in a respectable dictionary. The terms refer specifically to gourmet bouquet construction and I decided it would be helpful to have our own dictionary.

Bloom To drop the vegetables into ice water to allow them to curl into various shapes resembling real flowers.

Crisping The science and practice of keeping vegetables fresh and crunchy.

Feathering Making tiny fine slits at the ends of the petal of the vegetable flower, creating a feather-like appearance.

Filler Foliage Long, leafy vegetables such as parsley or bronze lettuce used to

the chilled, skewered flower. Hold the flower over the pan that you used for heating the gelatin, so the pan will catch the drippings. When the flower is completely covered, very gently shake off the excess. By the time you have finished glazing the flower, the gelatin has probably begun to set, leaving a thin, smooth, shiny coating. It is important to work rapidly when using gelatin glazes, for gelatin sets quickly; if it cools too much, it begins to set and is not liquid enough to spoon over the flowers. At the same time if it is too warm, it will not jell after reaching the flower. Sometimes it may be necessary to reheat and cool the gelatin mixture several times in order to coat all of the flowers. The short time span between the cooling and setting period is when quick spoonery is essential.

give the bouquet a fuller, more authentic-looking shape.

Floral Pick A slender wooden stick, green in color, with a thin wire attached to one end, used to support filler foliage.

Ribbons Thin strips of vegetables in various shapes and lengths.

Scallop To cut the edge of a vegetable into ornamental lines so that the edge has a pattern of hills and valleys.

Scissory The skillful use of scissors in cutting vegetable leaves to resemble flower petals.

Sniffery Hidden fragrance enhancers designed to entice the olfactory sense.

Stamen The protruding center of a flower.

Stickery Edible ornaments which protrude from the bouquet for visual interest and flavor.

Toothpickery Artful dexterity with regard to the placement of toothpicks. A most necessary and respected art.

Tuber A large, rounded root vegetable. In our bouquets, it refers to beets, rutabagas, and turnips.

Wedge A V-shaped cut, either vertical or horizontal.

Wiring Vegetables Wiring filler foliage to a floral pick by gathering several leaves into a small bunch and joining them to the pick by wrapping the wire tightly around them. (The wire should spiral down the pick. Make sure the wire end is secured tightly to the pick.)

2

A Seasonal Shopping Guide

A listing of appropriate bouquet components and suggestions on how and when to select them.

When I walk through the produce section of a market and see the colorful array of vegetables displayed, my thoughts inevitably turn to ways of transforming them into fresh and vibrant bouquets.

This chapter is designed to help you make full use of the many vegetable textures, colors, and shapes available and to answer any questions you might have concerning selection, seasonal availability, storage, and nutritional value. Each vegetable listing also includes the flowers and accents that are fashioned from it.

Before you go out to shop for vegetables, refer to seasonal availability. This will help you purchase the most vibrant, tasty, and economical flowers. Your bouquet may even assume a seasonal character, since your vegetable choices can change with the seasons.

If you are using whatever vegetables you already have on hand, then scan the list and become inspired by what you can do with them!

When preparing the vegetables for the bouquet, I use a washing solution which can be purchased at most health food stores. This helps remove chemical residues ordinary washing may leave.

Number of calories and amounts of carbohydrates are based on a 100-gram (3½-ounce) serving size.

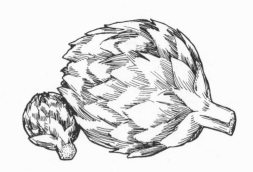

Artichoke (Large and Miniature)

Selection When using a large artichoke for the leaves of vegetable flowers, choose one that is heavy for its size. In both large and small artichokes, look for the greenest leaves, as free from blemish and brown spots as possible. The leaves should be tightly compacted around the head of the artichoke. Spreading leaves indicate age and an artichoke that is tough and bitter.

Storage Place immediately in the crisper.

Availability Peak season is March through May.

Nutritional Value An excellent source of iron; 20 calories; 9.9 grams of carbohydrates.

Use Large artichoke as leaves for flowers (see page 143); small artichoke as stickery (see page 143).

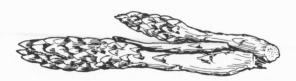

Asparagus

Selection Look for firm, well-formed, rounded spears with compact tips. Asparagus spears are generally purchased in bunches.

Storage Wrap in wet paper towels and keep in the refrigerator. Asparagus should be used as soon as possible.

Availability Peak season is March through June.

Nutritional Value An excellent source of vitamin C, niacin, thiamine, vitamin A, and iron; 27 calories; 2.2 grams of carbohydrates.

Use Container for a bouquet (see page 53).

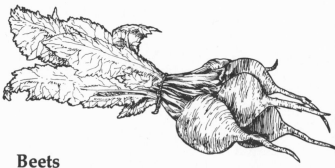

Beets

Selection Choose beets that are deep red in color and have smooth skins. The roots should be slender and firm and the tops fresh and green. Beets are generally sold in bunches.

Storage Beets will stay fresh in the refrigerator. Cut off the greens about an inch above the beet. Keep the beets in a plastic bag until ready to use. Keep the greens for use as filler foliage.

Availability Peak season is June through August, but they are available all year round.

Nutritional Value A good source of potassium; 43 calories; 9.9 grams of carbohydrates.

Use Flowers—tulip, poinsettia, carnation (see pages 125, 106, 121); beet tops as filler foliage (see page 88).

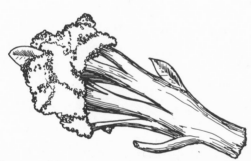

Broccoli

Selection Look for broccoli that is firm and dark green in color, with compact little clusters. Avoid clusters that are spread apart or yellow. These are signs of age.

Storage Keep in the refrigerator.

Availability Peak season is October through May.

Nutritional Value An excellent source of vitamin C, niacin, thiamine, riboflavin, vitamin A, iron, phosphorus, and calcium; 32 calories; 5.9 grams

of carbohydrates.

Use Container for a bouquet (see page 55).

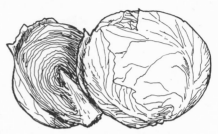

Cabbage

Selection Look for cabbage that is firm and heavy for its size. The leaves should be compact, and the head should feel solid. The coloring should be a rich green or maroon red and the head should be free of blemishes.

Storage Keep in the refrigerator.

Availability Year-round.

Nutritional Value An excellent source of vitamin C; calories—red 31, white 24; carbohydrates—red 6.9 grams, white 5.4 grams.

Use Flowers—lily, iris (see pages 110, 111).

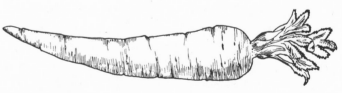

Carrots

Selection Look for firm, smooth carrots, rich in color.

Storage Carrots will store well in the refrigerator.

Availability Year-round.

Nutritional Value An excellent source of vitamin A; 42 calories; 9.7 grams of carbohydrates.

Use Flowers—pansy, lily; stamens (see pages 98, 100, 129, 130).

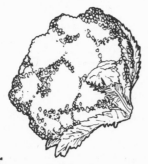

Cauliflower

Selection Choose cauliflower that has compact, white to creamy white little florets and is free of any discolored spots. If the leaves are still attached, they should be green and crisp.

Storage Keep in the refrigerator.

Availability Peak season is September through November.

Nutritional Value An excellent source of vitamin C and iron; 27 calories; 5.2 grams of carbohydrates.

Use Container for a bouquet, stickery (see pages 52, 139).

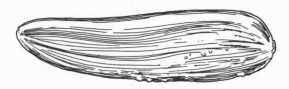

Cucumber

Selection Look for a firm, well-shaped cucumber with the largest circum-ference. The firmness is especially important here, since a soft cucumber will be bitter.

Storage Keep in the refrigerator.

Availability Year-round.

Nutritional Value An excellent source of iron; 15 calories; 3.4 grams of carbohydrates.

Use Container for a bouquet; skins as stemmery (see pages 53, 138).

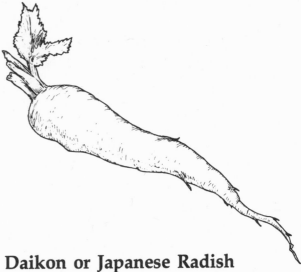

Daikon or Japanese Radish

Selection The diakon radish is often used in Oriental cooking. Look for a large, white root somewhat resembling a parsnip. The daikon should be firm, white, and free of scars or discoloration.

Storage Keep in the refrigerator.

Availability Year-round.

Nutritional Value Particularly high in vitamin C; 19 calories; 4.2 grams of carbohydrates.

Use Flowers—daffodil, daisy, rosette (see pages 100, 110, 116).

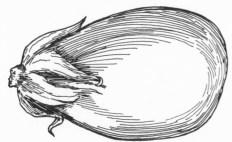

Eggplant

Selection Look for eggplants which are firm and have smooth skins. They should be a rich shade of purple. There are various shapes available, such as the European and Oriental eggplant. Since we are using the eggplant as a container, the larger, rounded one is most suitable.

Storage It is preferable to store this vegetable at approximately 50 degrees.

Availability Year-round, with a peak in late summer.

Nutritional Value Medium potassium; 25 calories; 5.6 grams of carbohydrates.

Use Container for a bouquet (see page 54).

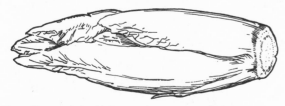

Endive (Belgian or French)

Selection Endive has small, elongated stalks with white leaves that become a pale green at the ends. Look for small, well-formed heads that are firm and crisp.

Storage Keep in the refrigerator in a plastic bag.

Availability In the summer months.

Nutritional Value Medium potassium; 15 calories; 3.2 grams of carbohydrates.

Use Flower—exotic endive (see page 107).

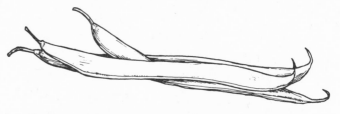

Green Beans, Snap Beans, or String Beans

Selection Look for beans that are firm, rich in color, and free of blemishes. Crispness is especially important, since the beans will be used in the bouquet as stemmery and will be eaten raw.

Storage Beans may be kept in the refrigerator and should be used soon after purchase.

Availability May through October.

Nutritional Value Good source of vitamin A; 32 calories; 7.1 grams of carbohydrates.

Use Stickery (see page 137).

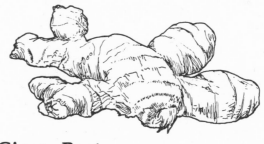

Ginger Root

Selection This brownish root, which seems to resemble a piece of plumbing, should be firm when you purchase it. You won't be needing very much for the bouquet, so if you are buying it for that purpose only, select a small piece. In addition to its use as sniffery in the bouquet, ginger root can enhance a wide variety of foods such as salads and fruit desserts.

Storage If you buy a small amount, there won't be much, if any, to store; however, it will keep well in the refrigerator.

Availability Year-round.

Nutritional Value An excellent source of iron; 49 calories; 9.5 grams of carbohydrates.

Use Sniffery (see page 148).

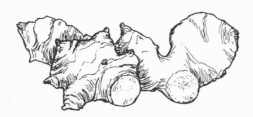

Jerusalem Artichoke or Sun Choke

Selection This is a small, brown root resembling ginger root. It has a crunchy texture and a nutlike taste. When purchasing, look for firmness.

Storage These can be kept in a plastic bag in the refrigerator.

Availability Late summer through winter.

Nutritional Value An excellent source of

niacin, thiamine, iron, phosphorus; 16.7 grams of carbohydrates.

Use Stickery (see page 141).

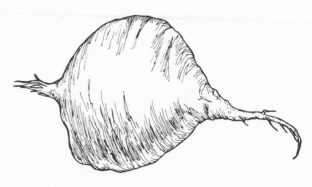

Jicima

Selection This is a large, brown root, somewhat resembling a brown potato, but larger. It is important to select a firm jicima so that it will be crunchy. In addition to its use in the bouquet, it can be sliced in salads and is sometimes considered a fruit. In any case, the taste is sweet, refreshing, and crunchy.

Storage Keep in the refrigerator. Cover cut pieces tightly with plastic wrap.

Availability Spring and summer months.

Use Star (see page 111).

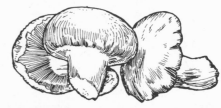

Mushrooms

Selection Look for brown, cream colored, or white caps which are smooth, firm, and closed.

Storage Mushrooms will keep well in the refrigerator.

Availability Year-round.

Nutritional Value An excellent source of niacin, riboflavin, thiamine, phosphorus; 28 calories; 4.4 grams of carbohydrates.

Use Stickery (see page 144).

Onions (Boiling Onions, Shallots, Chives, and Scallions)

Selection Boiling Onions: These should be firm, white, small, and rounded (for the nicest chrysanthemums).

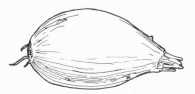

The skins should be papery thin and free of any soft spots. Avoid those which show signs of sprouting.

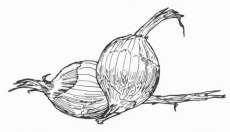

Shallots: These are very small, round onions. The outer covering is brown and papery; when this layer is removed, a light purple layer is revealed. Look for firm, small onions. Chives: These are a crisp, green vari-

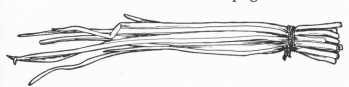

ety of onion used primarily for seasoning. Look for dark green, crisp, dry shoots which are free of blemishes. These are usually purchased in small bunches. Scallions: These are the variety of onion which have a white, elongated bulb at one end

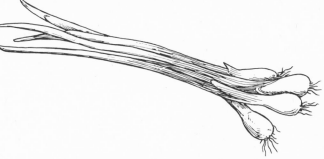

and long green shoots at the other. Look for well-formed, white bulbs which are firm and free of blemishes. The green shoots should be crisp and dry.

Storage Store boiling onions and shallots in a cool dry area. This will help prevent decay and sprouting. (Stored in this manner, onions will last for an indefinite period of time). Chives and scallions can be stored in the refrigerator. To keep them dry and to keep the aroma from spreading to other foods, store in an airtight, moisture-proof plastic bag. Use within a few days.

Availability Most types of onions are available year-round.

Nutritional Value High in vitamins A and C and iron; Onions: 38 calories, 8.7 grams of carbohydrates; Shallots, Chives, Scallions: 27 calories, 5.5 grams of carbohydrates.

Use Onion as flower—chrysanthemum; Shallots as sniffery; Chives as stickery; Scallion end as stemmery and white portion as onion curl (see pages 115, 147, 143, 140).

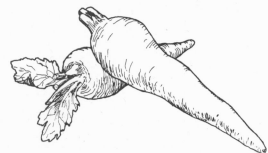

Parsnips

Selection Choose a firm, well-formed root that is cream color to a very light yellow.

Storage Parsnips will remain fresh in the refrigerator.

Availability Year-round, but peak season is October through April.

Nutritional Value An excellent source of vitamin C, thiamine, phosphorus; 53 calories; 12 grams of carbohydrates.

Use Flowers—pansy, petal flower, gardenia (see pages 101, 103).

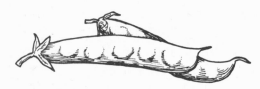

Peas (China Peas or Snow Peas)

Selection These are delicate little peas in a thin-shelled pod, sweeter than the larger variety. Look for a bright green pod which is smooth skinned and free of blemishes.

Storage Keep in the refrigerator.

Availability Peak season is March through June.

Nutritional Value An excellent source of vitamin C, thiamine, phosphorus; 53 calories; 12 grams of carbohydrates.

Use Stickery (see page 139).

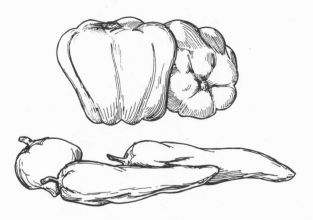

Peppers (Red and Green Bell and Chili)

Selection Look for smooth, firm, unblemished skins. They should be heavy for their size. Those peppers which have fully matured turn a brilliant red.

Storage Keep in the refrigerator.

Availability Peak season is June through September, though they are available year-round.

Nutritional Value Red Bell Peppers: An excellent source of vitamins A and C; 31 calories; 7.1 grams of carbohydrates. Green Bell Peppers: An excellent source of vitamin C; 22 calories; 4.8 grams of carbohydrates. Red Chili Peppers: An excellent source of vitamin C, niacin, thiamine, vitamin A, potassium, and iron; 65 calories, 15.8 grams of carbohydrates. Green Chili Peppers: An excellent source of vitamin C and niacin; 37 calories; 9.1 grams of carbohydrates.

Use Stickery (see page 138).

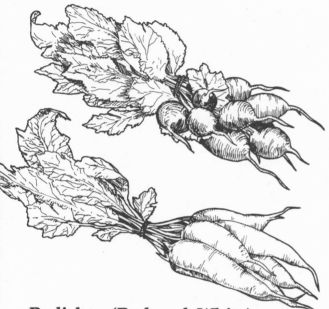

Radishes (Red and White)

Selection Red and white radishes are sold in bunches; select those that have fresh, green tops and are firm and free of blemishes or nicked spots. A variety of shapes and sizes of the red radish can be used in the bouquet. The larger and more unusual the shape, the more interesting the flower will be. Select small, well-formed white radishes. They should resemble small carrots and have firm, blemish-free skins.

Storage Store in an airtight plastic bag. Do not use radishes that are soft, since the resulting flowers will be soft and spongy.

Availability Red radishes are available year-round. Their peak season is May through July. White radishes are available from early spring through summer.

Nutritional Value Particularly high in vitamin C and iron; 17 calories; 3.6 grams of carbohydrates.

Use Flowers—radish blossoms, sweet pea, crocus, tulip, spray, clown (see pages 93, 113, 112, 126, 114, 97).

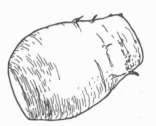

Rutabaga

Selection A rutabaga resembles a large turnip, but is light yellow in color. Choose large rutabagas that are heavy for their size and firm with smooth skins.

Storage Keep in a plastic bag in the refrigerator.

Availability Peak season is October through March.

Nutritional Value Particularly high in niacin and vitamin C; 46 calories; 11 grams of carbohydrates.

Use Flower—three-petaled tulip, tuber tulip, Herbie the Frog (see pages (123, 125, 78).

Squash (Banana, Crooked Neck, Summer, Zucchini)

Selection Banana Squash: This squash is generally displayed cut in pieces. Look for a good, rich, yellow-orange

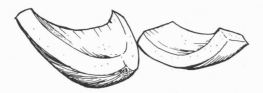

color, and squash that is heavy for its size. Crooked Neck Squash: This is a medium to small yellow squash which has a narrow, curved neck.

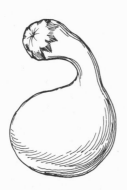

Since it is used in the bouquet as stickery, select firm, smooth squash with clear, bright yellow skins. Summer Squash: These are light green in color with natural, round ridges resembling a kind of flower. Look

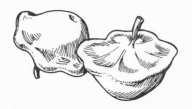

for firm, smooth skins. For the bouquet, select smaller, round summer squash. Zucchini: Choose zucchini that are firm and rich green in color, with smooth skins. For use as a container, select the largest in length and circumference.

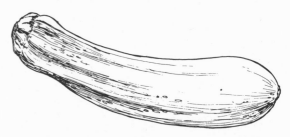

Storage Keep all squash in the refrigerator, banana squash and zucchini in an airtight plastic bag.

Availability Although banana squash is a winter squash and crooked neck is a summer squash, both are sometimes available in the spring. Summer squash and zucchini are available during the spring and summer months.

Nutritional Value Banana Squash: Particularly high in vitamin A; between 50 and 60 calories; 15 grams of carbohydrates. Crooked Neck Squash: High in vitamin A; 15 calories; 3 grams of carbohydrates. Summer Squash: High in vitamin A; 14 calories; 3.1 grams of carbohydrates. Zucchini: High in niacin; 17 calories; 3 grams of carbohydrates.

Use Banana, crooked neck and summer squash as stickery; zucchini as a container for a bouquet (see pages 139, 142, 53).

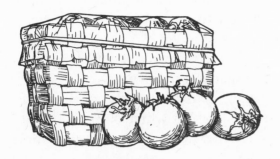

Tomatoes (Cherry)

Selection Cherry tomatoes are a small, sweet variety of tomato and are generally sold in little baskets. Look for firm, round tomatoes with smooth skins, rich and red in color.

Storage Keep the tomatoes in a cool area at about 50 degrees. If this is not possible, refrigerate and use soon.

Availability Tomatoes are available year-round, but their peak season is June through August.

Nutritional Value Particularly high in vitamin C; 22 calories; 4.7 grams of carbohydrates.

Use Stickery (see page 144).

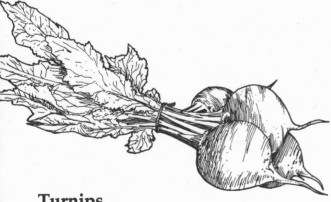

Turnips

Selection Choose turnips that are small to medium in size and of various shapes. Look for firm turnips with smooth skins and avoid those with deep scars. The greens should be fresh and crisp.

Storage Remove the tops for use as filler foliage. Place the turnips in a plastic bag in the refrigerator.

Availability Found year-round, their peak season is October through March.

Nutritional Value High in vitamin C; 30 calories; 6.6 grams of carbohydrates.

Use Flowers—tulip, peony, carnation, camellia, lily (see pages 125, 124, 121, 119, 118).

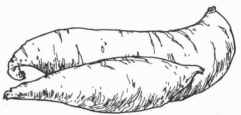

Yams

Selection Yams are the sweet variety of potato. The outside skin is a brownish orange. Inside, the yam is a light orange. Look for a firm, well-formed yam that is large in circumference. In the bouquet, yams are used to fashion rosettes, so the larger they are in circumference, the easier they will be to work with. As you become more familiar with making the yam rosette, you can vary the size of the finished flower by selecting a yam which is smaller in diameter.

Storage Keep in a cool, dry place. It is preferable not to store them in the refrigerator.

Availability Year-round.

Nutritional Value Raw yams are particularly high in potassium and thiamine; 101 calories; 23.2 grams of carbohydrates.

Use Flower—rosette (see page 116).

Root vegetables such as potatoes, carrots, parsnips, onions, and turnips can be stored up to several weeks. However, the longer the vegetables are stored, the lower their nutritional value is. So for the best nutritional value, it is best to purchase vegetables close to the time of use. Vegetables which keep best out of the refrigerator are eggplant, onions, and yams.

3

Gourmet Gadgetry

*An introduction to the tools and equipment used in
bouquet artistry.*

In this chapter, I'd like to share with you information about some of the gadgets I have found helpful in constructing the bouquet. There are descriptions of what these gadgets look like, what they are used for, and where they can be purchased. With a few exceptions, these gadgets can be found in the most modestly supplied kitchen. They are simply regular household items used in some irregular ways. While specific gadgets are suggested, I would like to emphasize that the key to using these suggestions is improvisation. My improvisational gadgetability was born of impatience. When I was creating, I didn't have the time or the inclination to drop everything and run to the store for what I needed. I simply looked around me and used what I had. You may come up with a creative use for something that is not at all associated with its original purpose. (If you do, would you please let me know?)

The gadgets are separated into two groups. The first group includes the essentials, the key tools needed in flower fashioning. The second group contains the auxiliaries: they act as supports and offer assistance in actual bouquet construction. These auxiliaries are not used in every bouquet but are helpful in con-

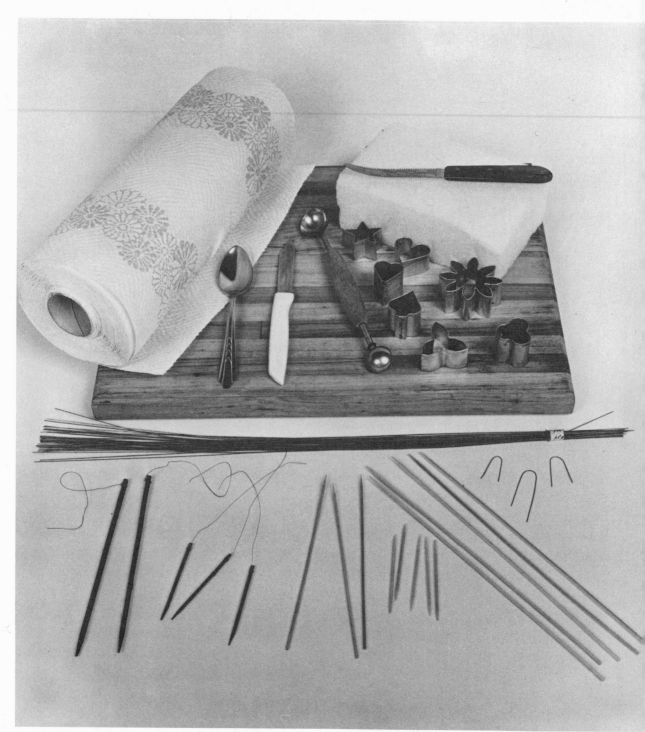

Front: 6" floral picks, 3" floral picks, wooden skewers in assorted lengths, wire affixers. *Above:* 22-gauge wire. *On cutting board:* paper towels, grapefruit spoon, paring knife, melon baller, hors d'oeuvre cutters, Styrofoam®, grapefruit knife.

structing certain bouquets, such as the bouquet A Condiment Christmas, which uses a base constructed from Styrofoam®.

The Essentials (listed in order of necessity)

Paring Knife

The paring knife is a small, thin, flexible-blade knife used for cutting small objects and for detail work. I recommend a small, very thin blade. The particular knife blade I use seems to have a great effect on the intricacy of my flower. The thinner the blade the more detail I am able to achieve. I also find that it takes a little while to find just the right-fitting handle. I suppose this is much like finding the right tennis racket. This may not make much difference at first, but as you become more proficient, these points become more important. A good thing to keep in mind is the comfort and ease with which you can handle each tool.

Ice Water

Ice water is an essential part of vegetable artistry. It is the culinary equivalent of time-lapse photography. This is where the real wizardry and magic take place. For ice water is what makes the vegetables bloom. Almost before your eyes, radishes become roses, onions become chrysanthemums, and daikons become daisies.

Grapefruit Knife

The grapefruit knife has a curved blade with a serrated edge. In the bouquet, it is used to cut around curved areas. Just about any grapefruit knife will do. However, I recommend one with a less flexible blade, since this will give you a little more leverage when working with fruits such as pineapple.

Melon Baller

Generally this tool is used for making little melon balls. It has a half-sphere at each end, with a handle in between, enabling you to scoop and scrape out portions of the vegetables. It's pretty handy for getting around small curved surfaces and has a large and small end so you can switch, depending on the size of the vegetable. Melon ballers can be purchased at supermarkets and gourmet supply shops.

Grapefruit Spoon

A grapefruit spoon is a spoon with a serrated edge. This is used mostly to scrape and scoop. Since you want to make sure that the handle won't come off in mid-scoop, a grapefruit spoon with a sturdy handle is best.

French Knife

The French knife has a large, straight blade. If you don't have a French knife, any large knife will do. The important thing is that the blade be thin. This will aid you in making thin slices. This knife is used to make *very* thin slices for such vegetable flowers as the turnip Easter lily and the yam rosette.

Toothpicks

There are several kinds of toothpicks. I recommend the round ones. They are sturdier and won't break and splinter under slight pressure, a very important consideration when working with food.

Wooden Skewers

Wooden skewers are long wooden sticks that come in various lengths. In purchasing these, keep in mind that the length of your skewers plays an important part in determining the height of your bouquet. Skewers can usually be purchased at your local grocery store in 12", 10", or 6" lengths.

Hors d'Oeuvre Cutters

These are small versions of cookie cutters. They are used for cutting condiments such as pimiento or cheese and come in a variety of shapes. They are just the right size for very little hands that want to add their creativity to the bouquet. Incidentally, children love working with these little cutters and can be happily occupied for hours, provided, of course, that they feel theirs is an important contribution. Hors d'oeuvre cutters can be purchased at a supermarket or gourmet supply shop.

Daisy Cookie Cutter

This is a regular cookie cutter in the shape of a daisy. It is used for a variety of vegetables. In The Gourmet Garden, it is used to make daisies from jicima as well as from any of the tuber vegetables.

Kitchen Scissors

Kitchen scissors are scissors which have been set aside for kitchen use only. They can be any size that is easily handled.

Paper Towels

Having moist paper towels on hand during the cutting procedure is helpful for minor cleanup, but more important they are used to keep the finished bouquet fresh until serving time.

Spray Bottle

The spray bottle is filled with ice water and used to give the bouquet a final refreshing mist just before serving. It doesn't have to be any particular kind of spray bottle, just one that emits a fine spray.

The Extras

Styrofoam®

When using floral picks in a deep hollow container, such as a decorative porcelain bowl, cut a layer of Styrofoam® 1" thick to fit into the bottom of the container. Floral picks with the filler foliage are then stuck into the Styrofoam® until it no longer shows, and a nice full and tight appearance is achieved on top. Styrofoam® is used also as the base for the bouquet A Condiment Christmas.

Floral Picks

A floral pick is a slim, green, wooden stick with a thin wire attached to one end. This little piece of wood and wire is usually used for the filler foliage. The wire portion is actually wound around the vegetable, and the wooden shaft is then placed in the container. This little aid is most valuable, since it allows us a much wider range of vegetable choices by adding support to those vegetables which otherwise would be too delicate. Floral picks can be purchased from most craft or floral supply shops. They come in lengths of 3″ and 6″. When selecting the floral picks, do so with the height of your bouquet in mind.

22-Gauge Wire

This thin wire is used for the stems of some of the vegetable flowers and lends a soft curving line to the bouquet. The use of the wire is optional and not required until you get into some fancy fashioning. I have found it to be a handy household item just to have around, in any case. 22-gauge wire is also used to make wire affixers. Like the floral picks, the 22-gauge wire can be purchased in most craft supply stores or from the local florist.

Wire Affixers

Wire affixers are used for attaching filler foliage to Styrofoam®. They are shaped like a U and are inserted first through the core of the filler foliage, then into the Styrofoam®. This is done in one swift, easy motion. The wire affixers are easy to make. Cut the 22-gauge wire into 1″ to 1½″ lengths with wire cutters or scissors. Then bend the wires into a U shape. These affixers may be purchased ready made, but I must confess that I don't know what they're called. And besides, I advocate doing it yourself, especially since it's so easy. Wire affixers are used to arrange the Condiment Christmas tree and the lily pad mound for Herbie the Frog.

Cellophane Wrap

This wrap is used to give the bouquet a festive appearance, especially when it is presented as a gift (see page 81). I usually use colored cellophane, which can be purchased in most party supply stores. Clear plastic wrap will do just as well, if you top it off with a bow.

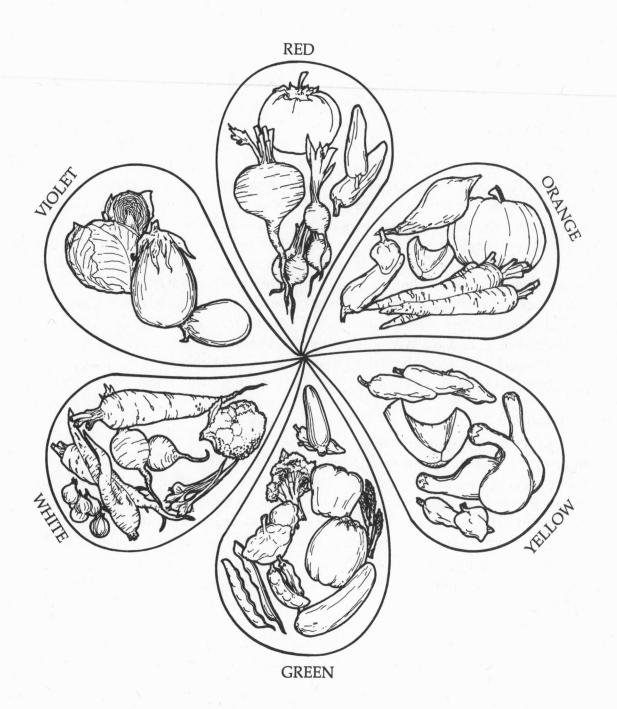

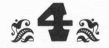

Color Concoctions

A palette of natural vegetable tints to add color to your bouquet.

This chapter is all about color. Colorful vegetables are irresistible. I'm talking about the natural color of vegetables such as beets, carrots, and red cabbage. I like to vary and combine them. I like the impact of an orange carrot stamen combined with a beet tulip, or a yellow rutabaga perched atop a purple eggplant container. At the same time, why be limited to the realistic use of colors? Why not have, say, a blue onion chrysanthemum or a purple Easter lily? It is easy to do so by using natural fruit and vegetable derivatives. I discovered most of these derivatives after I realized that anything that stained me did a great job on the vegetable as well. (I'm sorry to say that adulthood hasn't provided an immunity to berry stains. I still get purple fingers and lips.) This chapter also deals with color harmonies; knowing color harmony is helpful in putting together an ornamental bouquet. For fingertip reference to natural vegetable colors, the color wheel is separated into categories of vegetables within the color spectrum and how they may be combined for greater color effectiveness.

Color Harmonies

Here are some very basic color harmonies which will give you some guidelines for using color combinations. You are certainly not limited to these harmonies, and I encourage you to try your own color combinations.

Monochromatic

A monochromatic color scheme is one that uses various shades and tints of a color, shade being a darker variation and tint being the lighter variation. Applied to our bouquet, that would mean picking a color and using several of its tones. For example, a beet, radishes, and some pink turnip peonies could be mixed in one monochromatic red bouquet. This color harmony produces a subdued, more uniform effect. The filler foliage will supply the depth of color needed in the background. (See the Cabbage Patch, Color Plate 6.)

Complementary

Complementary colors are those colors directly across from each other on the color wheel. This color harmony produces a vibrant and forceful effect that will electrify your bouquet. It is an effective harmony for the splash and excitement of summer. A dazzling example of this is a combination of yellow rutabaga tulips with grape juice–tinted crocuses. (See the Springtime Bouquet, Color Plate 2.)

Another example of complementary harmony is the green of the parsley background with the red tomatoes and cranberries in A Condiment Christmas. (See Color Plate 11.)

Analogous

This harmony, made up of colors close to each other on the color wheel—for example, yellow and orange or red and orange—also produces an exciting color combination. Some examples of vegetable combinations with analogous colors are beet tulips with carrot pansies or beet poinsettas with banana squash condiments. (See the Flower Fiesta, Color Plate 7.)

Warm and Cool Colors

Advancing colors—yellows, oranges, and reds—are those which are warm and have a tendency to stand out. Receding colors—blues, greens, and violets—are those which are cooler and stay in the background. When planning your arrangement, try to place the advancing vegetable colors at the focal point (the center of attention), while placing the receding colors toward the outside.

How to Use the Vegetable Color Wheel

The color wheel is a quick vegetable color guide. It is divided into groups of vegetables falling within a particular

RED
Tomatoes
Red Bell Peppers
Chili Peppers
Radishes
Beets

VIOLET
Red Cabbage
Eggplant
Shallots

ORANGE
Banana Squash
Carrots
Chili Peppers
Pumpkin
Yams

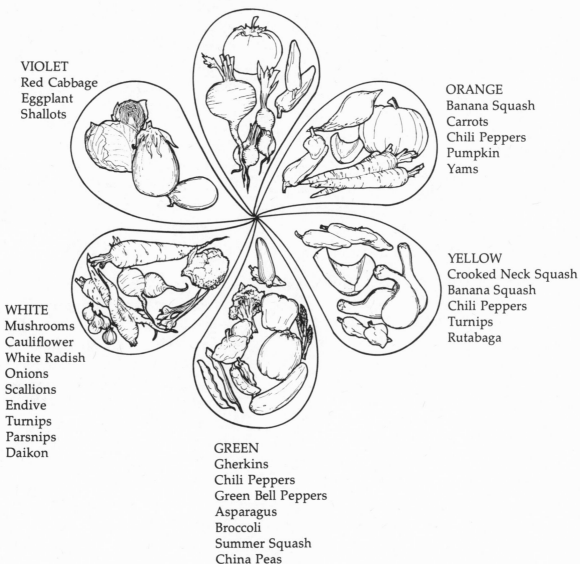

YELLOW
Crooked Neck Squash
Banana Squash
Chili Peppers
Turnips
Rutabaga

WHITE
Mushrooms
Cauliflower
White Radish
Onions
Scallions
Endive
Turnips
Parsnips
Daikon

GREEN
Gherkins
Chili Peppers
Green Bell Peppers
Asparagus
Broccoli
Summer Squash
China Peas
Green Beans
Zucchini
Cucumbers

color range. Now you can see at a glance all the vegetables in the particular color you selected.

STEP-BY-STEP

1. Select a color harmony from those offered on page 42 or feel free to use your own.
2. Glance at the color wheel and choose the vegetables falling within these color categories. Those vegetables in the white group may, of course, be colored to fit your color scheme. (See Coloring Vegetables, below.)
3. Refer to Chapter 2, A Seasonal Shopping Guide, for all of the different blossoms that can be fashioned from a particular vegetable. Then simply select the flowers you like and begin.

When making color selections, keep your table appointments in mind. Consider the possibility of matching your bouquet to your table accessories.

Coloring Vegetables

Cut, carve, and bloom all of the vegetables before coloring. This will allow a more even color distribution.

Red

Beet juice is an excellent source of red and pink colors. I use several techniques for achieving these colors; the quickest method is to slice a soft fresh beet and rub it over another vegetable such as a turnip. I have discovered that the softer

the beet is, the more juice it contains. If the turnip is carved to resemble a carnation and the beet slice is rubbed over the tips, the effect is very realistic; you will have produced a red-tipped carnation. Another method is to drop the other vegetable flowers into ice water that contains a beet tulip. While the tulip is blooming it shares its color with the other vegetables. The pink in the turnip peony (pictured in Color Plate 6) was achieved in this way. Use just enough ice water to cover the vegetables, allowing them to bloom. Too much water will dilute the beet juice, resulting in a weak tint of pink. This preparation, most effective with parsnips and turnips, should remain in the refrigerator overnight.

The beet brew is another method of extracting red from the beet. Boil several peeled beets in a small amount of water. When the beets are soft, pour them into a blender along with the water and set on liquify. This produces a puree. Drop the vegetable to be colored into the brew and allow to stand for about an hour. Store this home brew in a tightly-capped container in the refrigerator. It can be reused for tinting.

Indigo

Concord grapes, when they are in season, are a good source of purple. I use the skins for coloring parsnip petals because of the beautiful shade they produce. Drop about 1 cup of grapes into a blender and add 2 tablespoons of boiling water. Set the blender on liquify. Then strain whatever peels remain, pressing them with a spoon through the strainer. Cool the juice and then drop the vegetable into this juice and let it stand for about an hour.

Another shade of indigo is produced from concentrated frozen grape juice. Just thaw the concentrate and immerse the cut or carved vegetable in the undiluted juice for about an hour. Remove the vegetable and lightly rinse it to prevent juice drips.

Blue

Fresh, frozen, or canned blueberries are all natural sources of blue. Just throw them into the blender and set on liquify. Dip the vegetables to be colored in this blueberry bouillon. The length of time I leave the vegetables in the coloring depends on the shade I wish to achieve. Naturally, the longer the vegetable remains in the liquid, the darker it will become—up to a point. If you expect to leave the vegetables in the liquid for a long period of time, place them in the refrigerator.

Yellow

For yellow, I have relied on the natural color of rutabaga, yellow crooked neck squash, and banana squash. However, on occasion when I needed a strong yellow for a tulip, I have used yellow food coloring. This is the only artificial color I use. Some day soon, I hope to come across a natural source of yellow coloring that is safe and edible.

Orange

The only source of orange I use is, again, the natural one—carrots. I simply vary the cutting angles to produce different flowers which fool the eye; however, the tastebuds know it's the same natural crunchy raw carrot.

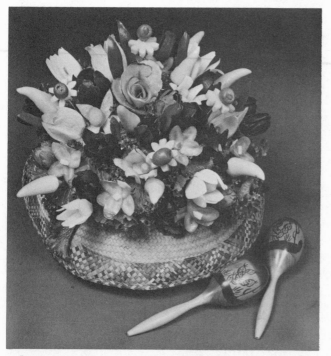

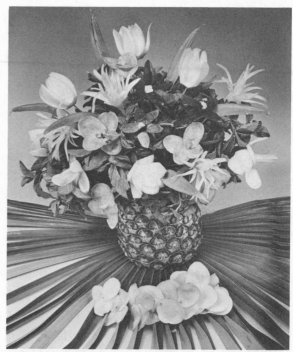

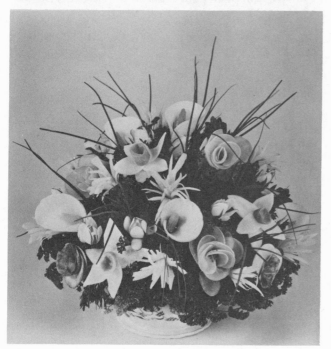

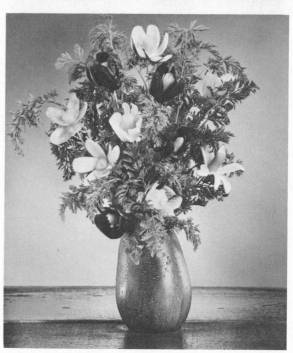

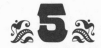

Containers and Bouquet Arrangements

Ideas for choosing imaginative containers and arranging exquisite bouquets.

A container is the vase for the bouquet. Many containers can be as edible as the flowers within. There are tips to learn on preparing these containers, keeping the fruit variety firm and the edible variety tasty, adding the little extra touches, and saving the situation if at first you don't succeed. Other containers can be fashioned from sundries in your home. Still others may be a cherished piece of china, a basket, or even a hat!

If I know the mood of the occasion, the first thing I usually do is scan my "container computer"; that is, I scan every-thing in sight, looking for just the right container. If edible or fruit containers are to be used, I begin thinking about the appropriate size vegetable flowers for that container. The selection process is usually determined by what is available. I find I'm most creative and feel the most satisfaction when my imagination is guided by what I call budgeted artistry, or how to make the most of what you've got. Variations and additions to your container can spark a special touch of interest and edible whimsy.

In this chapter we will also touch

lightly on selection hints as they pertain to fruit and vegetable containers. A more complete discussion is found in A Seasonal Shopping Guide, page 23.

An essential part of arranging a bouquet is its proportion; that is, the size of the bouquet in relationship to the container. I would like to emphasize that in this chapter I have touched only the surface of what your own ingenuity can develop and that these are merely guides showing you how possibilities can spring from improbabilities. I have found these particular containers suitable for most occasions. They are easy, imaginative, and, most important of all, fun to use.

Allow your imagination to take you to all corners of the house and every other area of your environment for these containers. You will find that you're able to create a container from things you never dreamed possible. The other day, I caught myself appraising the telephone as a suitable bouquet container. I quickly regained my composure as I thought of the consequences. Could you imagine if it rang during a party? I could just picture myself talking into a rutabaga.

Anything from discarded cottage cheese containers covered with colored foil to coffee cans covered with various colored ribbons can be used. Have you ever thought of using an old tea kettle? How about an old hat box or any other suitably shaped carton? All of these containers can be trimmed with ribbons, colored tapes, and foils. Even cellophane can be gathered around your container and trimmed with ribbon or yarn. Children are very imaginative with these kinds of suggestions and are most anxious to help in making containers.

Eggshells make interesting individual centerpiece containers. Simply save shells of eggs which were broken in half and used earlier. No need to trim the jagged edges unless you insist, in which case, this may be done delicately with small manicure scissors. Make a pedestal for the eggshell by cutting a disc ½" thick from a large carrot or daikon or any other suitable vegetable. Then simply scoop out the center of the disc with a cookie cutter. Place the pointed end of the eggshell in the center so that it rests snugly. Delicately fill the shell with the blossom end of parsley until snug enough to support the flowers on toothpicks. The small petal flowers are best suited for this kind of container, since they are the most delicate and practically weightless.

Collectible Containers

Collectible containers are fun and very easy to use, since very little preparation is involved. Simply select the most appropriate container and proceed. Keep in mind that the kind of container you use will set the mood of your bouquet.

If you would like your bouquet to enhance an elegant setting, choose the appropriate embellishments. I suggest silver, porcelain, or glass containers. A silver champagne bucket is beautifully displayed with the bouquet for an anniversary or other formal occasion and is large enough to hold a very large bouquet. For a touch of refinement, I have also prepared the bouquet in a large glass punch bowl. One of my favorite containers is a porcelain soup tureen (see Color Plate 4). It creates a homey, traditional effect and is perfect for a Thanksgiving dinner. A basket container adds a casual country air to an airy, light spring or summer bouquet (see Springtime Bouquet, Color Plate 2).

Sombrero Surprise

Have you ever thought of using a Mexican straw hat as a container for your bouquet? It immediately sets the stage for the festivities and brings out exclamations of surprise. Magnifico! Invert your sombrero and line only the deep portion with foil, or insert another container for firmness and retention of shape. Fill the hat in the usual manner with your favorite vegetable flowers (see Flower Fiesta, Color Plate 7).

Pedestal Containers

Pedestal containers of various heights are suitable for many different occasions and add a light feminine touch for ladies' functions such as luncheons and wedding showers. If you are using the pedestal container as a centerpiece for a sit-

down meal, be sure the large portion of the bouquet is well above or well below eye level. Craning necks, though humorous at times, are an indication that your beautiful bouquet is an obstacle rather than an attraction.

Fanciful Fruits

Have you ever considered using the rind of a fruit over again in a functional way that would add to your own creation? Rather than discarding used or leftover fruit peels, use them as the container for your bouquet. Use a portion of a round fruit which has been cut in half, since a wedge portion would not give your arrangement sufficient depth or support. Hollow out the remainder of any melon you wish. Allow a thickness of approximately 1". You may scallop the edges if you wish, or cut V shapes, creating a star-like pattern, or simply trim to leave a

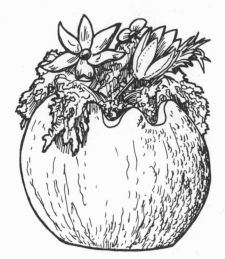

clean, smooth edge. Make sure to shave a small portion off the bottom so that the container will stand on its own. Refrigerate overnight or place in the freezer portion of the refrigerator for several hours. This will help refresh the fruit rind. Line the inside of the rind with foil and fill with some filler foliage.

Pineapple Pot

The rind of a pineapple is easy to use and generally will keep its freshness. To prepare the pineapple, cut off the top portion, leaving ¾ of the pineapple for the container. Hollow out the inside with a grapefruit knife, being sure to leave a wall approximately 1″ thick to assure firmness. Dry the inside with a paper towel. You may want to cut out small pieces at various levels of the pineapple so that pieces of filler foliage can

be inserted, creating greater interest. Turn it upside down and slice a thin portion off the bottom for stability. Refrigerate overnight or place in the freezer for several hours. Insert filler foliage and vegetable flowers.

Citrus Cups

Oranges and grapefruits may be cut at the top, leaving ¾ of the peel, or may simply be cut in half. To hollow out, use a grapefruit knife or grapefruit spoon, making sure to clean out all parts of the inside; that is, don't leave any grapefruit or orange. The peel of these fruits is pretty firm, but any excess fruit inside will produce sogginess. So remove everything down to the white of the peel. Stuff with filler foliage and small vegetable flowers.

Edible Containers

These are my favorite of all containers, since they can be eaten along with the vegetables, leaving nothing but the wooden skewers at the end of your meal. Your guests will surely admire your cleverness and practicality, and will probably want to eat your cups and saucers as well.

Bread Basket

Any uncut, hard, crisp bread of thick consistency (such as sheepherder or pumpernickel) makes a wonderful container (see Italian Antipasto Artistry,

Color Plate 1). I suggest a round or elongated shape. A hard crust is essential so the skewers will be held firmly in place. Slice a thin sliver off the top and hollow out with a grapefruit knife, leaving a wall about 3″ thick, so the sides and bottom will not collapse. Try lining the inside walls with cream cheese or another favorite spread. Next put in the filler foliage, making sure to insert it tightly, and then add the vegetable flowers. A touch of cream cheese applied around the edges with a pastry tube is a delightful complement to your bread. Try sprinkling chopped chives on top of the cream cheese.

Marshmallow Magic

Marshmallows are fun to use and come in a variety of colors. The trouble with using them is that they frequently find their way to my mouth before they reach the container. Assembling this container is much like playing with tinker toys. I am thoroughly convinced of its therapeutic value, since once I am absorbed in its assembly, everything else is forgotten. If you are a child (and who isn't?) you'll enjoy this one.

Get some good thick toothpicks. Start with a form, preferably a small one, like a cottage cheese container. Begin by fitting a toothpick between two marshmallows and pressing in equally from both sides so that the toothpick does not show, but is equally inserted in each marshmallow. Press another toothpick half way through the side of one of the marshmallows and follow this with another marshmallow and so on until you have circled the container and the last marshmallow is affixed to the first. Now begin the next row up. Repeat the procedure with one additional step; that is, place a toothpick half way through the top of a marshmallow in the existing circle and stick another marshmallow on top of the remaining portion of toothpick. Then proceed as with the first circle. Repeat both of these steps until you have reached the desired size and shape.

There will be some variation in the shape of the final container, since the marshmallows themselves are not equal in shape. However, we can allow for creative license in this instance, particularly since it's a very authentic-sounding excuse, and no one will know it was unintentional. This will be our secret.

You may wish to fill in the shape with pieces of firm fruit such as apple or pineapple, placed in various positions using the same method of toothpickery. It is best to leave the original container inside, as the softness of the marshmallow will not hold the weight of various vegetable flowers. Fill this container with any of the filler foliage you choose and proceed to insert vegetable flowers.

Vegetable Containers

Green or Red Pepper Pots

Slice the top quarter off the pepper, making sure you leave a large enough opening to fill the pepper with ease. Turn it upside down and make another thin slice on the bottom to stabilize the centerpiece. Hollow out the inside; then proceed to fill with filler foliage. Tightly pack the filler foliage and top off with a more delicate petal flower vegetable.

Casual Cauliflower

This vegetable is easy to use and requires little preparation. Select a medium to large cauliflower, making sure the white portion is clean and that no brown spots are visible. Just a word here about brown spots; they have a definite effect on the taste buds. I have known guests to circumvent an entire bouquet due to one tenacious brown spot. Slice off the bottom portion close to the root, being careful not to cut the root off. This is done so that the arrangement won't wobble, spilling vegetables, cauliflower, and your creative efforts. If, after all this, your cauliflower still wobbles, try sticking several toothpicks through the bottom at various strategic locations. If you get carried away, simply turn the cauliflower over and use it as a toothpick

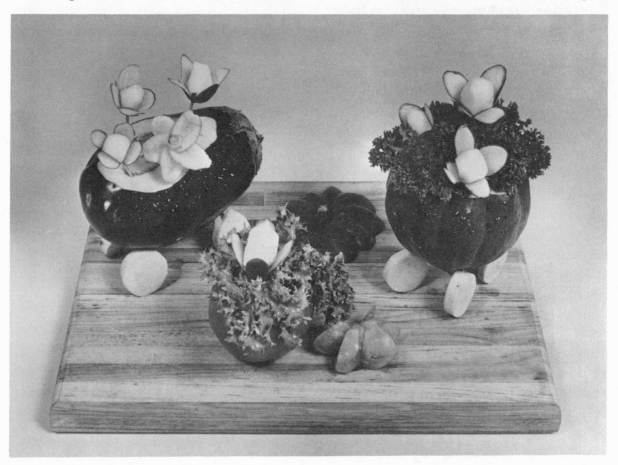

Left: Eggplant Carriage. *Center:* Tomato Cup. *Right:* Cinderella Squash.

holder, or discard and proceed to the next container. I suggest using the smaller vegetable flowers in a variety of colors. To fill in the arrangement, add filler foliage on flower picks.

Zucchini Boat

Select the zucchini or hothouse cucumber largest in circumference that you can find. This will give your bouquet greater stability. Shave off a thin slice from the bottom portion, turn over, and cut a thicker slice off the top. This is where the vegetable flowers will be placed. Choose from the smaller, more delicate of the vegetable flowers. Place on toothpicks and arrange along the length of the zucchini or cucumber. Fill in with filler foliage for greater fullness and interest.

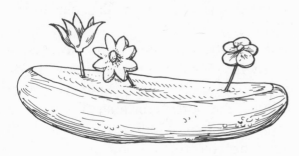

Concentric Cabbage

The colorful red cabbage is easy to work with, keeps well, and requires very little preparation. I use red cabbage because of its vivid color; however, if you have regular green cabbage on hand, please feel free to use it. Place the cabbage with the core side down. Cut off about ⅓ of the cabbage and hollow out, leaving a thickness of about 2" to the outside wall

all around the cabbage. Fill with tied, washed bunches of parsley or any other leafy variety of filler foliage. Whatever filler foliage you use, the key is to be sure to pack it tightly so that your bouquet will be firm and your vegetable flowers held in place securely.

Squash Cup

Any kind of squash will do and all can be prepared in the same manner. Simply cut off the top portion, exposing a large enough area to insert the vegetable flowers easily. Leave at least ¾ of the squash intact, and cut a thin slice off the bottom for stability. Fill the squash with filler foliage; then proceed with your choice of medium size vegetable flowers.

Cinderella Squash

To form a Cinderella Squash, simply add four carrot discs from a carrot which is very large in diameter to a round squash. The discs should be approximately 1½" thick if they are to support the squash carriage and be attached at the bottom with toothpicks. If they are to be attached at all four sides, the discs may be much thinner. Again attach with a toothpick and whimsically top off with a black olive in the center. Children enjoy the story book enchantment of the Cinderella Squash.

Asparagus Accents

Asparagus stalks make a most unusual and easy-to-use container. When the stalks have served their purpose as a

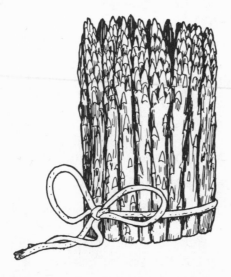

container, they can be served another day as a cooked vegetable. Special hints: select firm, fresh asparagus stalks, securely tied in a medium to large size bunch. Pay particular attention to the color. It should be a good rich green the entire length of the stalk. A white color at the tip may indicate toughness. Gather several bunches of asparagus stalks and estimate the size that you would like your container to be by the number of bunches you are holding.

The night before you assemble your bouquet, crisp your asparagus by untying the bunches. Wash each bunch thoroughly and wrap in the wet paper towel. The asparagus can then be stored overnight in the refrigerator. This method will add crispness and keep your vegetable fresh. Sometimes there is a variation in the length of the asparagus. If you wish to even this out, you may, of course, cut them all the same length from the bottom. I like the natural uneven

look, so I leave them as they are.

The following morning, when preparing your asparagus container, gather up all the stalks and tie them neatly with the most brightly colored ribbon or yarn you can find. This part always reminds me of wrapping a package. (I was always the one to get my finger tied in the middle of the bow.) You might find another hand helpful. However, I discovered my own ingenuity while caught in strange contortions when no help was available. (It *can* be done.) The next step is simply to fill the top, first with the filler foliage and then with the vegetable flowers. If you wish to vary the height of your bouquet, simply use wire cutters to cut the wooden skewers to the desired length, but cut from the flat end instead of the pointed end. You may also use toothpicks, if you like.

A variation of Asparagus Accents, if you wish to use fewer asparagus stalks, is to arrange the stalks next to each other around the outside of a small basket or other round container, and garnish with a bright, colorful ribbon.

Eggplant Elegance

Eggplant usually stores well and will remain fairly fresh for a reasonable length of time. The main consideration when selecting this vegetable as a container is to choose a fairly large one with a smooth, firm skin and good color. Cut off the top portion containing the stem so that you still have a good ¾ of the eggplant left. Now turn the eggplant

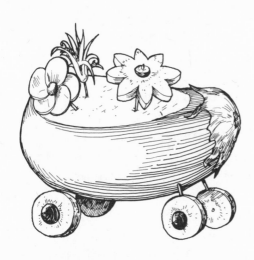

will give your bouquet a wilted look and surely alienate your guests. Crisp in the same manner as the asparagus. The number of bunches you select will depend again on the size you would like your finished container to be. Put several bunches together and tie securely with ribbon. Fill with any kind of vegetable flowers, since this is a very sturdy container that will support flowers of all sizes.

over and slice off a thin portion of the bottom so that the arrangement will stand firmly. Then add your filler foliage, followed by the flower vegetables.

Another use of the eggplant is to make an Eggplant Carriage. For this, purchase a medium size, curved eggplant. Lay it on its side so that the curved ends are up. Cut out a round portion close to the top, nearer the fat portion, leaving the stem intact. Next, cut from a very wide carrot four slices about 1½" thick for wheels and use toothpicks to attach them to the sides of the eggplant. Place a black olive in the center of each wheel. Proceed to fill the carriage with vegetable flowers; top with a bow and serve chilled. This is an excellent container for a baby shower or a children's party (see photograph, page 52).

Broccoli Vase

Select broccoli that is firm and rich in color. Be especially cautious about brown spots on the blossoms, as they

Tomato Cups

I would recommend the use of extra large tomatoes if they are used as a centerpiece and medium sized if used for individual servings. For a centerpiece, cut a star shape out of the stem end of the tomato. Next, fill with short pieces of parsley, again making sure the parsley is tightly packed. Top this off with a selection of small, delicate, vegetable flowers, placed on toothpicks. For individual servings, select medium to small tomatoes and cut the same as for centerpiece use. Make additional shallow wedges running the length of the tomato, but make sure you don't pierce the inner wall. Load a pastry

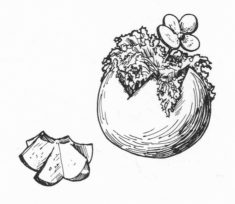

tube with cream cheese and fill the wedges; this will convey a festive I-went-to-a-lot-of-trouble look when really you didn't. I promise, no one will know but you and me. Fill the top in the same way as directed for the tomato centerpiece.

Arranging Bouquets

Concentric Construction

One of the considerations when putting your bouquet together is the shape it will take. You might be wondering *why* the shapes of these bouquets are generally symmetrical, *how* I am able to arrange them in this shape, *where* the various components should be placed, and *when* the bouquets should be arranged.

Why? Placed in a symmetrical shape, the vegetable flowers are conveniently accessible from all sides. Symmetry is perhaps the easiest and fastest of the floral shapes to achieve with a minimum of handling. Since our flowers are to be eaten, not only is it important for our guests to be able to help themselves easily but also the less the flowers are handled after construction, the better. Other shapes require additional materials and the kind of elaborate handling which is better left for nature's flowers. Symmetry supplies balance and a certain formality which adds elegance to the bouquet.

How? Considerable latitude can be exercised in the construction of symmetri-cal shapes. The design can be varied by arranging the vegetable flowers loosely (widely spaced) or tightly (ingredients touching); the latter technique resembles a continental bouquet. In this kind of arrangement, flowers of various sizes and colors are placed very closely together. The filler foliage plays an important part in permitting this kind of placement. The more tightly the filler foliage is fitted into the container, the more closely the ingredients can be placed. The filler foliage may be long-stemmed mustard greens in a large container—which produce a large, spectacular arrangement (see Cabbage Patch, Color Plate 6)—or the watercress inserted tightly into a small, dainty container—which results in a small, dainty bouquet (see Pansy Picnic, Color Plate 3). When constructing the symmetrical bouquet, place the ingredients so that they are evenly distributed throughout. Look down on it from above to make sure there aren't any stray blossoms popping out, then step back from it. If it looks pleasing to you, give yourself a pat on the back and have a leftover. If, however, you would like to change the appearance, do so by simply rearranging the ingredients, being careful to handle only the skewers. Each bouquet seems to have a personality all of its own. Therefore, it's almost impossible to create two exactly alike.

Occasionally, other shapes and modifications of symmetry develop, such as a modified rectangle, square, or oblong.

This is perhaps due to the shape of the container. If you are using a zucchini container, for example, the placement of skewered blossoms along its natural, oblong curve will modify the symmetry of the bouquet. If this happens, WONDERFUL! If you like it, continue to use the same technique of arranging this newly formed shape.

Where? The filler foliage establishes the height and density of your bouquet. Insert the filler foliage tightly into your container to give the bouquet a look of abundance as well as to support the vegetable flowers. At times it is necessary to use Styrofoam® in the bottom of the container for added height when the rim of a large container extends beyond the top of the filler foliage (see the Cabbage Patch, Color Plate 6).

The emphasis of the Gourmet Bouquet is on the unique appetizing quality of the flowers rather than the principles of floral design. Since the bouquet incorporates a quality of improvisation, arrange the blossoms by following this same technique—one I call Fit-The-Blossom-into-An-Open-Space. Begin by placing the largest, most brightly colored blossoms at the focal point or center of interest (see Flower Fiesta, Color Plate 7). You may have several of these large, outstanding blossoms in one bouquet; just arrange the rest of the blossoms around this focal point, fitting each blossom into an open space until your bouquet is completely full.

When placing stemmery or stickery into the bouquet, keep in mind that their purpose is to accent or sometimes break up the symmetry. For the most pleasing effect, place them at regular intervals throughout the entire bouquet (see the Easter Bouquet, Color Plate 4).

Place the condiment capers and sneaky sniffery randomly among the vegetable blossoms.

When? Construction of the bouquet should be completed just before serving time. For the freshest bouquet, arrange it as close to serving time as possible—I recommend about ten to fifteen minutes before. This will give you enough time to enjoy yourself while constructing your bouquet, and give it a final ice-water misting.

When Flowers Have a Mind of Their Own

Have you ever wondered how florists make their bouquets stay in place and hold their shape? Occasionally, special aids are enlisted in their craft, and these same aids can be borrowed for the construction of some of our bouquets, such as A Condiment Christmas. I refer to these aids as auxiliaries. They help support the blossoms and expand the possibilities for bouquet arrangement. These auxiliaries are not necessary for every bouquet; in fact you need not use them at all, but it's helpful to know they are available.

To use the *floral pick,* hold it beside the bottom or core of the filler foliage, stemmery, or sniffery and wind the little wire in a spiral around both the vegetable and the pick. It's just that simple. This attaches the vegetables to the sharp-pointed picks, enabling you to place them exactly where you want them to be. This is sometimes referred to as wiring.

Wire affixers are thin, small pieces of wire, shaped into a V. They are particularly handy when working with Styrofoam®, as they allow us to affix filler foliage to it. (See A Condiment Christmas, page 76.) To use the affixers, hold the core of the filler foliage up against the Styrofoam® and push an affixer through core and Styrofoam® in one motion. Begin at the bottom and affix each new layer on top of the previous one in order to conceal the wires.

Styrofoam® gives special support in constructions such as A Condiment Christmas and Herbie the Frog. When using several pieces of Styrofoam® be sure to secure all pieces to one another with extra long wire affixers (make them by extending the length of the wire). To cover the Styrofoam® with foliage, use wire affixers of normal size.

Shape and Height

A general guide for choosing the size and shape of your container is that the actual arrangement should be 1½ to 2 times taller than the container itself; this will give you the best proportion. Keep in mind also that the larger, heavier vegetable flowers will require a larger, heavier container. For example, a pumpkin container is appropriate for the rutabaga tulip. The carrot pansy is more suitable to the zucchini container. The shape and height of the container you select will depend greatly on the theme of the occasion as well as on the particular kind of gourmet bouquet that it will hold.

The bouquet may be a spectacular addition to a buffet table; in this case, the only limitation on the height and width of the bouquet and container is the size of the buffet table and the amount of space available. Remember your bouquet is edible and you'll want your guests to enjoy your creative efforts, so do have it conveniently located. Using your good judgment will lead you to the appropriate bouquet and the right container.

6

A Bouquet
for All Seasons

---

*A step-by-step guide to fashioning and serving
gourmet bouquets.*

You may be wondering just when to use a particular bouquet and how to combine the wide choice of ingredients. In this chapter, all the bouquet elements are combined in various ways to produce holiday, seasonal, and international bouquets. Because of the almost infinite possibilities, I think it will be useful to have a guideline showing which ingredients to combine as well as which steps I use for the construction of each bouquet. Different cultures, customs, and languages have always been fascinating to me. This, along with the notion that tastebuds seem to transcend cultural barriers, is what inspired me to incorporate international bouquets in

this chapter. (Perhaps the U.N. should exchange bouquets?)

I offer these bouquets as a guideline; I would like to emphasize that the ingredients need not be limited to the ones I have chosen to use. Nothing says you can't mix cultures. You can mix any ingredients and even create a smorgasbord bouquet. (What could be more international than that?)

Serve your bouquet on a buffet or dinner table alongside an assortment of dips. Some guests, captivated by your artistry but unfamiliar with the bouquet idea, may need an encouraging "Help yourself, it's all edible. Pull out a blossom and dunk it in the dips." The bouquet can be an elaborate hors d'oeuvre or can take the place of chips served with a dip. It can replace a salad or be a meal itself. Or, it can be for display only, as an inventive substitute for cut flowers, to add a whimsical touch to any occasion.

Suggestions for each of these uses are offered in this chapter. No matter how the bouquet is served, you can be sure it will generate excitement.

Bachelor Bouquet

This bouquet is especially designed for those who wish to have elegance with minimal preparation. It is made up entirely of radish blossoms and requires little in the way of preparation other than cutting and ice water blooming.

INGREDIENTS

Container Basket
Filler Foliage Parsley
Vegetable Flowers Radish blossoms
Special Hints One radish blossom design may be used throughout the bouquet if you prefer. This bouquet may be as small or as large as you like, so vary the size of the bouquet and the container to change the effect.

STEP-BY-STEP

1. Cut and bloom the radish blossoms. About four bunches are sufficient for the bouquet pictured; this includes reserve blossoms.

2. While the flowers are blooming, tightly fit the parsley into the basket.
3. Skewer the flowers.
4. Place the flowers in the bouquet.
5. Give the bouquet a final misting of ice water and serve.

Though this bouquet is made entirely of radish blossoms, it can still be the main attraction at a romantic candlelight dinner. Try several different containers such as glass or even a silver wine basket to set the mood. If you wish, you may even use one radish blossom design throughout the entire bouquet. This bouquet complements the most elaborate or the simplest of meals. Try serving the Bachelor Bouquet beside a puffy cheese omelette. The textures and colors combine to give just the right touch of elegance and simplicity with a minimum of preparation.

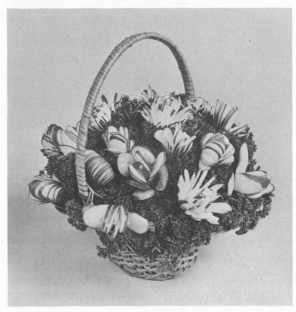

Bachelor Bouquet ready to serve

Italian Antipasto Artistry

COLOR PLATE 1

This bouquet contains virtually everything you might find in an Italian antipasto salad. Whenever I think of Italy, it brings to mind red colors, (predominant in this bouquet), prosciutto, mozzarella, salami, pasta, fine Italian wine, and spumoni, all of which can be incorporated into the evening's meal.

INGREDIENTS

Container Sheepherder Bread Basket
Filler Foliage Parsley
Vegetable Flowers Radish tulip with carrot spray stamen, radish daisy with carrot disc stamen, beet tulip with carrot spray stamen
Condiment Capers Marinated artichoke hearts, pimiento poppy with carrot tip stamen (use carrot disc to prop it up), salami rosette with olive and cream cheese ornaments
Stickery Bread sticks and chives

STEP-BY-STEP

1. Cut all the vegetable flowers and bloom them in ice water.
2. While the flowers are blooming, assemble and skewer the condiments. Then place them in the refrigerator to preserve freshness.
3. Wire the chives and breadsticks.
4. Prepare the bread by cutting out the center (See Edible Containers, page 50.)
5. Fill the bread with parsley.
6. Skewer the vegetable flowers and place them in the bouquet along with the condiments and stickery.

A dip I enjoy serving along with the bouquet is made with plain yogurt, fresh dill weed, sweet basil, fresh minced garlic, and kimmil. Add these seasonings to suit your taste and serve it chilled.

Springtime Bouquet

COLOR PLATE 2

This bouquet contains all the splendid colors and vibrant freshness of springtime. The basket offers country charm; the greenery adds lacy fullness. All together they make a quaint bouquet reminiscent of old world enchantment.

INGREDIENTS

Container Oval basket with handle
Filler Foliage Parsley
Flowers Beet and turnip tulips, three-petaled rutabaga tulip, daikon daffodil, radish crocus
Stemmery Cucumber peels (See page 138 for wiring instructions.)
Special Hints See Chapter 4, Color Concoctions, for crocus coloring. Glaze the vegetable flowers including the stemmery if your bouquet is to keep till the following day.

STEP-BY-STEP

1. Cut and bloom all the vegetable flowers.
2. While the flowers are blooming, prepare and chill the coloring you wish

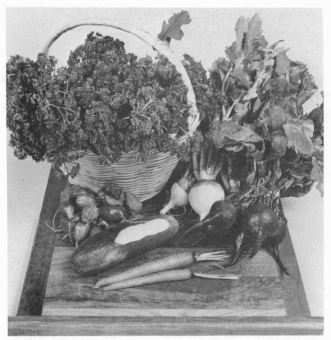

Ingredients

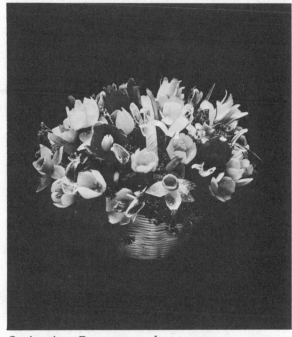

Springtime Bouquet ready to serve

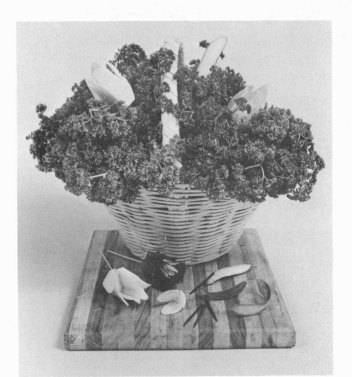

Steps 4 and 5

to use.

3. Place the flowers in the chilled coloring and let stand till the desired effect is achieved.

4. Place the crisped parsley in the basket close together, since this will shape your bouquet and securely hold the flowers in place.

5. Skewer the vegetable flowers and glaze if necessary. Then place them in the bouquet putting the large brightly colored blossoms in the center. Then arrange the rest of the blossoms in a symmetrical pattern until the basket has a colorful fullness.

6. Now arrange the stemmery around the bouquet wherever you think it needs an accent.

7. Give the bouquet a final ice water misting. This will not affect glazing.

I love mixing seasons with these spectacular spoofs by placing a Spring Bouquet on my coffee table in the middle of winter. The comments and exclamations are almost as delightful as the joy and brightness brought into the room by the bouquet.

Pansy Picnic

COLOR PLATE 3

The picnic pansy baskets are suggested for a luncheon or any casual setting, perhaps at a card party when a low calorie snack is welcome. Recycle baskets from a recent fruit purchase, so that you'll have several bouquets to place strategically on a coffee table, dinner table, or on the card table during snack time.

INGREDIENTS

Container Fruit basket lined with foil and trimmed with ribbon

Vegetable Flowers Parsnip pansy, radish crocus, radish sweet pea, radish tulip

Filler Foliage Watercress

Special Hints Glaze the vegetable flowers if your bouquet is to be maintained till the following day.

STEP-BY-STEP

1. Cut and bloom all of the vegetable flowers.
2. While the flowers are blooming, pre-

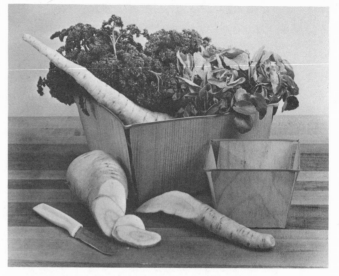

Ingredients

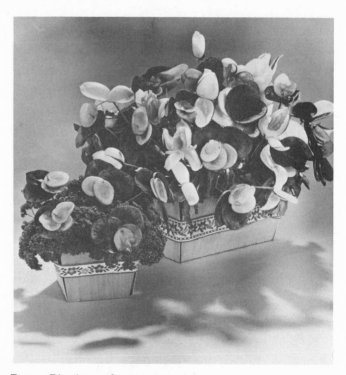

Pansy Picnic ready to serve

pare and chill the vegetable coloring you wish to use.

3. Place the vegetables in coloring until the desired shade is achieved.
4. Place the crisped watercress tightly in the basket.
5. Skewer the vegetables; glaze, if desired, and place them in the bouquet.
6. Give the bouquet a final ice water misting.

Since the filler foliage is watercress, you can use it in a salad after it has been used in the bouquet. The picnic pansies go well with a low-calorie dip made with plain yogurt, garlic powder, and a touch of paprika for color.

Stickery Chives
Special Hints If your Easter Bouquet is to be a display bouquet, glaze the vegetable flowers.

STEP-BY-STEP

1. Cut all the vegetable flowers and bloom in ice water.
2. Immerse bloomed vegetables in the desired vegetable coloring.
3. Wire the chive stickery and refrigerate.
4. Tightly fill the container with crisped parsley. Lightly mist with ice water.
5. Skewer all flowers; glaze, if desired, place in the bouquet.
6. Add the chive stickery.
7. Give the bouquet a final misting and

Easter Bouquet

COLOR PLATE 4

The Easter Bouquet pictured was designed primarily as a display bouquet. It makes a light spring addition to the holiday table. All of the ingredients in the bouquet may be eaten; however, when constructing a bouquet *specifically* for eating, add condiments.

INGREDIENTS
Container Porcelain soup tureen
Filler Foliage Parsley
Vegetable Flowers Turnip Easter lily, daikon daffodil, white radish spray, daikon rosette (fashioned the same way as the yam rosette), beet carnation, parsnip pansy, radish blossom #2 and #3, radish tulip

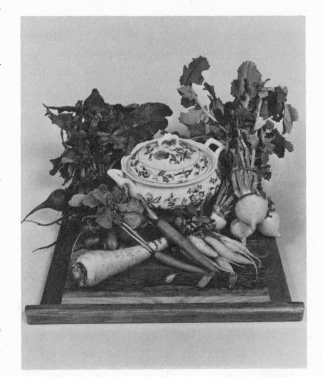

Ingredients

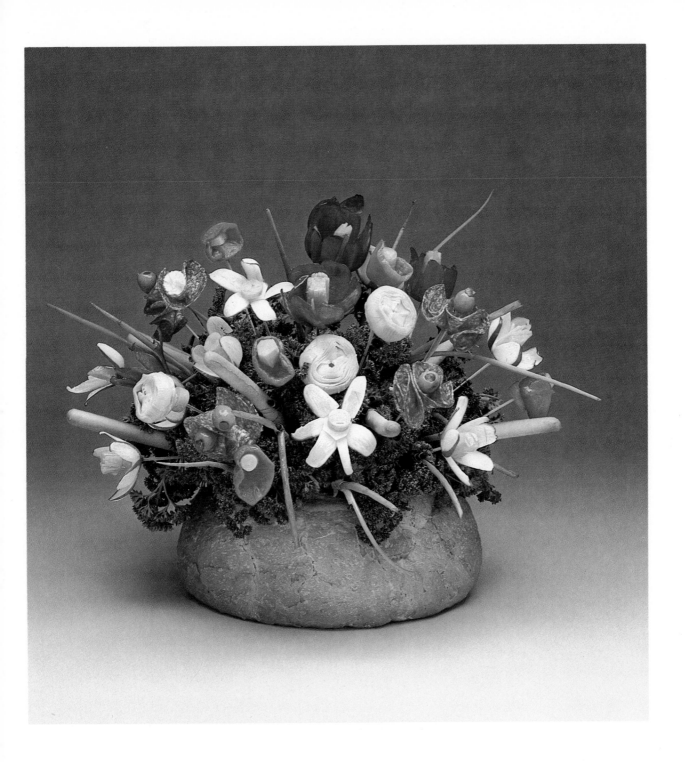

Color Plate 1, Italian Antipasto Artistry (page 61)

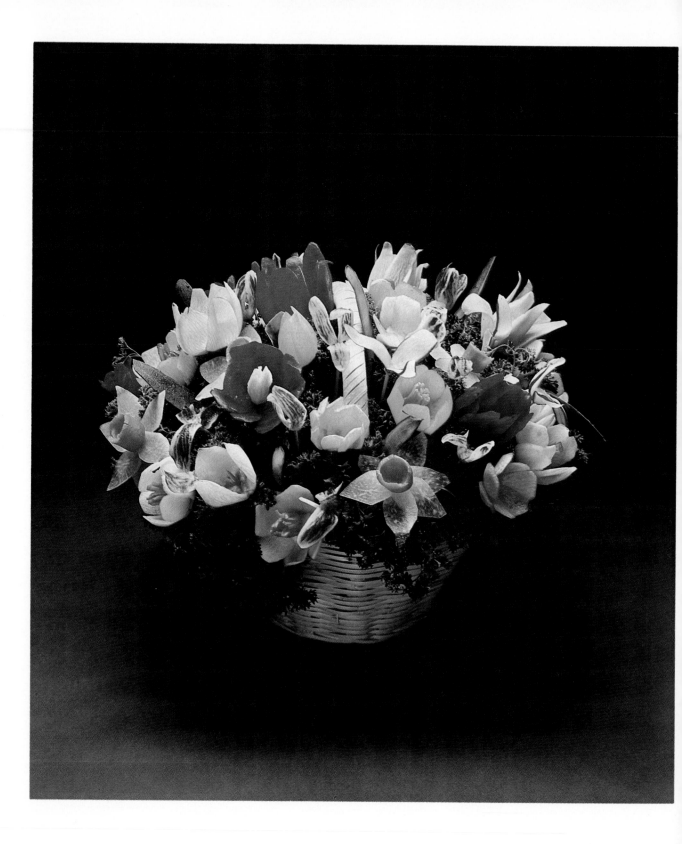

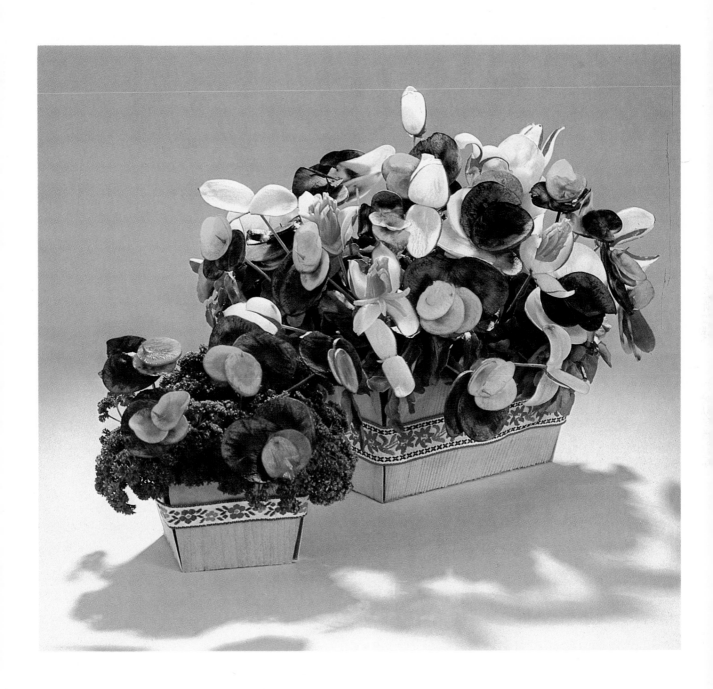

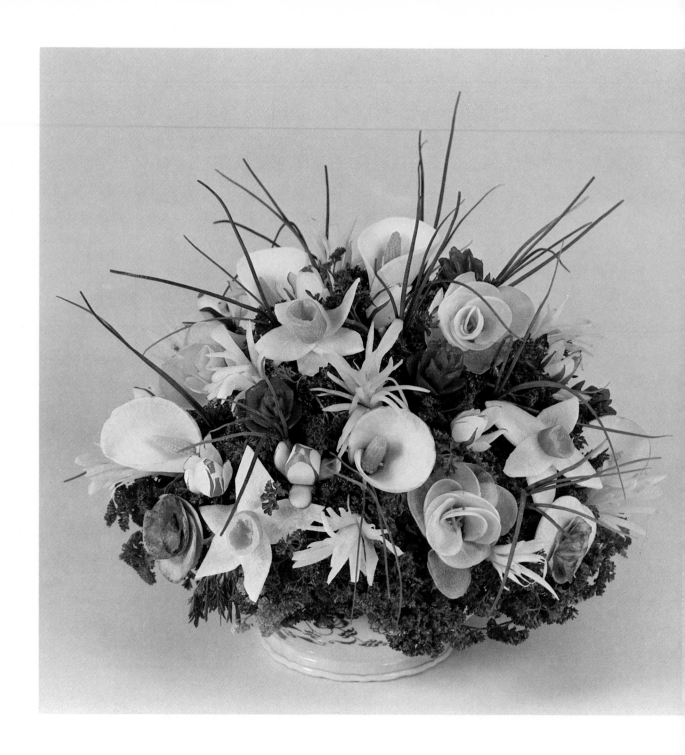

Color Plate 4, Easter Bouquet (page 64)   *Color Plate 5,* Eggplant Extravaganza (page 65) ➡

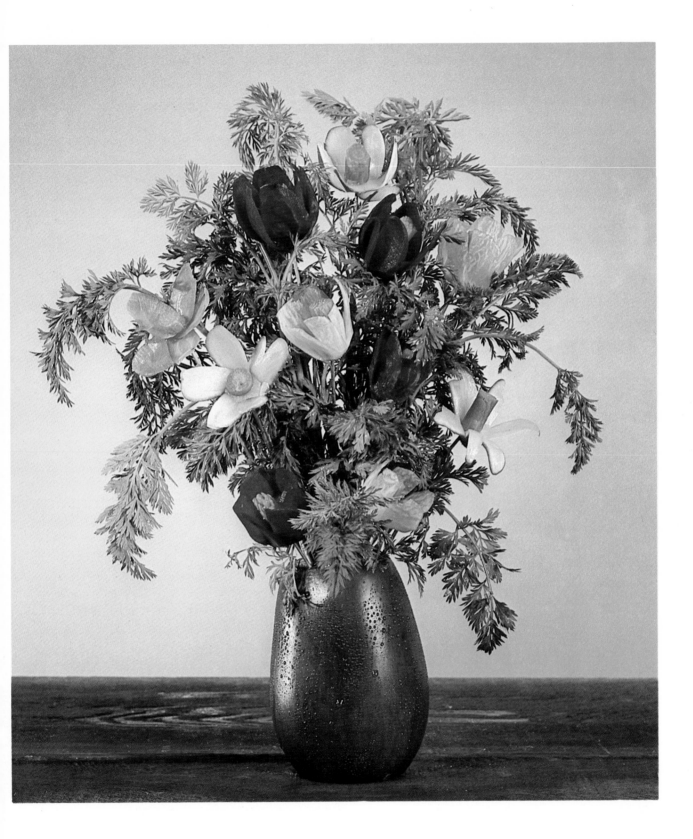

Color Plate 6, Cabbage Patch (page 67)

Color Plate 7, Flower Fiesta (page 69)

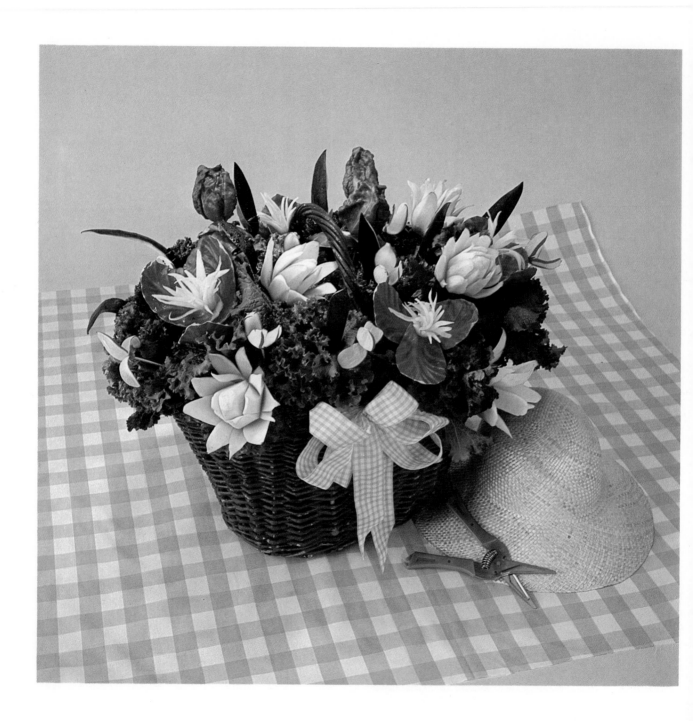

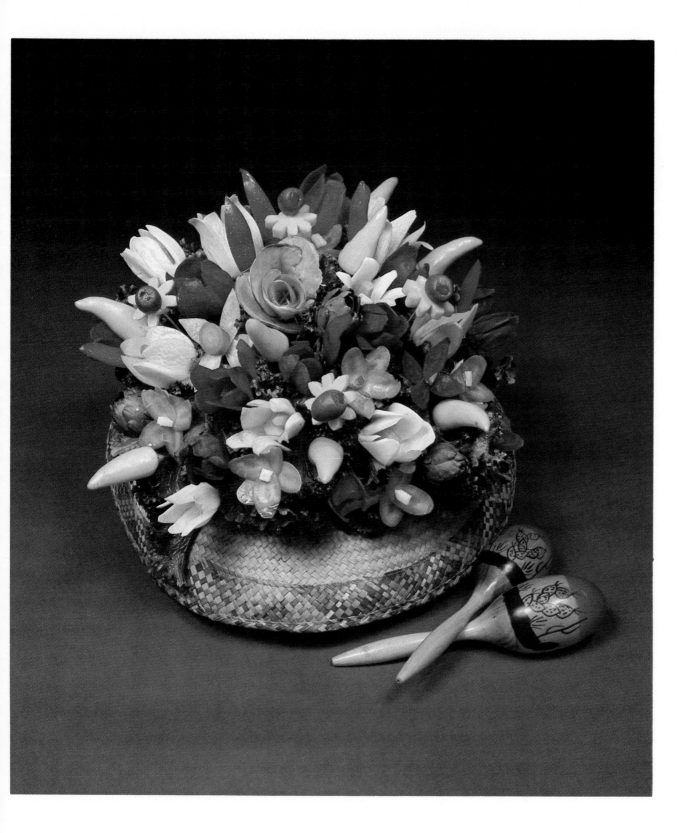

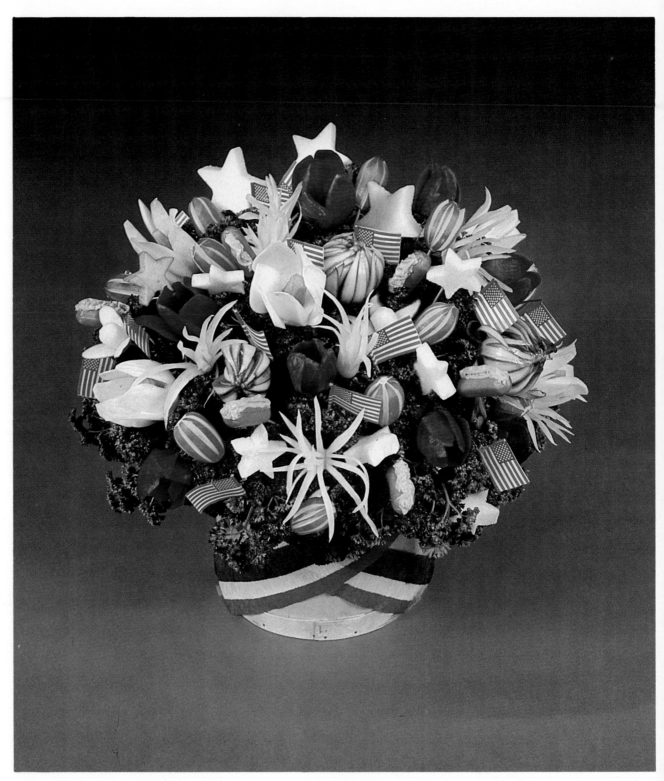

Color Plate 8, Stars and Stripes (page 70)

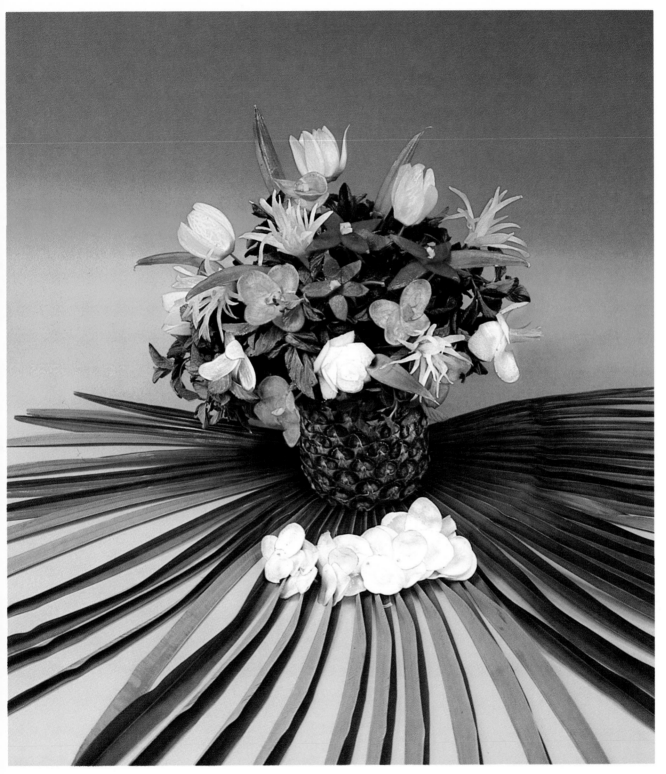

Color Plate 9, Hawaiian Holiday (page 72)

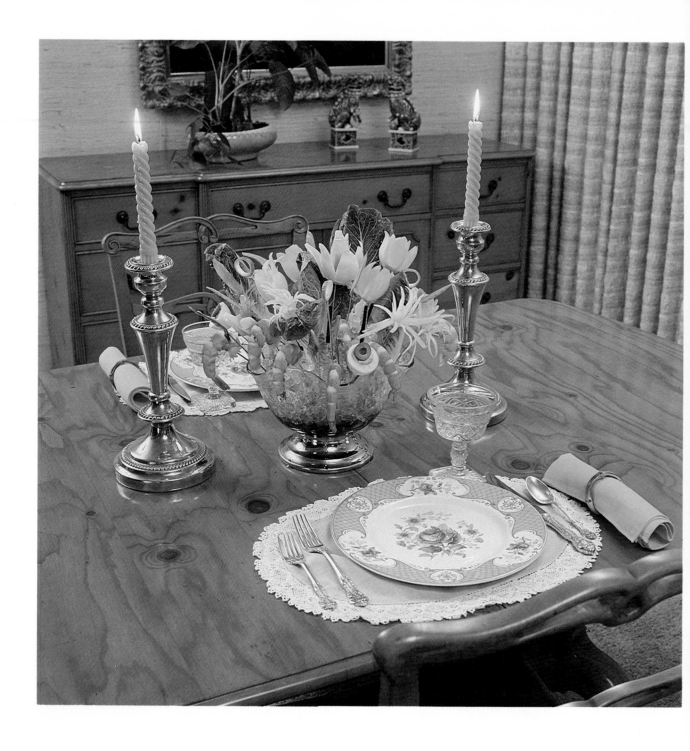

Color Plate 10, Buffet in a Bouquet (page 74)　　　　*Color Plate 11,* A Condiment Christmas (page 76)▪

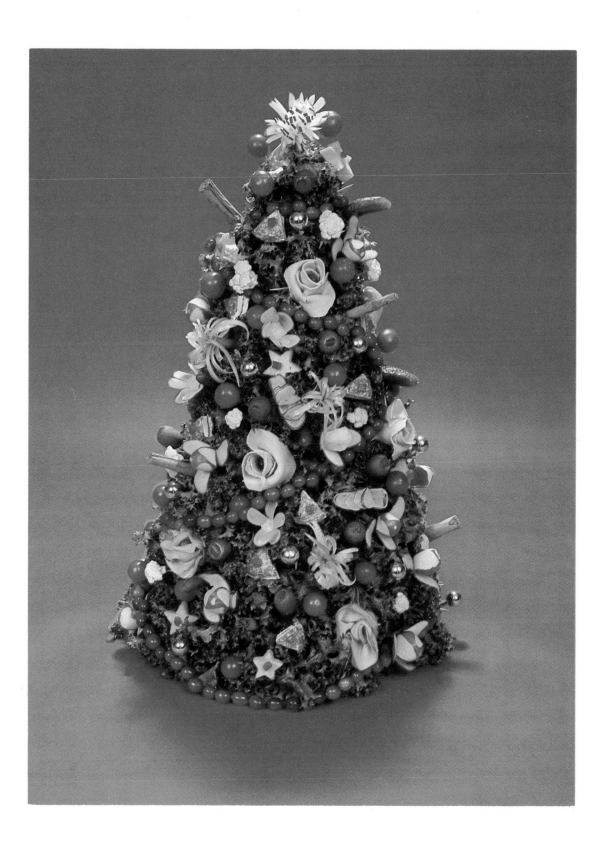

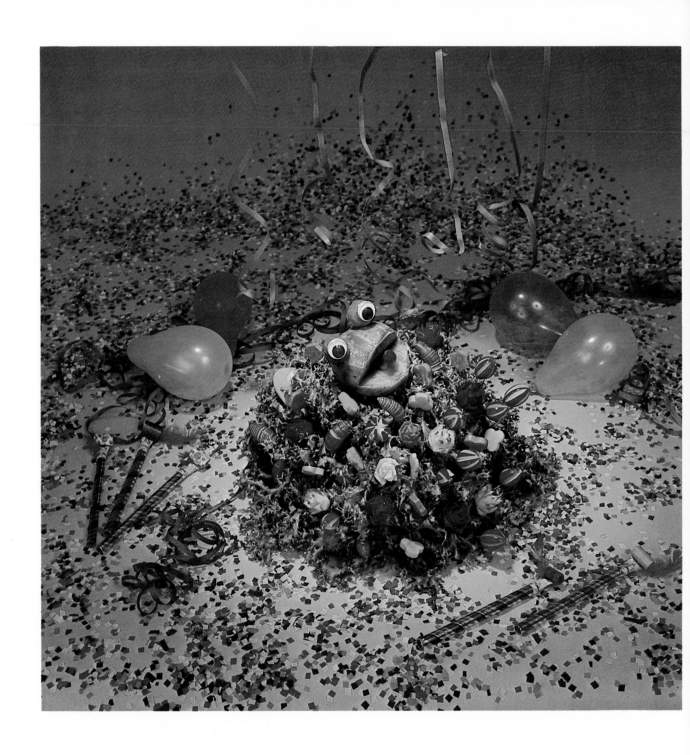

Color Plate 12, Herbie the Frog (page 78)

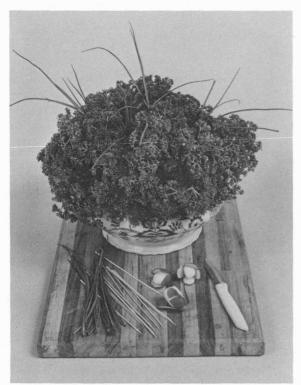
Steps 4, 5, and 6

place in the refrigerator or cover with cold, moist paper towels until serving time.

You can serve this bouquet as a salad with the traditional Easter dinner. Add condiments, if you like, and serve with this zesty dressing: Blend cream cheese with mayonnaise until creamy (the consistency of salad dressing). Add sharp grated cheese, dried bits of bacon, and just a dash of dried mustard. Mix well, chill, and serve. The guests may serve themselves all through dinner, dipping the elaborate salad in the dressing. This salad adds spice not only to your dinner, but to the conversation as well.

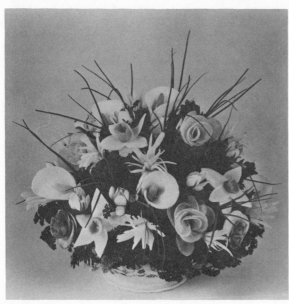
Easter Bouquet ready to serve

Eggplant Extravaganza
COLOR PLATE 5

The Eggplant Extravaganza is just the right centerpiece for a Greek theme. Surround this bouquet with stuffed grape leaves, black olives, Greek bread, moussaká, and Greek wine. When the evening's festivities have ended, you have the added bonus of an eggplant container than can be used for another meal. You have displayed not only your artistry, but your practicality as well.

INGREDIENTS
Container Eggplant Elegance
Filler Foliage Carrot tops
Vegetable Flowers Beet tulip, turnip tulip, radish tulip, radish daisy, carrot lily

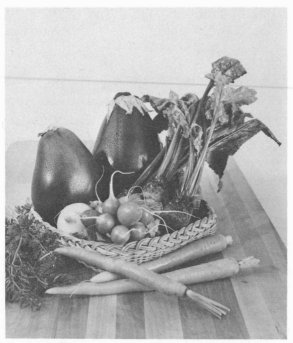

Ingredients

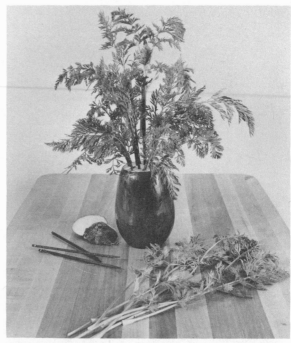

Step 3

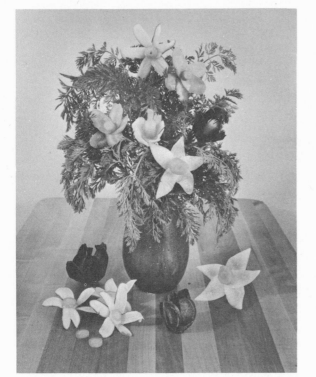

Step 4

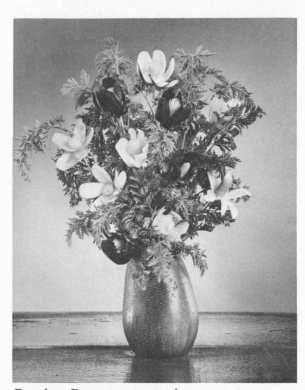

Eggplant Extravaganza ready to serve

Special Hints 10″ and 6″ skewers are used to give this bouquet a variation in height. The carrot tops are wired on floral picks (see page 22 for wiring information) to give them support and secure them in the eggplant container. Glaze the flowers if they are to last until the following day.

STEP-BY-STEP
1. Cut and bloom all the flowers.
2. Cut a small slice off the bottom of a medium to large eggplant so it has a sturdy base.
3. Use one to two bunches of crisped carrot tops, and wire them to floral picks in small bunches according to their length. The height of the foliage should be 1½ to 2 times the height of the container. Establish the appropriate height with a small bunch of the longest carrot tops. Then proceed to stick the wired carrot tops into the eggplant container until the foliage has a graceful, abundant appearance.
4. Skewer the vegetable flowers with skewers of various size. Glaze if necessary. Then place them in the bouquet at varied heights and angles.
5. Give the entire bouquet (including the container) a final ice water misting. Ice water will not disturb the glazing.

A tasty Mediterranean dip to serve with the Extravaganza is made with ground chick peas (these may be canned), a dash of olive oil, and garlic

salt. Add the seasonings to taste, and serve the dip chilled.

Cabbage Patch
COLOR PLATE 6

This casual summer bouquet, which looks as though it were freshly picked, was assembled for display from vegetables that had lost their flavor and crispness. If your vegetable crisper is like mine, an occasional forgotten vegetable will suddenly appear looking as if it has seen better days. No need to throw it away; recycle it into a display flower. Just cut and bloom the flowers, then glaze them to preserve their appearance till the following day.

INGREDIENTS
Container Willow basket
Filler Foliage Mustard greens
Vegetable Flowers Cabbage iris and lily, turnip peony, radish crocus and sweet pea
Special Hints Styrofoam® was used at the bottom of the container along with 10″ skewers to help support the larger blossoms.

STEP-BY-STEP
1. Cut all the vegetable flowers and place them in ice water to bloom.
2. While the flowers are blooming, cut a 3″ thick piece of Styrofoam® and fit it into the bottom of the basket.
3. Glaze the flowers after they have fully bloomed.

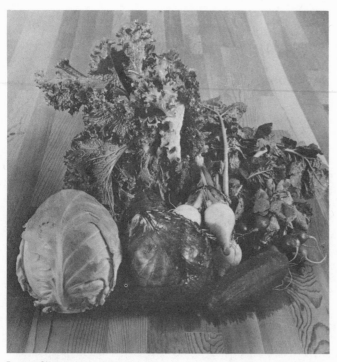

Ingredients

4. Fill the basket with filler foliage.
5. Skewer the vegetables using the 10″ skewers.
6. Place the flowers in the bouquet and attach a gingham bow to the front of the basket.

Be sure to inform your guests that although this bouquet is made of vegetables, it was designed for display rather than eating. Prepare for questions and compliments when your guests find you've cleverly transformed what otherwise would have come to a less artful end.

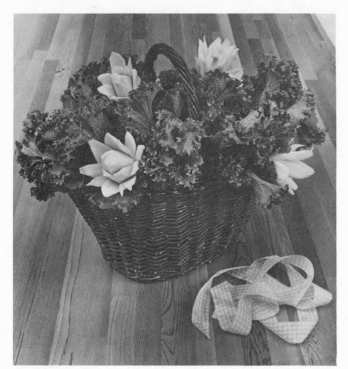

Steps 4 and 5

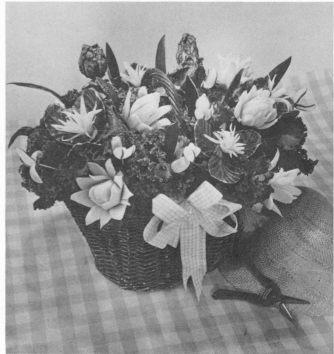

Cabbage Patch ready

BOUQUET BASICS

Flower Fiesta

COLOR PLATE 7

The colors used in this bouquet bring out the gaiety and lively spirit associated with the traditional fiesta. If your occasion is a special one with a cultural theme, display the colorful Flower Fiesta on a buffet table with a brightly colored tablecloth of corresponding colors. Serve miniature tacos, chilled sangria, and an assortment of dips. The visual impact of the bouquet will take care of the rest. The maracas, by the way, are not edible.

INGREDIENTS

Container Sombrero Surprise

Filler Foliage Mustard greens

Vegetable Flowers Beet and turnip tulips with carrot spray stamens, daikon daffodil, carrot pansy, yam rosette, daikon daisy

Condiment Capers Cheese daisy with olive; yellow chili peppers

Stickery Red peppers, miniature artichokes

STEP-BY-STEP

1. Cut all the vegetables and place them in ice water to bloom.
2. Cut out all the cheese daisies, skewer, and refrigerate.
3. Wire the red peppers for stemmery, skewer the miniature artichokes and chili peppers, and place these in the refrigerator.
4. Prepare the container (see Sombrero Surprise, page 49). Place a small but deep cardboard box under the deep

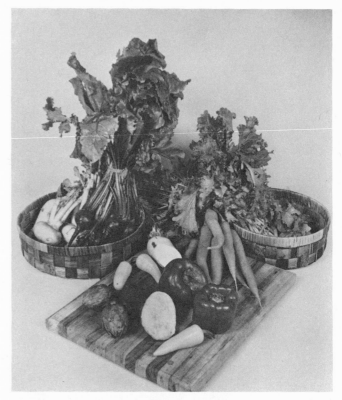

Ingredients

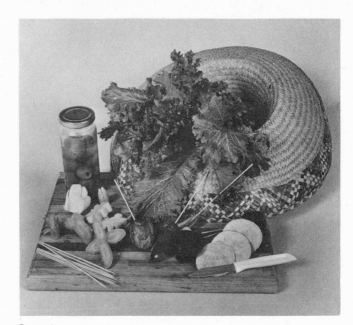

Step 4

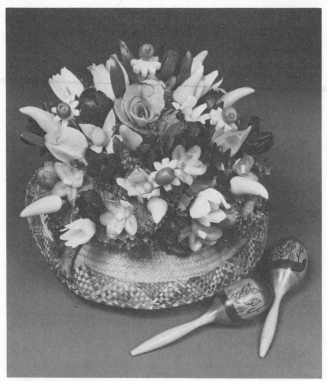
Flower Fiesta Ready to serve

Stars and Stripes
COLOR PLATE 8

What Fourth of July celebration is complete without hot dogs, stars, flags, and sparklers? These are all artfully and edibly incorporated into the bouquet in the traditional red, white, and blue.

INGREDIENTS

Container Old wooden cylinder

Filler Foliage Parsley

Vegetable Flowers Turnip tulip with carrot tip stamen, beet tulip with carrot spray stamen, onion chrysanthemum, white jicima star, white radish spray, radish blossom #1, and radish blossom #2

Condiment Capers Cocktail hot dogs with mustard

Special Hints Mustard can be applied to the cocktail hot dogs with a pastry tube to produce squiggles. The white radish sprays suggest sky rockets and sparklers. The stripe effect is achieved with radish blossom #1.

STEP-BY-STEP

1. Cut all the vegetable flowers and place them in ice water to bloom. After the blooming, put the desired flowers in vegetable coloring.
2. Prepare the container. For this container, strips of crepe paper are applied in a crisscross pattern around the wooden cylinder; hold the crepe paper in place with 2-sided tape.
3. Fill the container tightly with crisped

portion of the hat for greater stability; then fill the hat tightly with the mustard greens. When this is completed, spray lightly with ice water.

5. Skewer the bloomed vegetables, then fill the sombrero with vegetable flowers, condiments, and stickery.
6. Give the bouquet a final misting. If room permits, place it in the refrigerator or cover it with cold, moist paper towels till serving time.

A favorite dip to serve along with the bouquet is made of sour cream, guacamole, a dash of cayenne pepper, and a small bag of crumpled corn chips for crunchyness. Mix this well, refrigerate, and then serve.

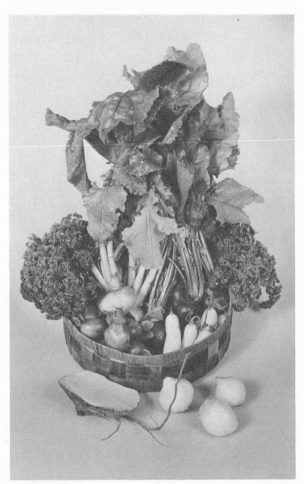

Ingredients

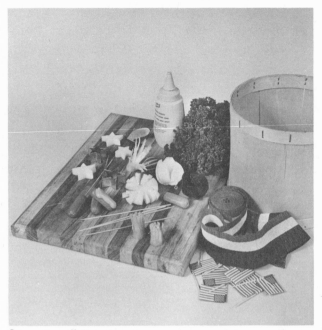

Steps 1 and 2

parsley and spray with a fine mist of ice water.

4. Skewer the vegetables and place them in the bouquet.
5. Skewer the cocktail hot dogs and squeeze the mustard squiggles on. Then place the hot dogs carefully in the bouquet.
6. Finally, insert the paper flags.

The Fourth of July brings to mind celebrations, family gatherings, and picnics.

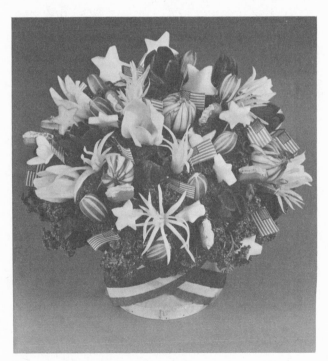

Stars and Stripes ready to serve

A BOUQUET FOR ALL SEASONS

Bring the bouquet to the picnic. Serve it along with barbecued hot dogs, hamburgers, and plenty of lemonade. One dip I like to serve with this bouquet is made with cream cheese and sour cream whipped together in a blender until smooth and creamy. Add minced green pepper, a touch of tabasco, and garlic powder. Another dip, a favorite among youngsters, is made with crunchy granola. Add about ½ cup granola to a pint of the sour cream/cream cheese mixture. No need to mix anything else: just dip the vegetables and enjoy.

Vegetable Flowers Turnip tulip with carrot spray stamen, white radish spray, turnip camellia, miniature beet poinsettia, radish sweet pea, parsnip petal flower; at the bottom, parsnip gardenia

Stickery Pineapple spears

STEP-BY-STEP
1. Cut and bloom all vegetable flowers to be used. When flowers are fully bloomed, immerse in chilled vegetable coloring.
2. Prepare the pineapple container. (See

Hawaiian Holiday

COLOR PLATE 9

In this perfect luau centerpiece, the pastel colors and pineapple bring to mind the allure of the tropics. This bouquet can be used as a display centerpiece, exhibiting your culinary crafting. The Hawaiian bouquet is designed for just that purpose. The flowers may all be glazed to preserve their freshness throughout the entire evening and may even be intermingled with natural flower leaves or palm leaves as pictured. You may turn it into a more edible bouquet simply by adding condiments and stickery.

INGREDIENTS
Container Pineapple Pot
Filler Foliage Mint leaves

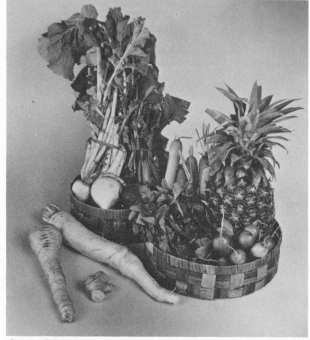

Ingredients

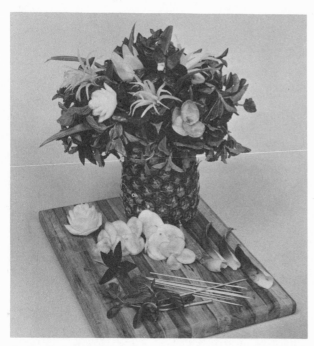

Steps 4 and 5

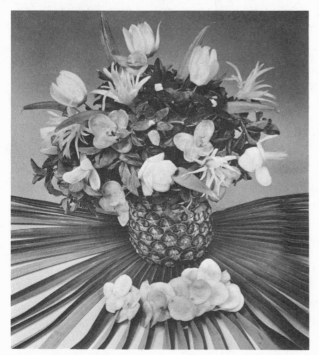

Hawaiian Holiday ready to serve

preparation instructions, page 50.) Save the spears and wire them for stickery.

3. Glaze the vegetable flowers after they have been fully bloomed and colored.

4. While the glaze is setting (this takes only a few moments), fill the container tightly with crisped mint leaves. The arrangement pictured requires three bundles.

5. Add the glazed vegetable flowers, then the pineapple spears for stickery.

To construct a flower lei, use a number of parsnip gardenias. Insert a toothpick in each flower. Now arrange the skewered flowers very closely in a circle around the centerpiece. This lei should be glazed for lasting freshness.

Display the Hawaiian Holiday at a luau. Arrange the buffet table with an assortment of barbecued meats, fish, steamed rice, and various tropical fruits, such as papaya and mango. Towards the end of the evening, remove the flowers from the pineapple container and slice it into small wedges. Add toothpicks and serve. I like to serve a creamy meringue along with the pineapple. This is made by beating 3 egg whites until stiff; add ½ cup sugar and a cap full of a sweet liqueur. Mix, chill, then serve. This is the confectionery equivalent of a cream dip. Encourage your guests to dip the pineapple in the meringue and enjoy the offerings of the tropics.

Buffet In A Bouquet

COLOR PLATE 10

Leftovers, a lack of time, panic, and a desire to make a strong, creative impression inspired this idea. One day while expecting a very special dinner guest, I realized that somewhere in the chaos of the week's scheduling I had lost a day. This special guest was due tonight, not tomorrow. I was frantic; the panic began. What to serve? Where would I find time to shop or cook? How would I ever dazzle him with my culinary expertise? I turned to the bouquet, since it had pulled me through so many other tight culinary spots. I couldn't serve *only* vegetable flowers, because I was going to serve vegetables anyway. Then it hit me. Why not make a *buffet* out of the bouquet? Well, I couldn't serve chateaubriand or cornish game hens on a stick: these undoubtedly would lose something in the translation. The next thing that came to mind was—sea food! It could all be skewered and didn't have to be cooked. Shrimp, scallops, crab chunks, fried potato rosettes, tomatoes, toasted garlic bread squares, greenery! It was complete. The evening would be saved; my guest would dine, if not elegantly, at least uniquely. The table arrangements, candle light, and wine were appropriate appointments. All made for an exciting meal. This bouquet should be named The Busy Person's Answer to a Fancy Dinner, for the bouquet simply unfolded, really without too much help

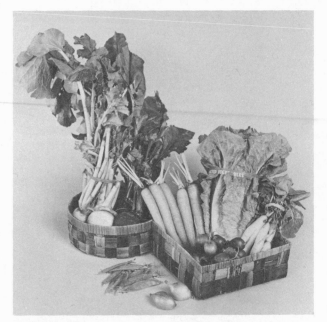

Ingredients

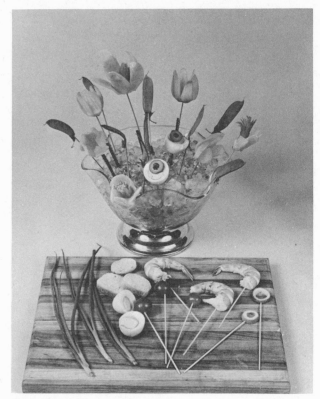

Steps 3, 4, 5, and 6

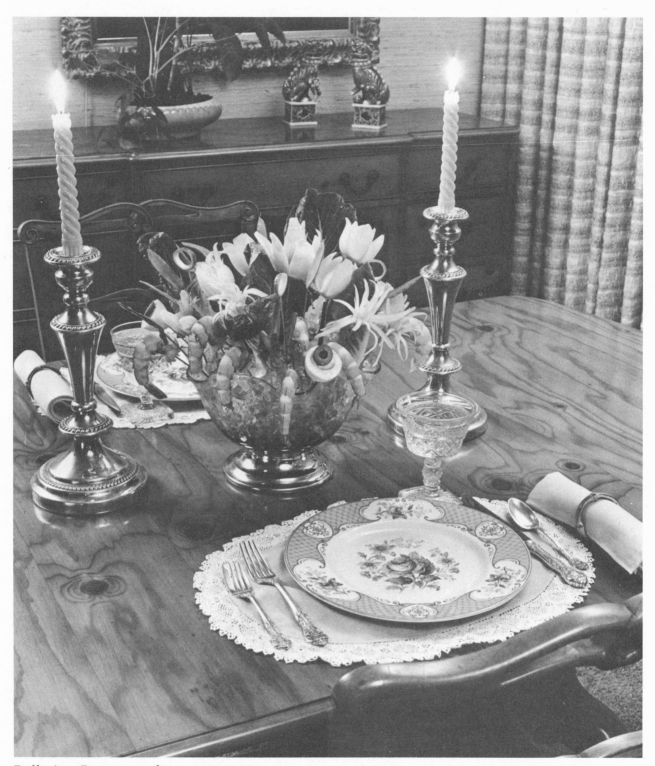

Buffet in a Bouquet ready to serve

A BOUQUET FOR ALL SEASONS

from me. The atmosphere was haled as elegant, and the bouquet ingenious and extraordinary.

INGREDIENTS

Container Glass bowl with a wavy rim and a small silver pedestal

Filler Foliage Romaine lettuce

Vegetable Flowers White radish spray and turnip tulip with carrot spray stamens

Stickery Hard-boiled eggs with olive slices, shrimp, china peas

Sniffery Shallots

Special Hints Since the container I used was glass with a wavy rim to suggest the sea, I added crushed ice with green coloring to add drama and keep the things chilled at the same time.

STEP-BY-STEP

1. Crisp the romaine lettuce.
2. Cut all the vegetable flowers and place them in ice water to bloom.
3. Skewer the shrimp and hard-boiled eggs, which can be leftovers. String china peas on a skewer.
4. Prepare the container by filling it with crushed ice and food coloring.
5. Pull apart the stalks of romaine lettuce and stick the core end deeply into the crushed ice.
6. Ten minutes before serving, skewer the vegetable flowers and place them, along with the stickery, into the crushed ice. Then place the entire bouquet in the refrigerator for a final chilling.

The colors of the sea bouquet highlighted the table appointments so that the dinner and dinnerware were color coordinated (I couldn't have done that with chateaubriand.) A yam rosette was placed at the side of each plate for an elegant bit of garnish. I served sour dough bread, butter curls, and tartar and cocktail sauces on the side. The result was an elegant illusion which required minimal panic and preparation time.

A Condiment Christmas
COLOR PLATE 11

This special Christmas tree is equipped to carry not only ornaments but condiments as well. It will keep your guests nibbling festively all evening. It can be constructed to accommodate any size party simply by varying the size of the Styrofoam® cone.

INGREDIENTS

Container Styrofoam® cone or discs of graduated sizes.

Filler Foliage Curly endive

Vegetable Flowers Radish blossom #6 (star at top of tree), radish tulip (fully bloomed), and radish blossoms #2, #3, and #4

Condiment Capers Olives, baby gherkins, turkey rollettes, salami stacks, banana squash

Stickery Cherry tomatoes, cranberry chains, cauliflower sections, onion curls

Sniffery Cinnamon sticks

Special Hints Use toothpicks instead of skewers for this one.

STEP-BY-STEP

1. Cut all the vegetable flowers and place them in ice water to bloom.
2. String the cranberries and refrigerate.
3. Skewer all condiments and stickery and refrigerate for freshness.
4. Prepare the container. If you are using Styrofoam® discs, place the largest one on the bottom; use three long wire affixers to attach each additional disc until they make a cone shape (see page 58).
5. After crisping the endive, attach it to the cone by placing the endive core

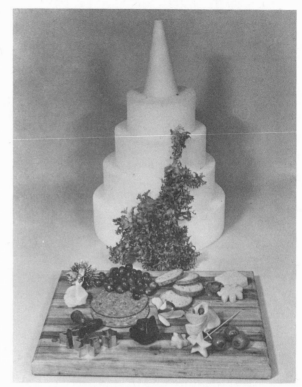

Steps 3, 4, and 5

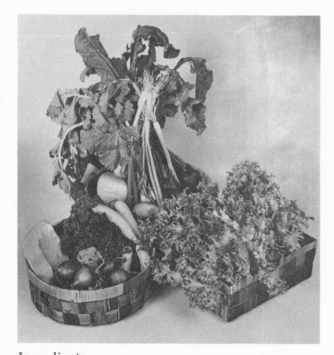

Ingredients

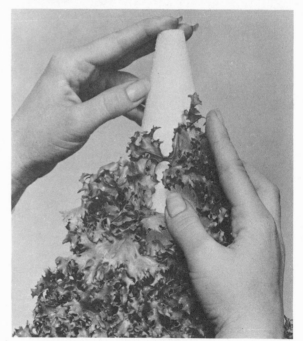

Step 5 (detail)

A BOUQUET FOR ALL SEASONS

77

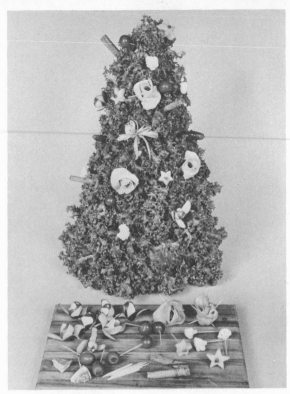

Step 6

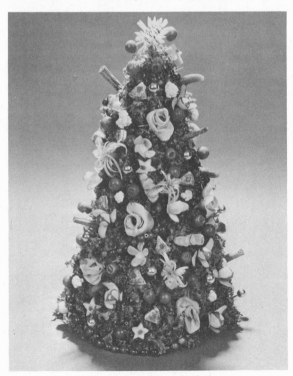

A Condiment Christmas ready to serve

against the Styfofoam® and pushing a wire affixer through both core and Styfofoam® in one swift motion. Work from the bottom up, being sure to cover the wires of the preceding layer. After the endive is fastened to the cone, spray it with ice water.

6. Skewer the vegetable flowers on toothpicks and stick them firmly into the tree. Then follow with condiments, stickery, and sniffery. Finally, encircle the entire tree with the cranberry chain.

Place this tree in the center of a buffet table along with egg nog. The cinnamon sticks in the tree add a special aroma of festivity. This is one Christmas tree which will certainly be remembered. Incidentally, this makes a delightful holiday gift.

Herbie the Frog
COLOR PLATE 12

Parents are always looking for something to capture the imagination of their children when it comes to eating vegetables. Why not present it to look like a creature they are familiar with? I must confess that a charming children's television show inspired this one. In a moment of whimsical delight, I found myself totally captivated by the little characters and I sat attentively listening and learning to spell. Well, that was when I knew one fellow in particular had to be immortalized in rutabaga. One day perhaps I'll come out with a complete line of edible vegetable creatures that children will recognize and that will make eating vegetables more appealing to them.

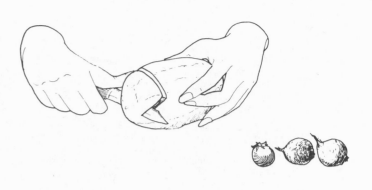

INGREDIENTS

Container Styrofoam® ball cut in half and a slightly larger disc for the base

Filler Foliage One bunch curly endive

Vegetable Flowers One large glazed rutabaga or turnip for the head, two small turnips for the bulging eyes, radish clown for the caterpillars, radish blossom #1 for the balloon flower, turnip and radish carnations, jicima in hors d'oeuvre cutter shapes, one cherry tomato slice for the tongue

Special Hints You can purchase puppet eyes at a toy store.

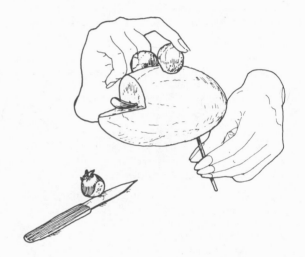

STEP-BY-STEP

1. Peel a large rutabaga and two small turnips.

2. Prepare the gelatin glaze as directed on page 20, adding some undissolved green gelatin to get a green color.

3. Holding the rutabaga with the root end horizontal, cut out a V-shaped wedge (for the mouth) at the opposite end. Then affix the turnip eyes with toothpicks and insert another toothpick at the bottom, where the neck would be. Then place this head for the time being in a piece of Styrofoam®.

4. When the glaze is sufficiently cooled, start spooning it over the head and eyes. Let it set—then recoat. Add the puppet eyes and slice of cherry tomato for the tongue while the gelatin coating is still slightly sticky.

5. Prepare the lily pad. Place the Styrofoam® dome on top of the Styrofoam® disc which acts as a platform. Start from the bottom and work up and around, attaching the endive leaves with a wire affixer (see page 58). so that each layer overlaps and hides the previous layer.

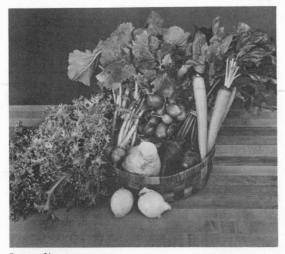

Ingredients

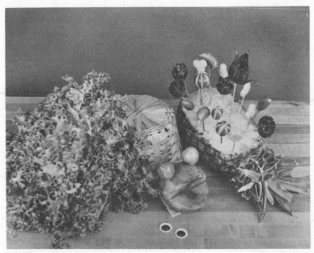

Step 4

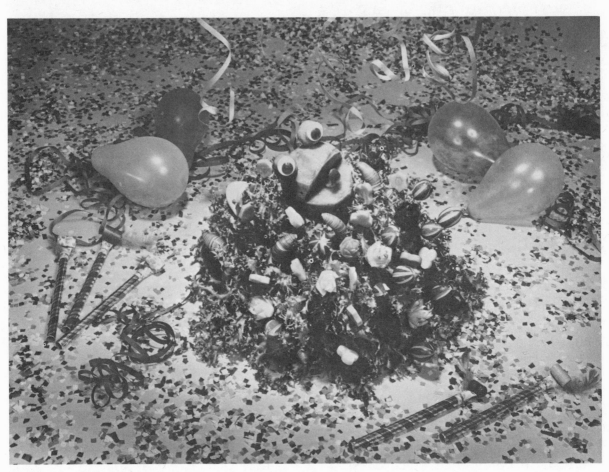

Herbie the Frog ready to serve

6. Skewer all the vegetables and place them in the lily pad.
7. Perch Herbie on top of the mound by sticking him into the top of the Styrofoam®.
8. Finally, mist the entire scene lightly with ice water and set the arrangement in the refrigerator until party time.

Bouquet Gifts

A bouquet filled with condiments and hors d'oeuvres makes a delightful gift. It certainly is more colorful than the usual bottle of wine or box of mints. During the holidays, I give little boxes of bouquets. (I used to bake cookies, but this is a pleasant switch. I get a little tired of baking all those cookies during the holidays. Besides, making the bouquet is much less fattening.) The most memorable gifts are still the ones you make yourself.

Boxing the Bouquet

If you are going to be giving away bouquets, you probably won't want to give away your fine procelain soup tureen with it. I suggest you get a small square box of sufficient depth to hold the bouquet and use it as your container. This can be decorated with ribbon or colored paper. Proceed to make the bouquet in the usual manner, being sure to construct it very securely. (You don't want any pansies popping out in the

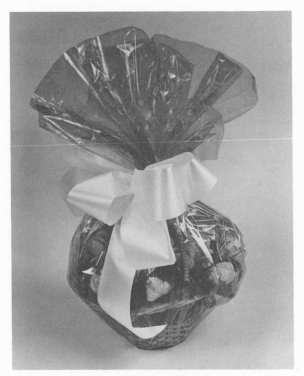

Colored cellophane and satin ribbon lend a festive touch to bouquet gifts.

middle of your presentation.) Give the bouquet a fine misting with ice water and leave it in the refrigerator for about ten minutes. To wrap, use colored cellophane to add to the festive appearance; this can usually be purchased at party shops. The length of the cellophane sheets you use will depend upon the size of the bouquet. Estimate its length so that it will extend about 5″ beyond the top of the bouquet. Place the bouquet in the center of the sheet of cellophane. Bring all corners to the top and gather them together. Tie securely with a wide ribbon, making sure to tuck in any straying pieces of cellophane.

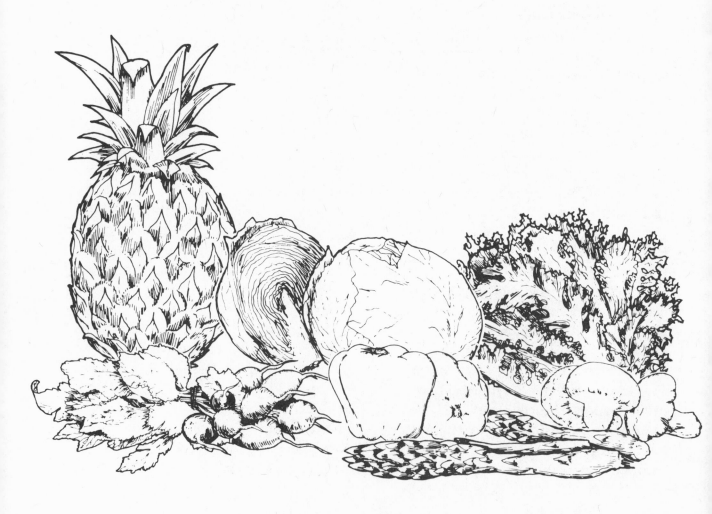

Part Two

THE GOURMET GARDEN

The magic secrets of vegetable artistry are unfolded in this section of the book. Here you'll find illustrated step-by-step information on each bouquet component—filler foliage (the first vegetables to go into the bouquet), vegetable flowers (from radish roses to tuber tulips), condiment capers (the skewered delicacies such as salami rosettes), stemmery and stickery (the accents and accessories of the bouquet), sneaky sniffery (the hidden fragrance enhancers), and finally, finery foldery (those special linen flowers designed to accentuate your table setting).

To make the most of The Gourmet Garden, I suggest that you first leaf through the entire section. Then, begin with filler foliage since it is the first to go in the bouquet, and proceed in order from there. The chapters are organized to follow the construction of the bouquet. (Before creating your bouquet, be sure to scan Chapter 2, A Seasonal Shopping Guide, to make the most of the ingredients you have on hand.)

While constructing these incredible edibles, do keep in mind that they are delectable illusions meant to delight the senses, not to imitate nature perfectly. The very first incredible edibles I made bore no resemblance to real flowers, nor even to these. No matter, for I had a wonderful time perfecting them (although I added an occasional reject to my salad bowl). The tulip, in fact, was fashioned by what I call an "artful accident." I thought I had made too deep a cut into one of the vegetables and was about to add it to a salad, when my imagination took over. I had no idea at the time, of course, that this was to become a tulip, but I had nothing to lose. I made another identical cut. Thus a tulip evolved.

Regard these flowers, if you will, as beginnings, guides meant to inspire you to create your own wonders. Your flowers need not be exact replicas of those pictured. After all, much of the beauty of art is born of the personal creative touch.

7

Filler Foliage

A greenery garden in which to plant your vegetable blossoms.

Filler foliage is the vegetable equivalent of the ferns and leaves used to accent a floral bouquet. They add shape, definition, and a touch of authenticity, and are the first to go in the bouquet. Since the filler foliage is made up of such things as spinach, watercress, and romaine lettuce, it is economically practical, for the filler foliage used in today's bouquet can be used in tomorrow's salad. For greater variety the filler foliage can be mixed so that there are several different textures in one bouquet. Carrot tops, for example, can be interspersed with parsley, or mustard greens with beet tops.

Each type of filler foliage is described below, with suggestions for seasonal displays and vegetable flowers appropri-

ate for them. The term *crisping* used in this chapter refers to separating the leaves and rinsing them thoroughly, then drying. Wrap the leaves in a moist paper towel and refrigerate. Some of the filler foliage, such as parsley and mint leaves, comes tied in bunches. Leave these tied and follow the same procedure as above. Crisping will help keep the vegetables fresh, preserve their texture, and enhance their appearance.

Bronze Lettuce

A brownish-tipped lettuce, the bronze lettuce gradually becomes greener towards the core. The leaves have a delicate, flowing shape. Because of its coloring, this kind of filler foliage goes nicely

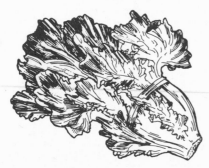

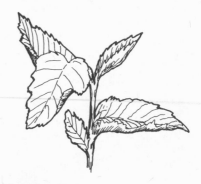

with a fall bouquet. Crisp, then gather several leaves back to back and wire them at the core or bottom. Place the floral pick next to the cores and wind the wire around both cores and pick. Place this piece in your container and repeat with as much lettuce as necessary to fill your container tightly.

Dandelion Greens

These greens are a timely addition to a spring wildflower bouquet. Medium to light green in color, they are available from about May to September. To use this vegetable as filler foliage, separate the stalks and crisp. Then put several of the stalks together and secure at the ends by wiring together with the floral pick. Place them in the container, continuing to fill your container in this way until it is filled snugly enough to hold the vegetable flowers. Incidentally, the ends of the stalks can be cut to any length before you wire the ends together.

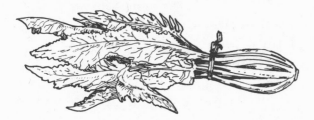

Mint Leaves

Because of their deep color, multi-leafed stem, and refreshing fragrance, mint leaves are a delightful filler foliage for a summer bouquet. Crisp this vegetable while it is still tied. Several bunches added together in a small-to-medium container make a perfect background for delicate vegetable flowers such as the turnip Easter lily or carrot pansy.

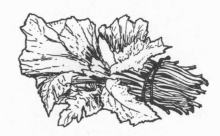

Mustard Greens

Mustard greens have a very hardy, frilly leaf in a vibrant shade of green. Crisp first. Because of the length and hardiness of the leaf, this filler may be used in several bunches or separated and wired with the floral pick and then placed in the container. Because it is firm and robust, it is a perfect filler for the Sombrero Surprise. It can support the weight of the larger variety of vegetable flowers.

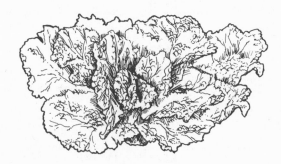

Savoy Cabbage

The savoy cabbage has a wide-leafed, elongated stalk and is a medium shade of green. This filler should be crisped before being inserted into the container. It can be used either in several bunches grouped together in a container—the quickest method—or placed separately, leaf by leaf. The wire picks are not necessary for this filler foliage.

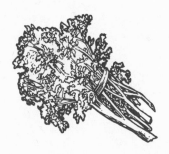

Parsley

I recommend this filler for a first bouquet. Parsley bunches are one of the easiest fillers to use. They are also usually the least expensive of all the filler foliage. Crisp, being sure to leave the bunches tied. Look for those bunches that have the longest, crispest stems. I use this filler when I have a very large bouquet and want to save time. Remember, the number of bunches used de-

pends on the size of the bouquet. I usually start out with about ten bunches for a medium bouquet and build from there.

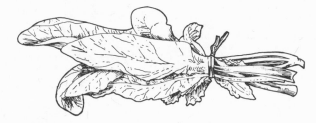

Spinach

Crisp the spinach leaves while they are tied in bunches. Several bunches in a small to medium container are very effective. The dark green color makes an impressive contrast with the brightly colored vegetable flowers.

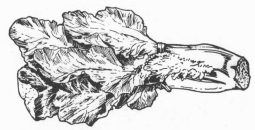

Romaine Lettuce

Romaine lettuce, like savoy cabbage, has a wide, elongated leaf. The leaves are quite tender and delicate in appearance. Crisp the romaine lettuce. Don't separate the stalks, since the entire head of lettuce can be used. Several bunches grouped together will do the job very well.

Salad Bowl Lettuce

Salad bowl lettuce is a very curly, soft-leaved lettuce. It is refreshingly green in

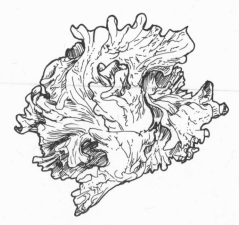

carrot tops. But if the container is a small one, such as an eggplant, the tops may be all you will need. Add the tops to the bouquet by wiring the leaves to a pick; or if parsley is used, simply insert the leaf into an available space.

color and delicate in texture, perfect for a spring or summer bouquet. This lettuce is crisped and used in its entirety. You will probably need several heads placed tightly in a container. Because of its delicacy, this filler foliage goes best with small to medium size vegetable flowers.

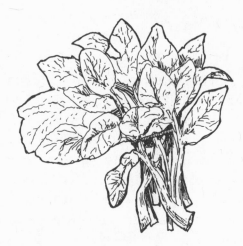

Watercress

Watercress makes an excellent filler for a small container. The leaves are dark green and delicate. When combined with a brightly colored, small vegetable flower, the effect is very pretty and appropriate, perhaps, for a ladies' luncheon or tea.

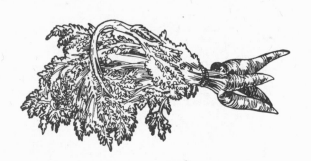

Turnip Greens, Beet Tops, and Carrot Tops

What a nice way to use the entire vegetable! No waste here. Simply cut the tops from turnips, beets, or carrots and crisp. These vegetables are best used as additions to fillers. Because of their rich color, I like to intersperse them with the other fillers to enhance eye appeal and reduce waste. A nice combination is parsley and turnip tops, or parsley and

Curly Endive

This is a curly, leafy vegetable with curving stalks coming out of a central core. It is these curving stalks that make this foliage perfect for affixing to Styrofoam®. Crisp. When it is ready for use, pull the stalks. Next insert the wire affixer through the core of the vegetable and push through the Styrofoam®. This filler foliage is used for the Condiment Christ-

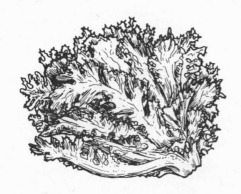

mas tree and for Herbie the Frog's lily pad mound. It is of a hardy nature and will remain fresh for a long time. When affixing the endive to Styrofoam®, be sure to start from the bottom and work up, so that each new top layer will conceal the layer under it. This filler foliage is actually reminiscent of a Christmas tree, since the tiny ends naturally curl up.

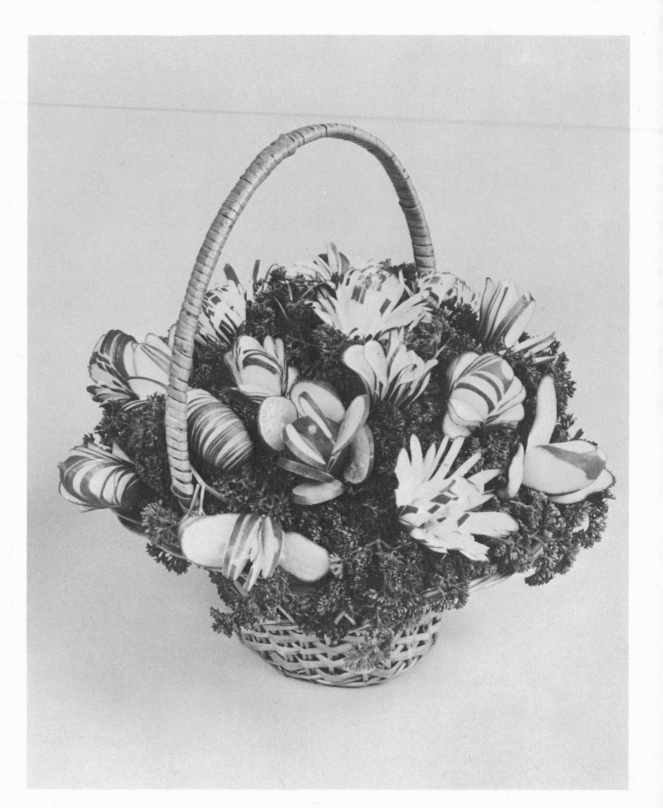

8

Please Eat the Daisies

A step-by-step guide to creating the vegetable flowers.

In this section are complete, illustrated, step-by-step procedures for fashioning all the bouquet blossoms. There are over thirty blossoms in all, and you need make only a few of these for your first bouquet. All of the flowers are categorized by the techniques used to fashion them and are graduated in order of difficulty, from the beginning get-acquainted radish blossoms to the Phi Beta Kappa of vegetable artistry, the Carve and Bloom group. An easy way to learn all of the flowers is to proceed from one group to the next, adding more flowers to your bouquet repertoire as you go along. To insure flower freshness and crunchyness, keep the blossoms in ice water or in the refrigerator until it is time to arrange the bouquet. When describing the blooming of flowers, I use terms such as *often* and *sometimes*. This is because some of these vegetables actually express their own unpredictable blooming preference, occasionally leaving me to wonder just who is the artist. So prepare for a delightful surprise in blooming. Incidentally, refer to Chapter 2, A Seasonal Shopping Guide, for information on how to select the various kinds of vegetables.

Suggestions are given with each blossom as to the shape of the vegetables, their coloring, and the gourmet gadgets used to prepare them. Also included is a section of petal patterns and special hints to make your first experience with vegetable artistry a complete success.

So have a good time! And remember, there is no waste; the blossoms you don't use in a bouquet, you can toss in a salad.

Flower Groups in Order (from simple to complex):
    Radish Blossoms
    Petal Flowers
    Fold-Open Flower
    Cut Flowers
    Cut and Bloom Blossoms
    Folded Flowers
    Carved Blossoms
    Carve and Bloom Blossoms
    Stamens

Radish Blossoms

This group of introductory flowers will acquaint you with such skills as paring with a knife and blooming with ice water. You can create an entire bouquet with just the radish designs found in this group. Your first try at vegetable artistry can produce results you can be proud of. (See page 60 for the all-radish bouquet.)

I have discovered that the secret of success in making these blossoms is to follow the shape of the radish. There is a design for almost any shape of radish, so guidelines are provided to indicate which shape radish should be used with each design. That way, you can use what

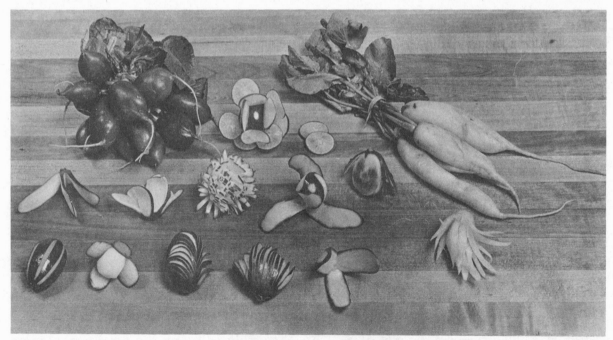

Front: Radish Blossoms #1, #2, #5, #4, Radish Crocus, White Radish Spray. *Middle:* Radish Sweet Pea, Radish Tulip, Radish Blossom #6, Radish Blossom #3, Radish Clown. *Back:* Radish Blossom #7.

you have on hand.

The gourmet gadgets needed for these blossoms are a sharp paring knife, ice water, and skewers. There are seven different radish blossoms in this section and a very special radish clown.

Radish Blossom #1

This little radish design seems to be a favorite among children. The alternate red and white wedges resemble hot air balloons. When the wedges are cut closer together, they have a striped effect as seen in the Stars and Stripes Bouquet, Color Plate 8.

Suggested Radish Shape Large and elongated

Special Hints Make shallow wedges. Be careful not to cut too deeply into the radish.

STEP-BY-STEP
1. Hold the radish with the stem down. Cut thin wedges in a vertical direction and discard the peels.

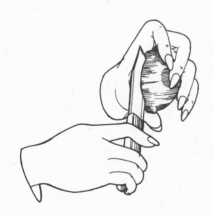

2. Continue in an alternating pattern all the way around the radish.

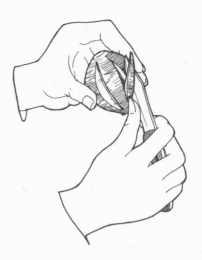

3. Rinse the radish thoroughly, then skewer and add to the bouquet.

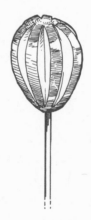

Radish Blossom #1 is used in Herbie the Frog, Color Plate 12.

Radish Blossom #2

Suggested Radish Shape Medium size, rounded

STEP-BY-STEP
1. Holding the radish with the stem end down, make four downward strokes all the way around.

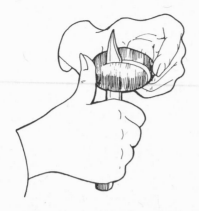

Radish Blossom #3

When fully bloomed, this radish often resembles an airplane propeller, which is what actually inspired its design.

Suggested Radish Shape Large and elongated

Special Hints Make smooth cuts from one end to the other.

STEP-BY-STEP

2. Peel and round off the top portion or, if you prefer, leave it as it is.

1. Hold the radish with the stem end down. Cut the petals on the diagonal. Starting at the top right, cut across to the lower left.

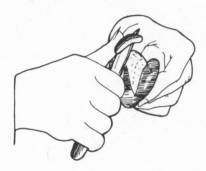

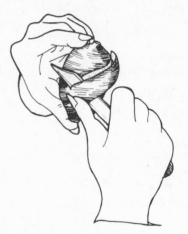

3. Place the radish in ice water to bloom. Skewer just before adding it to the bouquet.

2. Repeat two more times. Three petals are generally enough.

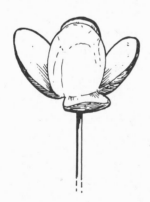

Radish Blossom #2 is shown in the Easter Bouquet, Color Plate 4.

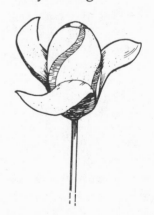

THE GOURMET GARDEN

3. Place the radish in ice water to bloom; then skewer at the stem end and add to the bouquet.

Radish Blossom #3 is seen in A Condiment Christmas, Color Plate 11.

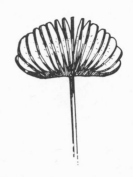

Radish Blossom #4

When fully bloomed, this design sometimes resembles an accordian. When a small elongated radish is used, it resembles a caterpillar, as in the mound for Herbie the Frog, Color Plate 12.

Suggested Radish Shape Elongated, any circumference
Special Hints Make very thin cuts, being careful not to cut all the way through the radish.

STEP-BY-STEP

1. Hold the radish horizontally. Make thin cuts as close together as possible. Begin at the tip of one end and continue cutting all the way across to the other end.

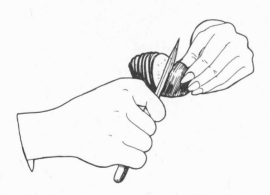

2. Place the radish in ice water to bloom; then skewer and add to the bouquet.

Radish Blossom #4 is used in A Condiment Christmas, Color Plate 11.

Radish Blossom #5

Suggested Radish Shape Very large and elongated
Special Hints Make thin slices, very close to each other.

STEP-BY-STEP

1. Holding the radish with the stem end down, start the first cut close to the bottom on the diagonal.

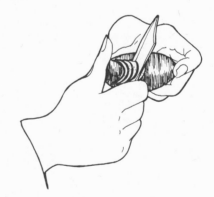

2. Make your next cut directly above the first, as close as possible to it. Continue until the entire row is completed.
3. Turn the radish and repeat two more times. Place in ice water to bloom. Skewer and add to the bouquet.

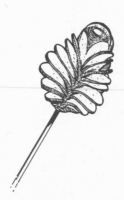

Radish Blossom #5 is used in the Bachelor Bouquet, page 60.

Radish Blossom #6

The inspiration for this radish came from a little sea creature. When fully bloomed, this design resembles a sea anemone.

Suggested Radish Shape Any size round radish

STEP-BY-STEP

1. Hold the radish with the stem end down. Cut a series of very thin slices all the way across.

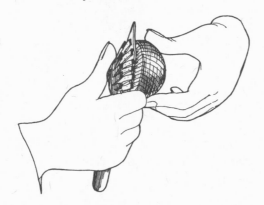

2. Turn the radish and press the cut ends together. Cut again making the same thin slices to produce a criss-cross pattern.

3. Place the cut radish in ice water to bloom; then skewer and add to the bouquet.

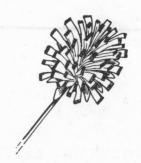

This radish blossom is seen as the star on the Condiment Christmas tree, Color Plate 11.

Radish Blossom #7

Suggested Radish Shape Two very large, round radishes

STEP-BY-STEP

1. Cut thin wedges all the way around the lower portion of one radish.

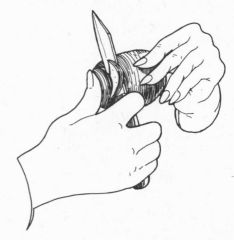

2. Repeat this step around the middle portion of the radish and progress to the top at alternate spaces.

THE GOURMET GARDEN

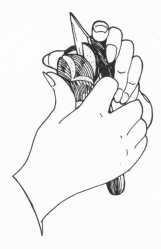

This design makes a good centerpiece flower for a small bouquet. It is found in the radish bouquet, page 60.

Radish Clown

This design added to a child's place at the table makes a delightful and appetizing surprise.

Suggested Radish Shape The largest, roundest radish you can find

STEP-BY-STEP

1. Slice off one side of the radish for the face.

3. Use the other radish (of approximately the same size) and cut discs ⅛" thick.

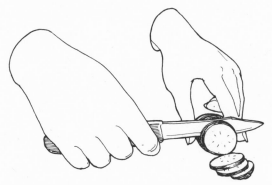

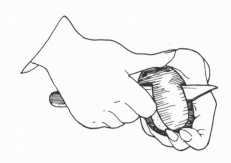

4. Fit a disc into each wedge. Wrap the blossom in a wet paper towel and refrigerate. Then skewer and add to the bouquet when ready for use.

2. To make hair, turn the radish so that the rounded side faces you. Now make tiny slices next to each other. Peel the slices up, being careful not to cut them off.

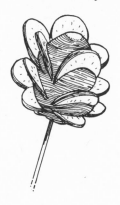

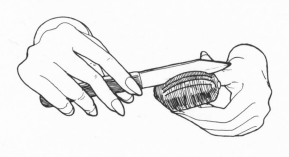

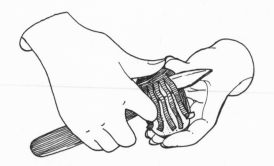

3. Drop the radish in ice water so the hair will curl. To give the clown a happy face, dip a thin-point brush in vegetable coloring and add eyes, a nose, and, most important of all, a happy smile.

Petal Flowers

This group of flowers is fashioned entirely of petals, that is, thin little slices of various vegetables. The petal shapes can all be modified by changing the cutting angles from vertical to diagonal. For easy shaping, petal patterns in actual sizes are included in this section. Incidentally, when children too young to handle a knife want to join in the making of petal flowers, just cut the petals out and let them do the rest. Though identifying these flowers botanically sometimes presents a challenge, the most imaginative blossoms are created this way; this is where the seeds of creativity are planted.

The most important technique for these flowers is making very thin slices. (See slivery slicing, page 19.) This technique will allow the petals to curl more realistically. The individual petals are first bloomed, then colored and skewered; finally, a stamen is added for realism. Complete directions for stamens are given on page 128. After they have been completely assembled, the blossoms are put back in ice water; this helps to shape and crisp them.

The gourmet gadgets used for this group are a French knife, a paring knife, skewers, and ice water. The flowers in this section are the carrot pansy, the carrot lily, the daikon daffodil, the parsnip pansy, the parsnip petal flower, the parsnip gardenia, and the beet poinsettia.

Carrot Pansy

Suggested Carrot Shape Medium to large size carrot. The size of the flower is determined by the circumference of the carrot.

Gourmet Gadgets Sharp paring knife, skewers, ice water

Special Hints Make vertical slivery slices.

STEP-BY-STEP

1. Cut five thin slices at the widest portion of the carrot. (See petal pattern, page 102.)

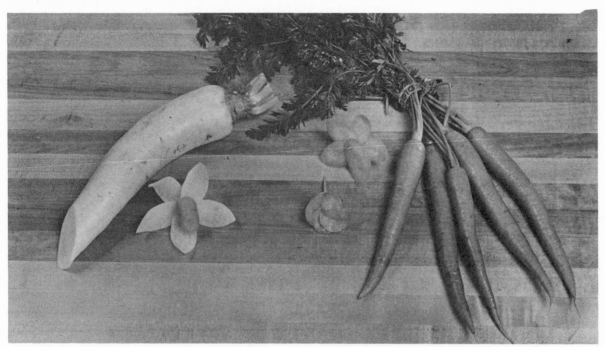

Left: Daikon Daffodil. *Above right:* Carrot Lily. *Below right:* Carrot Pansy.

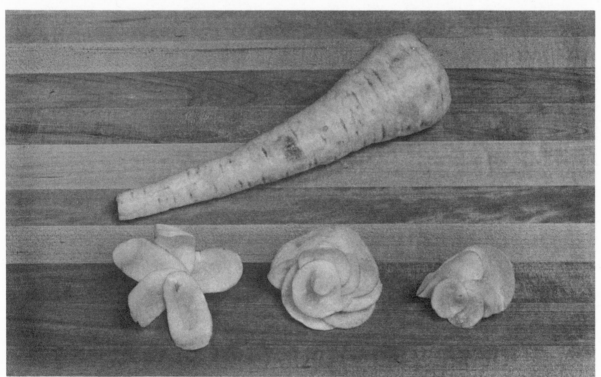

Left: Parsnip Petal Flower. *Center:* Parsnip Gardenia. *Right:* Parsnip Pansy.

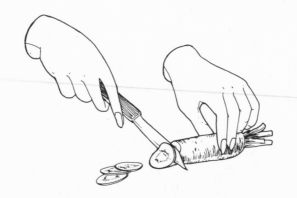

2. Place the petals in ice water.

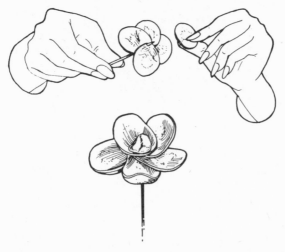

3. When the petals have curled, arrange them on a skewer to resemble a pansy.
4. Cut a small disc at the narrow end of the carrot and skewer it to the center of the pansy.

The carrot pansy is used in the Flower Fiesta bouquet, Color Plate 7.

Carrot Lily

Using the same procedure as for the carrot pansy, simply change the cutting angle from vertical to diagonal. (See petal pattern, page 102.) This will create a slight curving at the ends, and change the shape of the flower from a pansy to a lily. The carrot lily is seen in the Flower Fiesta bouquet, Color Plate 7.

Daikon Daffodil

Suggested Daikon Shape A straight daikon, large in circumference, is best.
Gourmet Gadgets Sharp paring knife, skewers
Special Hints Make diagonal slivery slices.

STEP-BY-STEP
1. Cut five thin slices on the diagonal.

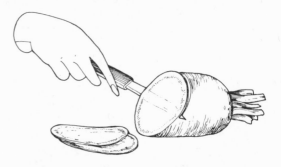

2. With a paring knife, cut out one of the slices to resemble a daffodil petal. (See page 105 for petal patterns.) This will be the pattern. Stack the remain-

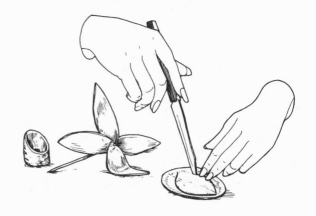

ing slices putting the pattern petal on top; then cut through all the slices, following the shape of the top petal.

3. Place the petals in ice water to curl.
4. While the petals are curling, make a stamen by cutting a 1″ to 1½″-long piece of carrot on the diagonal at its thickest portion. Hollow out the inside and make tiny slits around the top. Immerse in ice water to freshen and clean after handling.

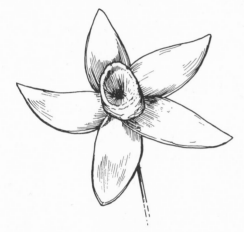

5. Arrange the curled petals on a skewer and top with the carrot stamen.

Daffodils can be made in various sizes by modifying the size of each petal (see the patterns on page 105) and adjusting the size of the stamen. The daikon daffodil is seen in the Easter Bouquet, Color Plate 4.

Parsnip Pansy

Suggested Parsnip Shape Use the widest, longest parsnip you can find.
Gourmet Gadgets Sharp paring knife, skewers, ice water
Special Hints Make vertical slivery slices.

STEP-BY-STEP

1. Cut *two* round, thin discs at the *widest* portion of the parsnip. (See petal patterns, page 102.)
2. Cut *three* round thin discs at the *small* portion.

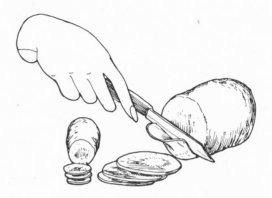

3. Bloom the petals in ice water and prepare two bowls of vegetable coloring. Yellow and purple make a realistic combination.
4. Dip the two large petals in purple coloring and the three remaining small petals in yellow coloring.
5. Skewer the two largest petals next to each other. Then skewer the remaining small petals so they are opposite the large ones.

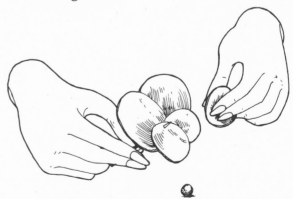

PETAL PATTERNS

Parsnip Pansy Petals

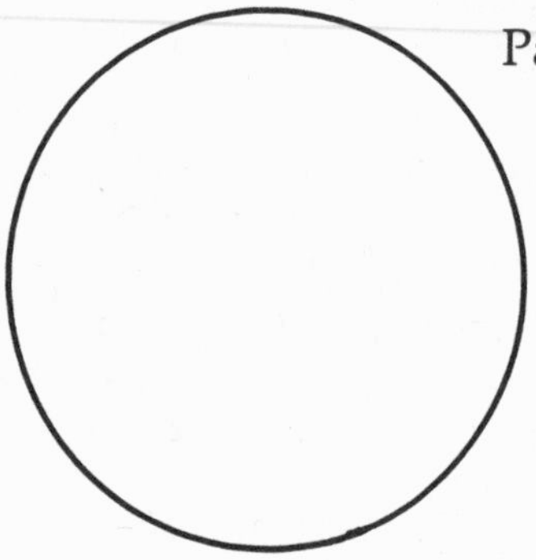

Large

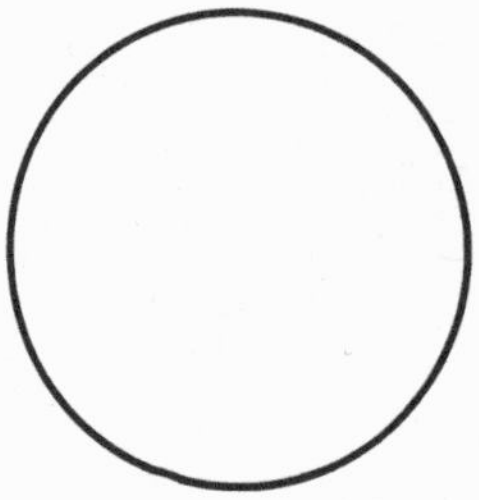

Small

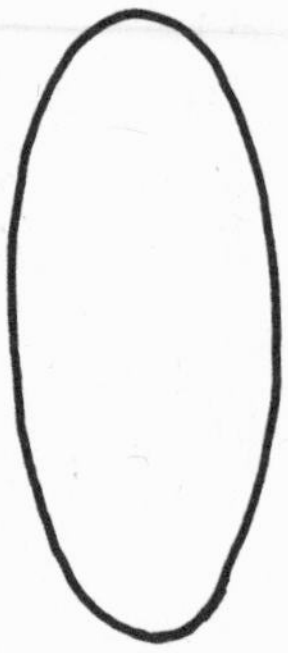

Parsnip Petal Flower

Parsnip Gardenia Petals

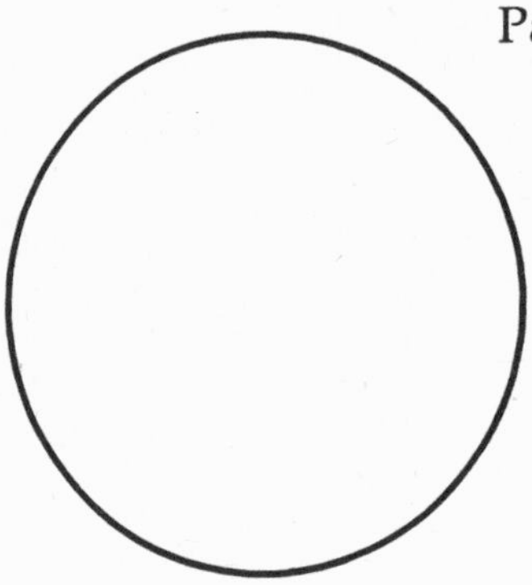

Large

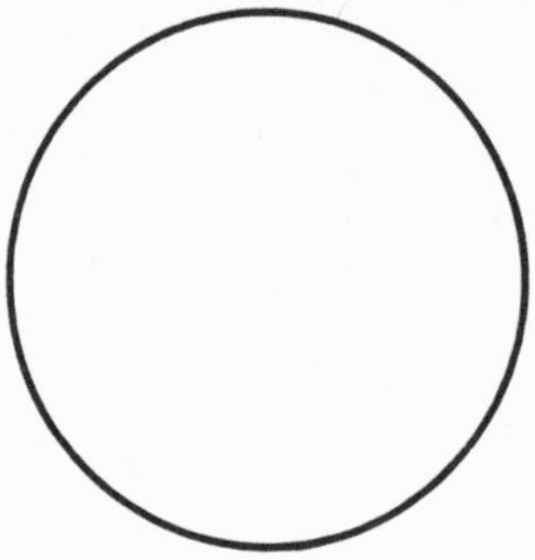

Small

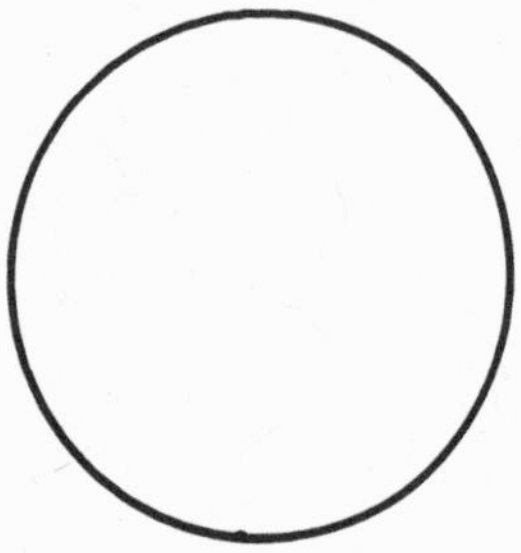

Carrot Pansy Petal

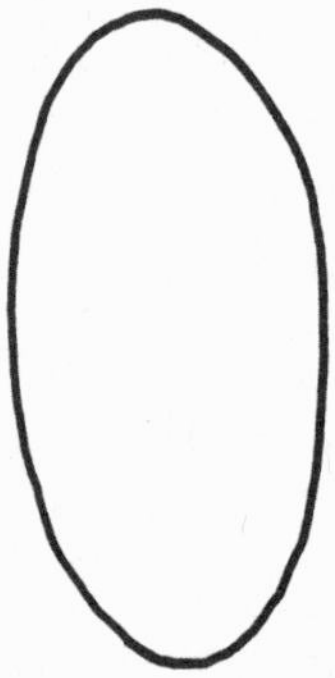

Carrot Lily

6. Top with a small parsnip disc or pea for the stamen.

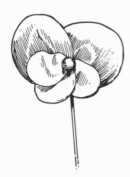

The parsnip pansy is featured in the Pansy Picnic bouquet, Color Plate 3.

Parsnip Petal Flower

Suggested Parsnip Shape Any size parsnip or leftover from the parsnip pansy

Gourmet Gadgets Sharp paring knife, skewers, ice water

Special Hints Make diagonal slivery slices.

STEP-BY-STEP

1. Cut six thin slices on the diagonal. Slice consecutively within any portion of the parsnip so the slices are uniform. Keep in mind that the size of your blossom is determined by just where you cut. (See petal patterns, page 102.)

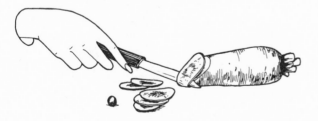

2. Place the individual slices in ice water to curl, then in vegetable coloring. Parsnips take particularly well to color. I suggest pastel colors for this blossom, light pink or yellow.
3. Skewer the individual petals, arranging them on the skewer in a circular pattern.

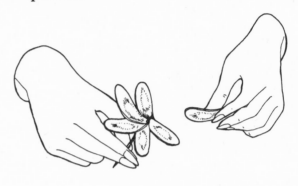

4. Use a pea or a small piece of parsnip for the stamen.

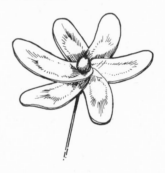

A version of the parsnip petal flower can be seen in the Hawaiian Holiday bouquet, Color Plate 9.

Parsnip Gardenia

Suggested Parsnip Shape The largest parsnip you can find

Gourmet Gadgets Sharp paring knife,

skewers, ice water
Special Hints Make vertical slivery slices.

STEP-BY-STEP

1. Cut six thin slices at the *wide* end of the parsnip. (See petal patterns, page 102.)
2. Cut six thin slices at the *mid* portion of the parsnip, producing smaller petals.

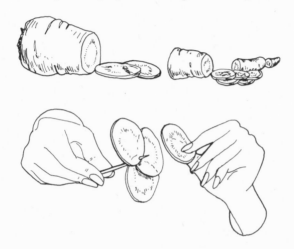

If you now have twelve thinly cut petals of two distinct sizes, you've got the idea.

3. Place the individual petals in ice water to curl.
4. After the petals have curled, skewer the *large* ones first in a circular pattern. To form this pattern, be sure to skewer the petals at the edges.

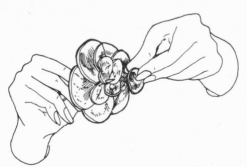

5. Skewer the smaller petals on top of the large ones, also skewering them at the edges.
6. To make a stamen, cut a small piece at the narrowest portion of the parsnip, then skewer it in the center of the petals. Place the completed skewered blossom in ice water for crispness until it's time to add it to the bouquet.

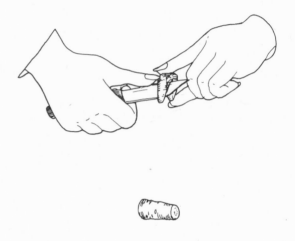

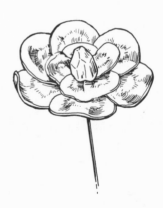

This is a good flower to use as the centerpiece of your bouquet. The parsnip gardenia is seen in the Hawaiian Holiday bouquet, Color Plate 9.

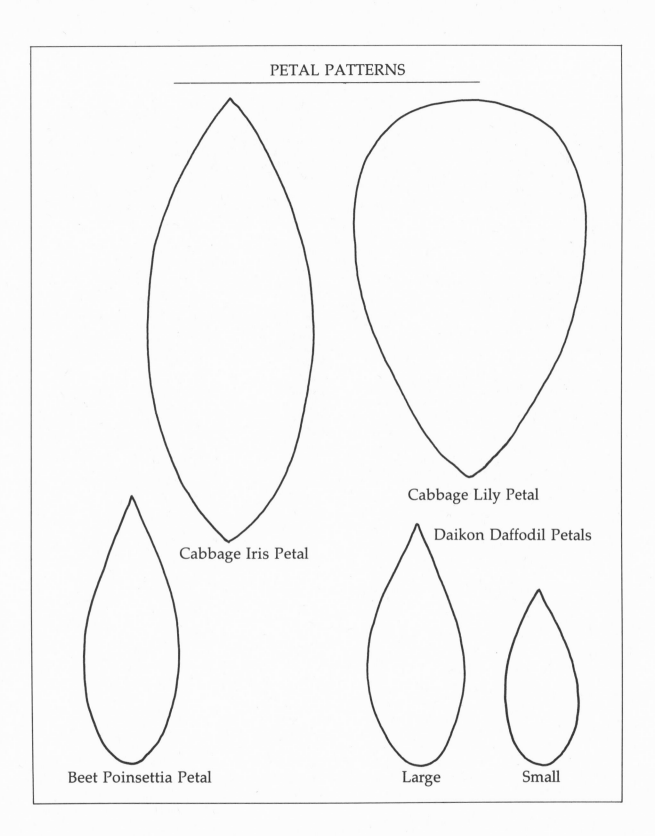

Cabbage Lily Petal

Daikon Daffodil Petals

Cabbage Iris Petal

Beet Poinsettia Petal

Large   Small

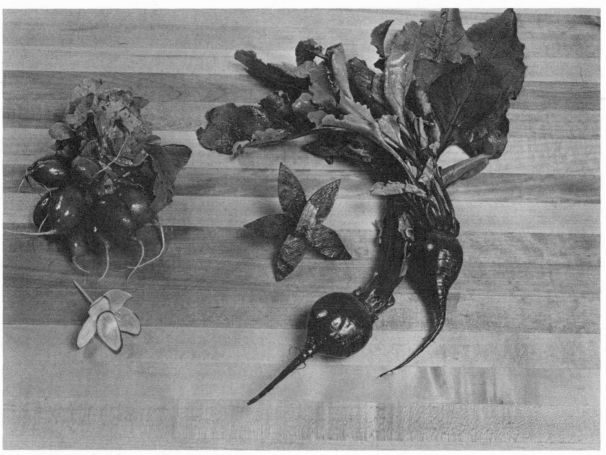

Left: Radish Petal Flower. *Right:* Beet Poinsettia.

Beet Poinsettia

Suggested Beet Shape A wide beet, large in circumference, is best.

Gourmet Gadgetry French knife, paring knife, skewers, ice water

Special Hints Make vertical slivery slices.

STEP-BY-STEP

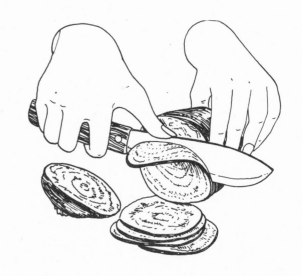

1. Using a very sharp French knife, make five thin slices.
2. Cut out the pattern of a petal on one beet slice with a paring knife. See page 105 for poinsettia petal pattern.

THE GOURMET GARDEN

3. Stack up all of the slices. Using the first petal as the pattern, place it on top of the stack and cut petal shapes with a paring knife.

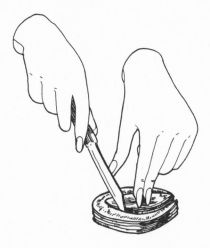

4. Place the petals in ice water, then skewer and top off with a carrot stamen.

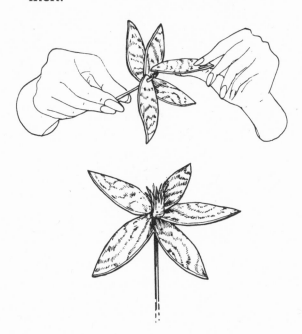

Occasionally, when cutting into a beet, you will find that it has an unusual pattern. This will enhance the appearance of your poinsettia and may even steal the show.

The beet poinsettia is shown in the Hawaiian Holiday bouquet, Color Plate 9.

The Fold-Open Flower

This blossom and technique require possibly the least amount of preparation of all the vegetable flowers. It is fashioned from Belgian endive. The leaves are tightly wrapped, three to four inches in length, and very light in color, coming from a central core at the very bottom.

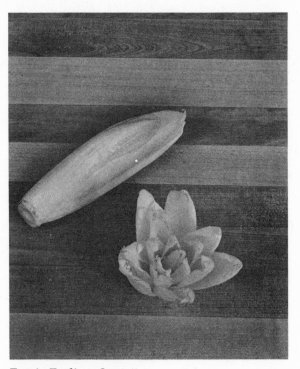

Exotic Endive, Step 1

Exotic Endive

Suggested Endive Shape A small to medium size, firm endive

Gourmet Gadgets Ice water, scissors, and skewers

Special Hints Take special care not to snap the leaves when unfolding them.

STEP-BY-STEP

1. Gently unfold the leaves of the endive as you might a rose.

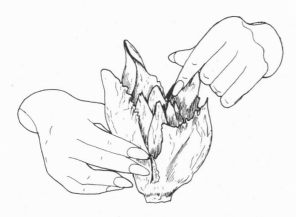

2. When you have opened the budding endive as far as it will go, place it in ice water. This will help it open even further to resemble an exotic tropical flower.

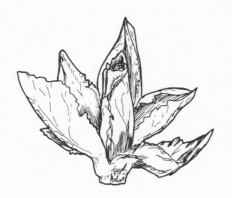

3. This step is optional. The leaves of the endive may be cut on the diagonal if they are too large for your bouquet, the remainder to be wired as stickery or tossed in a salad.

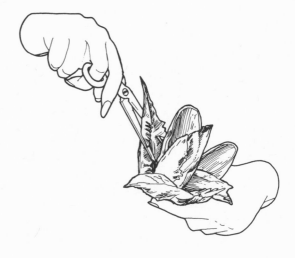

4. When the endive has bloomed, skewer it at the core and place it in the bouquet.

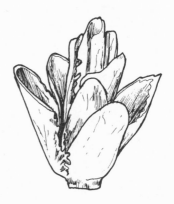

This flower is most attractive when left its natural color. The exotic endive is pictured in the Flower Fiesta bouquet, Color Plate 7.

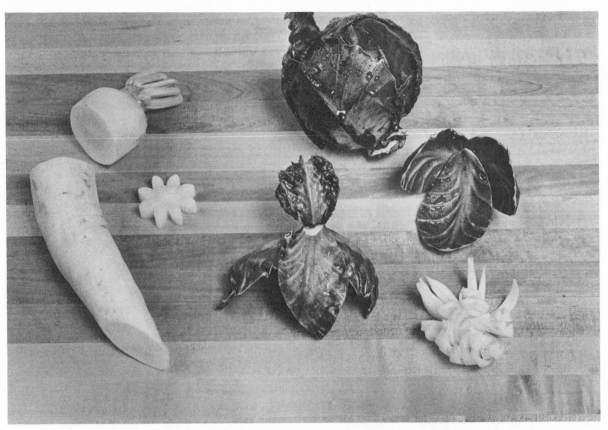

Left: Daikon Daisy. *Center:* Red Cabbage Iris. *Right:* Red Cabbage Lily petals with White Radish Spray stamen.

The Cut Flowers

This group of flowers is fashioned by two kinds of cutting. One technique, which I refer to as scissory, simply requires cutting cabbage leaves into a pattern. (Petal patterns for the cabbage flowers are included on page 105.) The other technique is as easy as cutting cookies; just cut the shapes out of jicima and daikon slices with hors d'oeuvre cutters. Since this technique doesn't require the use of knives, I recommend that it be done with the assistance of any eager young onlookers anxious to be involved. These flowers do not require ice water blooming, since they are fully bloomed by cutting. After each flower in the group is constructed, place it in ice water until time to add it to the bouquet. This will crisp the vegetable and freshen it after handling.

The gourmet gadgets needed for this group are kitchen scissors, hors d'oeuvre cutters, skewers, and ice water. The flowers found in this section are the red cabbage lily, the daikon daisy, the jicima star, and the red cabbage iris.

Red Cabbage Lily

Suggested Cabbage Size Medium size red cabbage or the remaining unused leaves of the cabbage iris

Gourmet Gadgets Kitchen scissors, skewers, ice water

Special Hints The techniques used are scissory and careful peeling of the cabbage leaves.

STEP-BY-STEP

1. Remove the core and peel the outer layers of the cabbage, being especially careful not to tear the leaves.

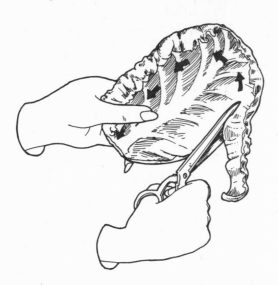

2. After peeling three leaves, cut them with kitchen scissors into the shape of rounded petals. See petal patterns on page 105.

3. Skewer the petals so they turn upward.

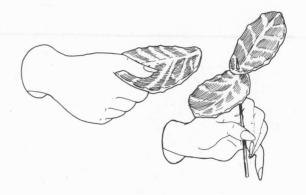

4. For the stamen, use a radish spray which has been colored pink.

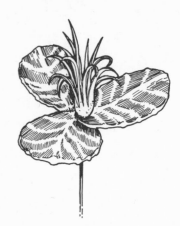

The cabbage lily is seen in the Cabbage Patch bouquet, Color Plate 6.

Daikon Daisy

Suggested Daikon Shape Select a daikon which is long and large in circumference.

Gourmet Gadgets Daisy cookie cutter

STEP-BY-STEP

1. Cut a ¼"- to ½"-thick slice at the widest portion of the daikon.

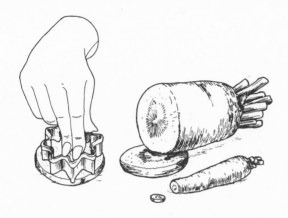

1. Slice the jicima into ¼"- to ½"-thick slices.
2. Place any shape hors d'oeuvre cutter on top of the slice and press down.
3. Skewer the jicima and store in the refrigerator until serving time.

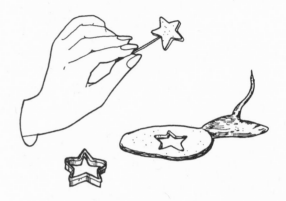

2. With a daisy-shaped cookie cutter, press down on the disc.

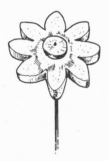

3. Skewer the daisy through the center and top with a carrot disc stamen. (See Stamens, page 128.) Refrigerate the daikon daisy and add to the bouquet just before serving time.

The daikon daisy is used in the Flower Fiesta, Color Plate 7.

Jicima Star

Suggested Jicima Shape Jicima resembles a very large potato that has been compressed at both ends. For our purposes, a medium size jicima is best.

Gourmet Gadgets French knife and hors d'oeuvre cutters

Star-shaped jicima are seen in the Stars and Stripes bouquet, Color Plate 8. This vegetable takes all of the vegetable colors well, and looks particularly irresistible in blue.

Red Cabbage Iris

Suggested Cabbage Size A medium size red cabbage will yield the most leaves.

Gourmet Gadgets Kitchen scissors, skewers, ice water

Special Hints The techniques used here are scissory and careful peeling of the cabbage leaves.

STEP-BY-STEP

1. Remove the core from a medium red cabbage. Carefully peel the leaves until you reach the center and have a tight, roundish, small ball of cabbage

left. This little ball will be the top of the iris.

2. Now for the rest of the iris, choose three of the remaining cabbage leaves and cut them into elongated leaves with kitchen scissors. (See petal patterns, page 105.)

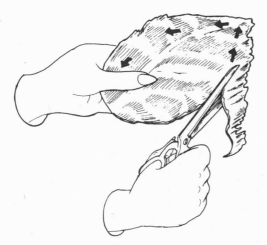

3. Skewer the three leaves first so that they point downward.

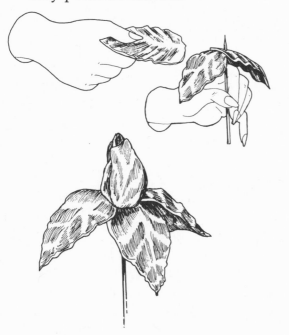

4. Add the center of the cabbage for the top and you have an iris. Save the remaining leaves for the red cabbage lily. Place the finished blossom in ice water for crispness.

The red cabbage iris is found in the Cabbage Patch bouquet, Color Plate 6.

The Cut and Bloom Blossoms

The two techniques used to fashion the blossoms in this group are *cutting* and *blooming*. These flowers all go through a complete metamorphosis in ice water. To assure full blooming, chill the ice water before putting in the flowers.

The gourmet gadgets needed are a sharp paring knife, skewers, and ice water; in addition, the crocus requires a grapefruit knife. The blossoms found in this group are the radish crocus, the radish sweet pea, the white radish spray, and the onion chrysanthemum.

Radish Crocus

Suggested Radish Shape The largest, most elongated radish you can find
Gourmet Gadgets Paring knife, grapefruit knife, skewers, and ice water
Special Hints The thinner the petals, the more realistically the crocus will bloom.

STEP-BY-STEP
1. Lightly peel the radish. (This step is optional.)

2. Hold the radish with the stem end down. Make one slice from the *top*, *outermost* edge of the radish down, but not competely through.

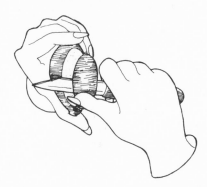

3. Repeat step 2 two more times, so that you have three petals.

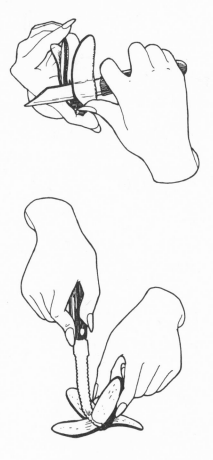

4. Using a grapefruit knife, cut the remaining center out at its core, taking care not to damage the other petals.

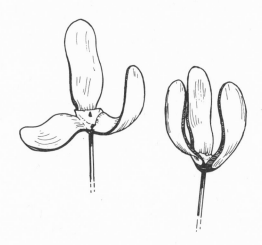

5. Drop the radish in ice water to bloom, and you will have a blooming crocus.

For a touch of authenticity, place the blossom in purple coloring, as recommended in Chapter 4, or use as a white blossom. This crocus is colored purple in the Springtime Bouquet, Color Plate 2.

Radish Sweet Pea

Suggested Radish Shape A large, elongated radish

Gourmet Gadgets Extra-sharp paring knife, skewers, ice water

Special Hints To achieve the curl required to indeed resemble a sweet pea, make the thinnest possible slices.

STEP-BY-STEP

1. Holding the radish with the stem end down, make one straight cut from nearly the center of the radish, cutting

all the way through so that you are left with a little more than half of the radish.

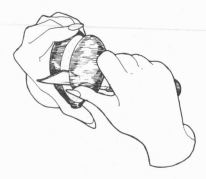

2. Turn the radish and make the same cut on the other side. Now you have a thin strip of radish with two flat sides left.

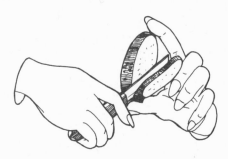

3. This is where skillful use of the paring knife comes in. Make three paper-thin slices down the center of the remaining radish and cut off the excess.

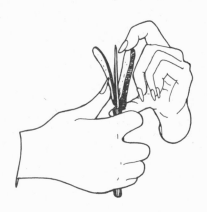

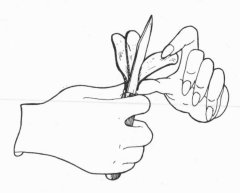

4. Drop the radish in ice water to bloom. When the petals begin contracting and curling, if the slices are indeed thin, you will have a sweet pea radish.

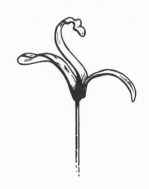

The sweet pea looks exceptionally pretty colored pink, though it is used in its natural color in the Pansy Picnic bouquet, Color Plate 3.

White Radish Spray

Suggested Radish Shape Long, straight white radish resembling a small carrot

Gourmet Gadgets Sharp paring knife, skewers, ice water

STEP-BY-STEP

1. Peel the radish lightly with a potato peeler.

THE GOURMET GARDEN

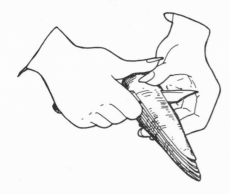

2. Holding the radish with the stem end down, make thin slices lengthwise, being careful not to cut through the radish.

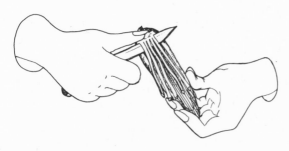

3. Turn the radish, holding all of the lengthwise strips together. Now cut again as in step 2, so that you have a crisscross pattern.

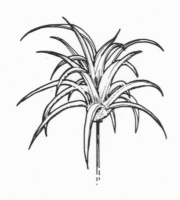

4. Place the radish in ice water to bloom,

then skewer at the stem end and add to the bouquet.

The radish spray, seen in the Easter Bouquet, Color Plate 4, is lightly tinted green. It is seen in its natural color in the Stars and Stripes bouquet, Color Plate 8, and is also used as a stamen, page 130.

Onion Chrysanthemum

Suggested Onion Shape Small boiling onion

Gourmet Gadgets Paring knife, ice water, and skewers

Special Hints Use a very sharp paring knife.

STEP-BY-STEP

1. Peel the onion. Hold it so that the point of the onion is on top.
2. Make the first cut using a rocking motion, directly down the center. Be careful not to cut completely through the onion.

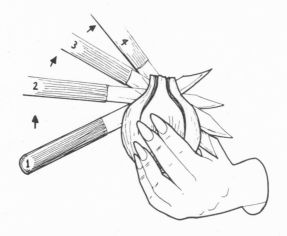

3. Turn the onion and repeat step 2. Do this several times until you have no more space to cut.

4. Place in ice water and watch your chrysanthemum bloom. Then place it in vegetable coloring. This blossom looks particularly striking in blue.
5. Skewer the chrysanthemum at the stem end and place in the bouquet.

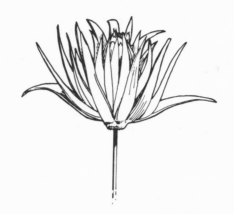

After this flower is in the bouquet, it continues to bloom on its own and even has a fragrance. The onion chrysanthemum is seen in the Stars and Stripes bouquet, Color Plate 8.

The Folded Flowers

The title of this section might suggest a kind of vegetable origami. Actually, the techniques used for fashioning these blossoms are much simpler. The key to these flowers is *thin slices.* The pliability necessary for making fancy folds is provided by the thinness of each slice. Once you have produced slivery slices, the rest is just a matter of folding and tooth-pickery.

The gourmet gadgets needed for these flowers are a French knife, toothpicks, ice water, skewers, and oil for frying the yam rosette. (This last item is optional, as the rosette may be eaten raw.) The flowers included in this group are the yam rosette and the Easter lily.

Yam Rosette

Suggested Potato Shape Select a large, long yam for your first rosette. This size will of course produce large petals, which are much easier to work with.

Gourmet Gadgets French knife, tooth-picks, skewers, and oil (optional)

Special Hints The rosette may be eaten raw or it may be fried in oil. When frying the rosette, skewer it first. This will enable you to pull it out of the oil quickly when crisp. To avoid soggy rosettes, heat the oil to between 340 and 360 degrees. This will assure crisp rosettes and minimize oil saturation. It is best to fry the rosettes the day they are to be served. However, they can be constructed the night before and stored in the refrigerator.

STEP-BY-STEP
1. Cut six to eight thin diagonal slices using the French knife. The number of petals you use will determine the size of your rosette. For your first rosettes, you may wish to make smaller blossoms by using fewer petals. After your first rosette masterpiece, add more petals to the next one to make it fuller.

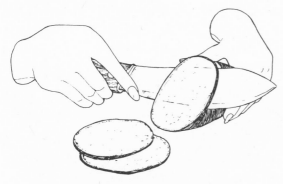

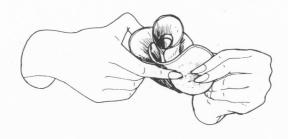

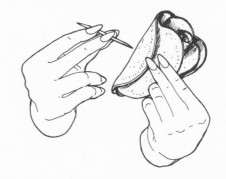

2. Wind your first petal around a pencil. Then remove the pencil and hold the petal so it won't lose its curl. The curl is the core of the rosette.

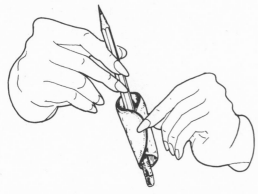

3. Arrange the remaining petals in alternate positions around the original curl. Be sure to have a firm hold on all the petals so they don't slip away from you as each new petal is added. This may sound a little tricky, but with the aid of toothpicks to fasten any slipping petal, it's easy.

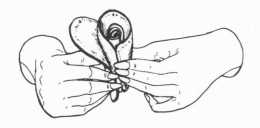

4. Fasten the rosette at the bottom with two crossing toothpicks, then skewer. You may find you need more than two toothpicks. This is perfectly all right. The appearance or taste of the rosette is not affected by the number of toothpicks used.

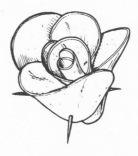

The yam rosette makes a wonderful centerpiece flower for any bouquet. It is pictured as a centerpiece in the Flower Fiesta bouquet, Color Plate 7.

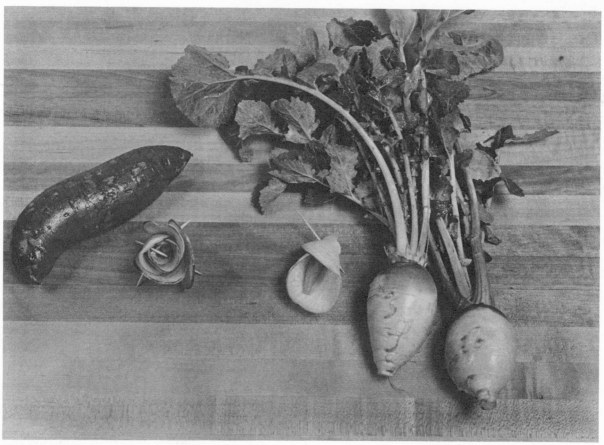

Left: Yam Rosette. *Right:* Turnip Easter Lily.

Turnip Easter Lily

Suggested Turnip Shape The largest turnip you can find
Gourmet Gadgets French knife, toothpicks, skewers, ice water
Special Hints The thinner the slices, the
  more pliable the petal.

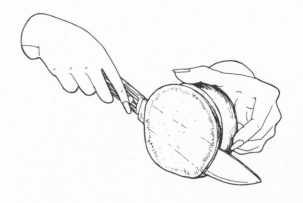

STEP-BY-STEP

1. Cut a slivery slice at the widest part of
   the turnip.
2. Fold the petal in a conelike manner.

THE GOURMET GARDEN

118

3. Place a miniature pickled corn in the center of the petal for a stamen.

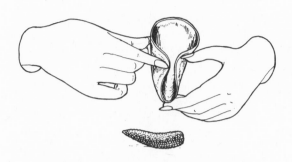

4. Fasten the petal by sticking the tooth-pick through the two front folds and through the miniature corn.

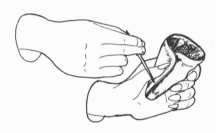

5. Place the blossom in ice water for crispness.
6. Skewer the lily just before placing it in the bouquet.

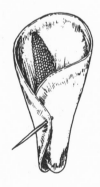

The turnip Easter lily is seen in the Easter Bouquet, Color Plate 4.

The Carved Blossoms

These blossoms are produced by actually carving beets and turnips into flowers with a paring knife. The important technique to remember is to make sharp, clean wedges. The step-by-step procedures for the carnation and the camellia are similar, with the exception of the cutting angle of the knife. This is fully explained with the instructions for each blossom. The blossoms need not bloom, for you have bloomed them by carving. To freshen the blossoms after handling, place them in ice water for a short time or simply rinse well under very cold running water and refrigerate.

The gourmet gadgets needed to fashion this group of flowers are a paring knife and skewers. Ice water is optional. The vegetable flowers in this section are the turnip camellia and the beet or turnip carnation.

Turnip Camellia

I recommend using a turnip for a characteristically white camellia; however, this carving technique can be applied to any tuber vegetable.

Suggested Turnip Shape Medium size, wide turnip
Gourmet Gadgets Sharp paring knife, skewers, and ice water (optional)
Special Hints When cutting wedges for the camellia, angle the knife blade towards the center of the turnip.

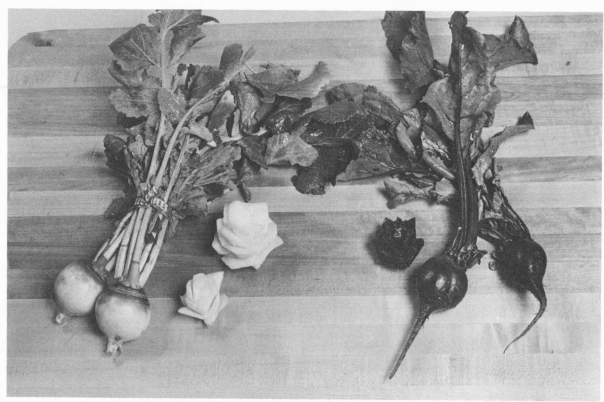

Left: Turnip Camellia. *Right:* Beet Carnation.

STEP-BY-STEP

1. Peel the turnip.
2. Hold the turnip with the stem end down. Make a small, inward cut at the lower third portion. Be sure not to cut through.
3. Repeat this step directly above the last one so that a wedge is formed and can be removed. Turn the vegetable and repeat this step 4 or 5 times. The number of wedges cut around the turnip depends on its size.

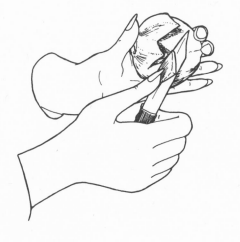

4. Now round off the top portion by cutting around it with a paring knife.

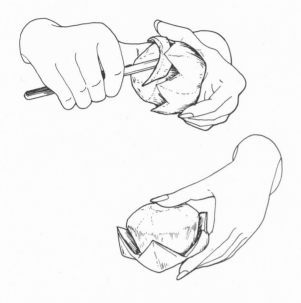

5. Begin making wedges again, this time in the middle of the vegetable, a tier above the last one.

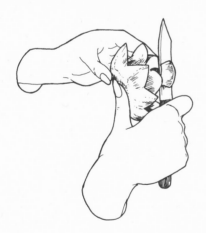

6. Repeat these steps until you have reached the top. Now make a small **V** cut at the top and you have a camellia. Place the camellia in ice water to freshen or run under very cold tap water. Skewer and add to the bouquet.

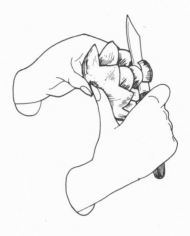

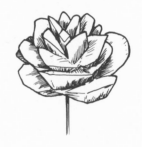

The turnip camellia is seen in the Hawaiian Holiday bouquet, Color Plate 9.

Beet or Turnip Carnation

Suggested Vegetable Shape Any size or shape beet or turnip can be used.

Gourmet Gadgets Sharp paring knife, skewers, ice water (optional)

Special Hints If your carnation is carved out of a turnip, a realistic coloring technique is to rub a freshly cut beet on the tips of the carved turnip. This technique will produce a red-tipped carnation.

1. Peel the vegetable.
2. Hold the vegetable with the stem end down. Make a small *downward* cut at the lower third portion. Be very careful not to cut through.
3. Make another cut directly above the last one so that a wedge is formed and can be removed. Turn the vegetable and repeat this step four or five times. The number of wedges cut around the vegetable depends on its size.

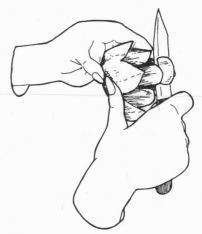

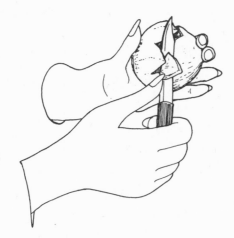

4. Now round off the top portion by cutting around it with a paring knife.

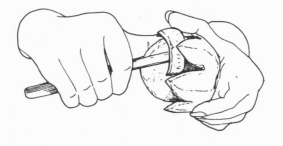

5. Begin making wedges again, this time in the middle of the vegetable, a tier above the last one.

6. Repeat these steps until you have reached the top. Make a small V cut at the top and your carnation is complete. Place the carnation in ice water to freshen or run under very cold tap water. Skewer and add to the bouquet.

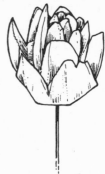

A beet carnation is seen in the Easter Bouquet, Color Plate 4.

Carve and Bloom Blossoms

This group of flowers requires two simple techniques: carving and ice water blooming. The carving techniques can

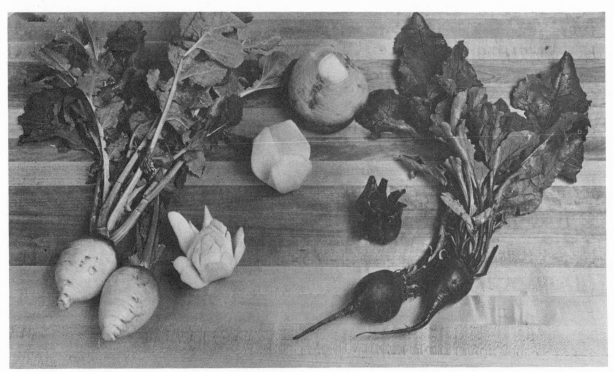

Left: Turnip Peony. *Center:* Three-Petaled Rutabaga Tulip. *Right:* Beet Tulip.

be used interchangeably for all of the vegetables in this section. For example, if you wish to make a three-petaled tulip but don't have the recommended rutabaga on hand, you can use a turnip or beet instead. Inside each beet, turnip, rutabaga, and radish there lies a tulip or peony just waiting to be released through the magic of your paring knife. So gather your gadgets and prepare to create.

The gourmet gadgets needed for these flowers are an extra sharp paring knife, a melon baller, a grapefruit spoon, a grapefruit knife, skewers, and ice water.

The flowers included in this section are the three-petaled rutabaga tulip, the turnip peony, the tuber tulip, and the radish tulip or daisy.

Three-Petaled Rutabaga Tulip

Suggested Rutabaga Size The size rutabaga you select will determine the size of your tulip, so select any size or shape that looks interesting.

Gourmet Gadgets Extra-sharp paring knife and grapefruit knife

Special Hints The rutabaga is a hard vegetable, so be sure your knife is extra sharp to penetrate its thickness.

1. Peel the rutabaga.
2. Hold the peeled rutabaga with the flat (stem) end down. Place the paring knife about ⅛" in from the edge closest to you. Now slice from the very top down, being careful not to cut all the way through.
3. Turn the rutabaga and repeat the same step two more times so that you have three petals and a middle portion.

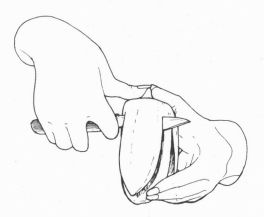

4. Using the grapefruit knife, cut out the middle portion.

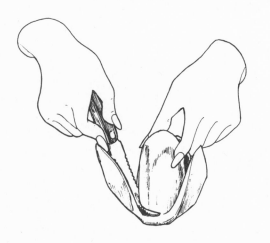

5. Drop the tulip in ice water. This will help crisp and freshen it, rather than bloom the blossom. Skewer just before adding to the bouquet.

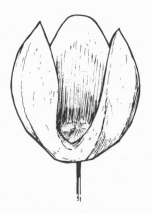

The three petal tulip is seen in the Springtime Bouquet, Color Plate 2.

Turnip Peony

Suggested Turnip Shape Any size or shape turnip is suitable for this flower.

Gourmet Gadgets Sharp paring knife and ice water

Special Hints This flower looks particularly nice when colored pink. See Chapter 4, Color Concoctions.

STEP-BY-STEP

1. Peel a turnip and hold it with the stem (flat) end down.
2. Start at the top and make a very thin slice all the way to the bottom, being careful not to cut through.
3. Make another slice just next to and slightly behind the first one, so that you have an overlapping effect. Con-

tinue the same procedure all the way around the turnip.

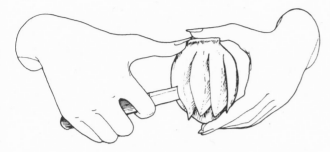

4. Repeat a second layer on the inside of the first.

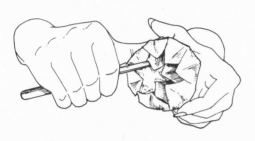

5. Proceed to cut another layer inside of the second. Make as many inside layers as you have room for. This will depend on the circumference of the turnip used. Generally, three layers are enough.

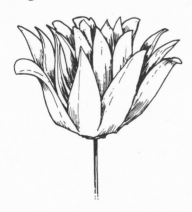

6. Place in ice water to bloom. Then,

skewer the bloomed peony just before adding it to the bouquet.

The peony makes a good centerpiece flower. It is pictured in the Cabbage Patch bouquet, Color Plate 6.

Tuber Tulip

Tulips can be fashioned from any of the large tubers—beets, turnips, and rutabaga. Vegetables cut using the tulip technique are remarkable. They actually transform in ice water, each flower expressing its own desired shape.

Gourmet Gadgets Paring knife, melon baller, grapefruit knife

STEP-BY-STEP

1. Hold the vegetable with the stem end down. Peel from the top down so that you have vertical indentations all the way around.
2. Start close to the top and make a slice all the way down, being careful not to cut all the way through.

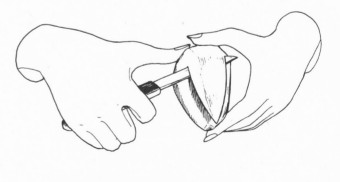

3. Make another slice just next to the first one. This time cut the slice out.

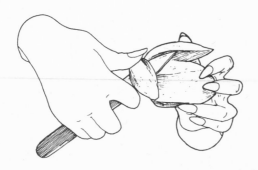

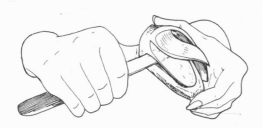

4. Now go to the top of the same place you cut out the slice, and repeat the step. Continue until you have gone all the way around the vegetable. What you have done is to create an indentation so that each slice is slightly behind and indented from the one before it.

5. Now you have a middle portion from which the rest of the petals are free.

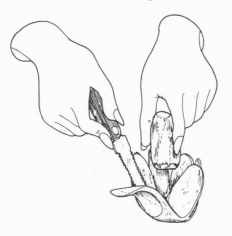

Cut out this middle portion, using a grapefruit knife, and follow by scooping out the remainder with a melon baller.

6. Place in ice water; when the tulip has bloomed, skewer and insert a carrot tip stamen. See Stamens, page 128.

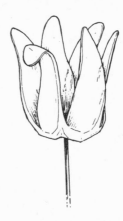

Tulips of all kinds are seen in the Springtime Bouquet, Color Plate 2.

Radish Tulip or Daisy

The radish tulip requires the same basic cutting technique as the tuber tulip, with a few minor changes and a special bonus. When radishes are cut in this way, they sometimes open fully to resemble daisies. How fully the radishes open seems to be determined by the length of time they are left in ice water and by how completely the center portion is scooped out. This flower is unique, as you have the choice of blooming it into a daisy or tulip simply by varying the blooming time. If you choose to have a tulip, remove it from the ice water when it reaches this stage. If you want a daisy, leave it in the ice water longer. I must confide, after working with these unpredictable little characters, that the degree of blooming time often depends on each radish's inclination. At times, after precise cutting and efficient scooping, the radish is determined to display its own special flower personality.

Suggested Radish Shape Medium size, rounded radish

Gourmet Gadgets Sharp paring knife, grapefruit knife and spoon, and ice water

STEP-BY-STEP

1. Hold the radish with the stem end down and slice off a thin piece.

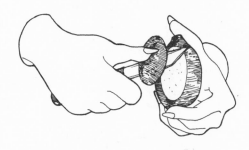

2. Start close to the top, slightly beneath the surface of the area just cut, and

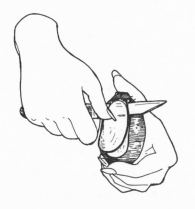

make a slice all the way down, being careful not to cut all the way through.

3. Make another slice just next to the first one; this time, cut the slice out.

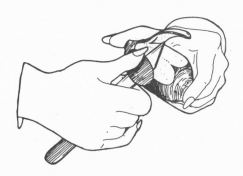

4. Go to the top of the exact place you cut out the slice, and repeat step 2. Continue until you have gone all the way around the radish. As in the tuber tulip, what you have done is to create an indentation so that each slice is slightly behind and indented from the one before it.

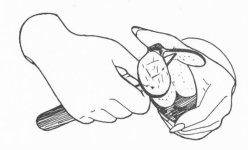

5. At this point, you have a middle portion from which the rest of the petals are free. Using a grapefruit knife, cut out this middle portion as completely as possible. Scoop out any excess radish with the grapefruit spoon. This will permit the radish to bloom fully, producing a daisy.

PLEASE EAT THE DAISIES

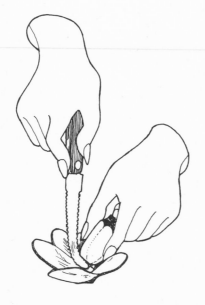

6. Place the blossom in ice water. When the radish has bloomed to a tulip skewer and place a carrot tip stamen in the center. Or when the radish blooms fully to a daisy, place a carrot disc stamen in the center.

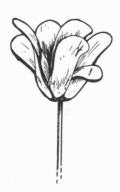

The daisy and tulip are seen in the Italian Antipasto Artistry bouquet, Color Plate 1.

Stamens

Stamens are a vital part of nature's flowers and add an accent of authenticity to ours. They are an optional step, since not all of our vegetable flowers have them. Although I have included flower suggestions for each stamen, the flowers and stamens are interchangeable and the combinations are limitless. All of the lengths and sizes given are merely guidelines for making the stamens. They may be any length, provided they are in proportion to the size of the flower. As an example, the radish spray is a large stamen and suits a large flower like the cabbage lily. Some of the stamens require blooming and may be bloomed along with the flowers; others require only cutting and skewering.

The gourmet gadgets needed are a paring knife and ice water. The stamens found in this section are the pickled corn stamen, the carrot tip stamen, the carrot spray stamen, the carrot disc stamen, and the radish spray stamen.

Pickled Corn Stamen

Miniature corn cobs make a tasty stamen for several different flowers. They require little in the way of preparation, other than opening a container. To vary the length of the corn, cut it off at the wide end, leaving the pointed end intact. Skewer the flower so that the tip of the skewer shows through the top. Then skewer the miniature corn cob at the

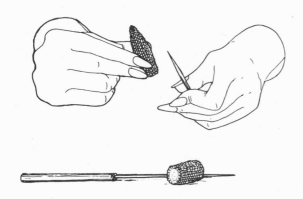

wide end. A corn stamen is used for the Easter lily (see Easter Bouquet, Color Plate 4). It is suitable for all the tulips and may be used for any of the petal flowers.

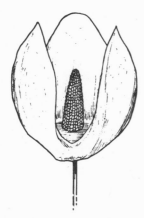

Carrot Tip Stamen

One of the most colorful stamens is made from the tip of a carrot. Cut the tip of a peeled carrot about 1" to 1½" from the end. The length of the carrot tip will depend on the size of the flower. If you are making a small flower, of course you'll want to use a shorter stamen. Rinse the stamen under cold water and skewer it to the center of the flower. The carrot tip stamen is used in the pimiento

poppy. (See Italian Antipasto Artistry, Color Plate 1.) This stamen may be used for any of the tulips or petal flowers. Simply adjust the length of the stamen to the size of the flower.

Carrot Spray Stamen

This is an easy but elaborate-looking variation on the carrot tip stamen. Make very thin slices the length of the stamen. Turn the carrot and repeat this step so that you have a crisscross pattern. Place the stamen in ice water to bloom along with the flowers, then skewer in the center of a blossom. The carrot spray stamen is used in the tulips pictured in the Eggplant Extravaganza, Color Plate 5.

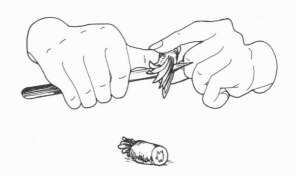

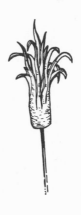

Carrot Disc Stamen

Not all stamens are protruding, and what could be easier than cutting a little carrot disc and skewering it to the center of a radish daisy. The carrot disc is used in the radish daisy pictured in the Italian Antipasto Artistry bouquet, Color Plate 1.

Radish Spray Stamen

The white radish spray is versatile; not only can it be displayed as a flower, but it can also be used as the stamen for the cabbage lily. (See the Cabbage Patch, Color Plate 6.) Because of its size, the radish spray stamen is best suited to a large flower. For complete directions for making the radish spray stamen, see the white radish spray, page 114.

Condiment Capers

Tasty additions to complement the flavor of your bouquet.

There is more to the bouquet than vegetable flowers, spectacular as these may be. Hors d'oeuvres, which until now have been limited to the platter, miraculously take their place among the vegetable flowers in the bouquet. What was once content to be a simple salami, a plain pimiento, a common cheese wedge is now transformed into a salami rosette, a pimiento poppy, or a charming cheese daisy.

Since the bouquet is edible, it is by no means limited to vegetables. When considering condiments, remember to include leftover meats such as roast beef or ham. When thinly sliced and rolled, these make lovely rosettes. Refrigerate the meat and cheese condiments as soon as they are fashioned into blossoms. Have plenty on reserve (I recommend about three per person). Add them to the bouquet just before serving time. Condiments not only enhance the appearance of your bouquet, they also complement the flavor of the vegetables.

Salami Stacks

Salami stacks are the most popular hors d'oeuvres. They have a tendency to disappear quickly, so keep enough in reserve to refill your bouquet. Spread cream cheese between two slices of salami. Spread another layer of cream cheese on the top slice and top with another slice of salami. You now have five alternating layers of salami and cream

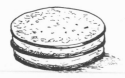

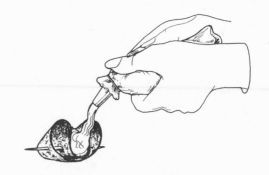

cheese resembling a double decker sandwich. Remember to spread the cream cheese evenly, about ¼" thick. Wrap the stack and set it in the freezer for about an hour until it is slightly hard. Then remove the stack and cut it twice until you have four wedges. Skewer each wedge and top with an olive or cocktail onion.

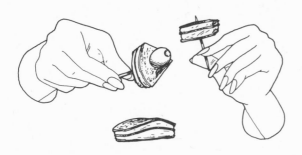

Salami Rosette

Fold a round slice of salami in half. Then, holding it at the bottom center, fold it again. Skewer with a toothpick through the center, topping with an olive or cocktail onion. For an added

touch of elegance, use a pastry tube to squeeze cream cheese into the center of your rosette, but be sure you do this *after* you have skewered the salami; otherwise, the rosette won't have the proper shape. Skewer the rosette through the bottom and place in the refrigerator. At serving time, place your chilled salami rosette in the bouquet. If you really want to get fancy, cut tiny wedges at the rim of the salami slices and then follow the above steps.

Peperoni Petals

Peperoni slices are a spicy essential. Slice pieces about ¼" to ½" thick, and

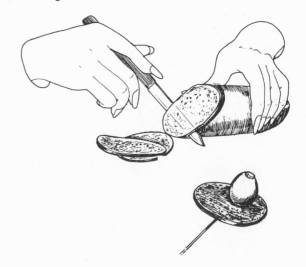

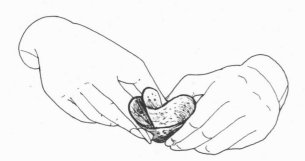

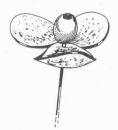

top with an olive. A variation is to skewer three very thin slices of peperoni sliced on the diagonal. Skewer the slices, arranging them like petals, and top off with an olive.

Pimiento Poppy

Place the whole pimiento on a cutting board. Cut off the end portion where the pimiento comes to a V. This V-shaped cone should be about 1" long from the tip up. Skewer a carrot disc first, to secure

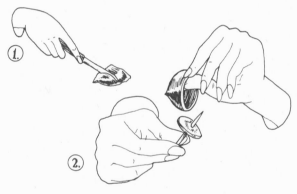

the pimiento and keep it from sliding. Then skewer the pimiento, topping it off with a carrot tip stamen. (See page 129 for stamen information.)

Banana Squash

Banana squash in the shape of little stars is a perfect addition to A Condiment Christmas. Cut a 1"-thick strip about 3" long. Brush lightly with butter and sprinkle with sugar. Brown the top in the oven for five minutes or until the butter and sugar melt. Heat the squash only enough to melt the butter and sugar—the squash itself should remain raw and crisp. When it is cool, cut with an hors d'oeuvre cutter. Skewer and re-frigerate until serving time.

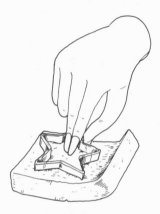

Cocktail Hot Dogs

These tiny little hot dogs make a very appetizing stamen for your flower. A very simple combination is made by cutting

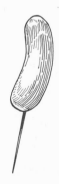

the hot dog in half and sticking one of the halves into a turnip or carrot disc. Skewer it lengthwise through the center. A variation is to use the whole hot dog: skewer it (again lengthwise) and add it to the bouquet. If you use enough of these, you will have something resembling an edible porcupine.

Turkey Rollette

Turkey is the prime ingredient here; get the kind that is pressed and sliced, not the kind that comes straight off the bird. Cut strips about 3" long and 2" wide.

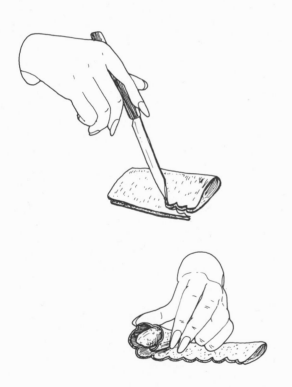

Scallop one edge (simply make an uneven, wavy line on one side with a paring knife). Place a very small sweet pickle at one end of the turkey slice and

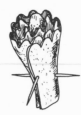

roll it up, allowing the scalloped edge to fold out. Secure with a toothpick, making sure to catch the left over end. Skewer and refrigerate. Arrange in the bouquet just before serving time.

Cheese

Different kinds of cheeses can be used and mounted in several different ways. One of my favorites is a hickory smoked cheese which goes well with salami or peperoni. Most hard cheeses are amenable to skewering. A quick, easy method is to cut squares of hard cheese and top with a colorful condiment. In keeping with the flower theme, you can slice the cheese about ½" thick and cut a flower shape with a daisy hors d'oeuvre cutter. One of the tastiest variations is to fashion a spreadable cheese, such as cream cheese, into a ball and roll it in chopped walnuts. Place the cheese balls in the freezer till they are hard. Skewer at serving time and place in the bouquet.

Not-So-Chilly Chili Peppers

Whole, small chili peppers in varying degrees of hotness can be purchased pickled. They come in a variety of colors and add a piquant, zingy touch to the

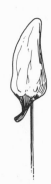

bouquet. Skewer at the stem end and place in the bouquet.

Marinated Artichoke Hearts

Whole marinated artichoke hearts tastefully enrich any bouquet. Simply

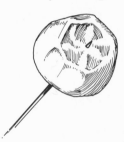

skewer, stick, and serve. Miniature sweet pickles, small green tomatoes, and any other skewerable condiments are also a welcome addition.

Miniature Gherkins

Skewer these miniature sweet pickles and place in the bouquet at various intervals.

Toasted Bread

Toast thick buttered slices of garlic bread. Cut the slices into various shapes with hors d'oeuvre cutters. Use the same cutters to shape salami or other meats. Place the meat on top of the bread and top with an olive. Skewer the stacks and distribute through the bouquet. To avoid sogginess, make sure the bread is thick and crisp.

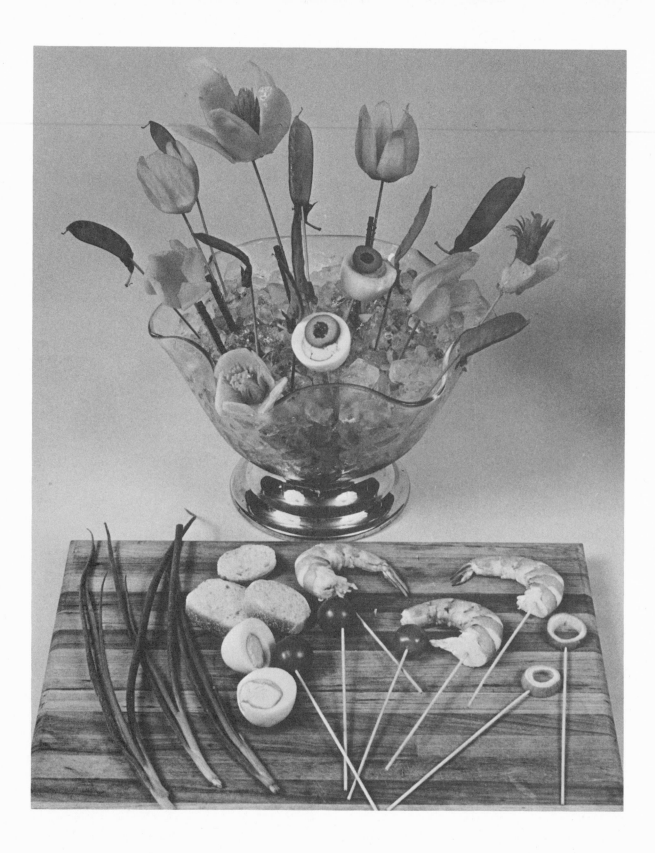

✣10✣

Stemmery And Stickery

Edible facsimiles of nature's leaves and stems to accent the vegetable flowers.

What flower bouquet is complete without stems and leaves? In this chapter are some of the edible facsimiles of Nature's own ornamentation. These colorful additions help break up the symmetry of the arrangement, adding interest, authenticity, and accent. Here, we are able to cleverly reproduce stems and leaves (without waste) from scraps, peels, and other edibles. Stemmery and stickery are of course optional. Your bouquet will be smashing whether or not you include them. However, they are the exceptional touches of imagination that extract the extra "ooh" or "ah."

String Beans

Wash and crisp the string beans (see page 85 for crisping instructions). Just before serving time, skewer lengthwise about a quarter of the way up from the end. Disperse the skewered string beans at various intervals throughout the bouquet. You might find that inserting the skewer only halfway into the string

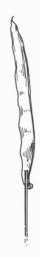

bean is not enough for your bouquet. If so, you can cut the bean down before skewering or simply skewer the bean further.

Cucumber Peels

The cucumber peel does not qualify as a stem; however, it makes a most authentic-looking bit of stickery. Cucumber peels may be used as leaves on the stems or they can be placed on skewers. Peel the cucumber with a knife (rather than a peeler); this will allow thicker

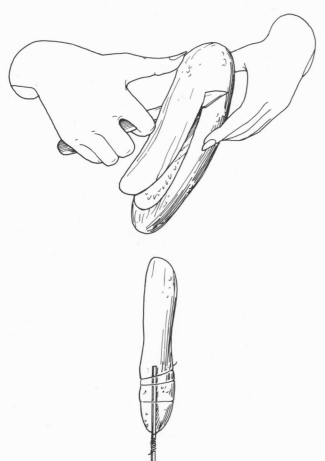

peels for firmer leaves. Now go the entire length of the cucumber, making the slices about ¾" to 1" wide. Place the slices on a cutting board and cut one end into the shape of a long, pointed spear. Attach the rounded end to a floral pick and add to the bouquet before serving time. Another method is to thread a skewer lengthwise into the peel, about halfway. Then add to the bouquet.

Red and Green Peppers

Red and green peppers are interchangeable as either stickery or leaves. The choice is yours and depends entirely on the way in which you cut the peppers. Hollow out the inside of the peppers from the core end and make 1" to 1½" slices from where the core was to the bottom. Go all the way around the pepper until it is completely cut. Thread it on the skewer straight up and down as stickery or thread two leaves crosswise to resemble the natural placement of leaves. Cut the pepper slices to simulate leaves and then skewer. Try mixing both red and green peppers in your bouquet,

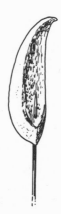

some to be used as leaves, others as stickery.

Green Summer Squash

This delightful little squash already has a natural cookie cutter shape at the edges. So to make use of this natural pattern, thinly slice the squash horizontally at the wide flowery part, making sure to include the intricate little convolutions. This results in a natural flower. Skewer the flower through the center and top with a cherry tomato or olive.

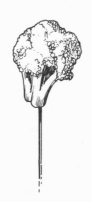

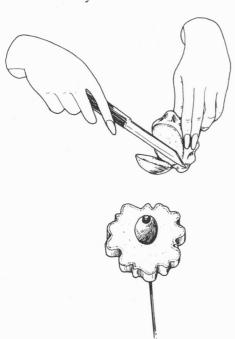

green stem left and skewer so that the white portion shows. Add this delicate little flower to your blossoming bouquet. You can use broccoli florets in the same way.

China Peas in Their Pods

These are a favorite with children, who seem to enjoy popping open the seams of the pods and chewing on the little sweet peas found inside. Crisp the pods and either wire on a pick and arrange in the bouquet or thread on a skewer one-third of the way at the stem end and place throughout the bouquet for easy picking.

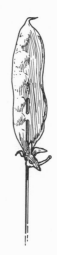

Cauliflower Sections

Small cauliflower florets on a skewer resemble tiny patches of candy tuft, a little flower having a lacy, feathery appearance. Cut small sections of the freshest, whitest cauliflower you can find. Trim the back so that there is not much of the

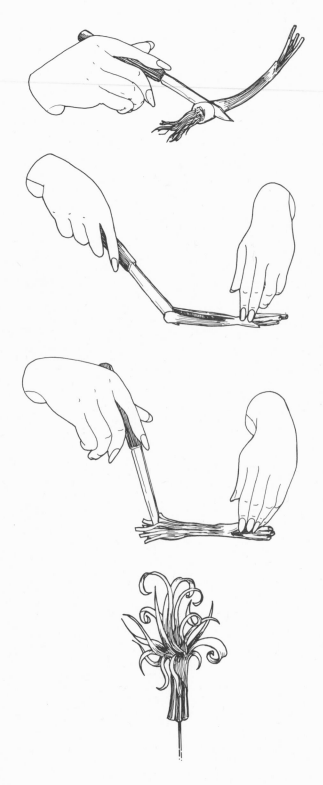

Onion Curls

To add a touch of Baroque extravagance, try adding feathered scallions. Place the washed scallion on a cutting board and trim the roots at the bottom edge of the white portion. Now make several lengthwise slices along this white (bulb) portion. Place the entire scallion in ice water, making sure it has enough room to bloom. Refrigerate for about one hour. Each scallion is now tipped with remarkable frilly curls. To skewer, cut off the green ends to about ½" above the very first cut. Since this green part is what keeps the whole thing together, be very careful not to cut at the wrong place. (A ½" misjudgment could leave you with a handful of loose onion curls.) Skewer the green end and place in the bouquet. Save the cut scallion greens; they can be used as stems to conceal the skewers. (See Scallion Ends.)

Scallion Ends

These are the ends left over from the onion curls, so if you followed my advice and kept the stems, you're all ready to go. Scallions make very authentic-looking stems, all in green, conveniently shaped for use, complete with a hollow space in the center for easy skewering. Crisp and cut to the desired length, thread the skewer through the inside of the scallion end, and top with a vegetable flower. Place in the bouquet where a part of the stem will show. This is very effective when used with loose, leafy

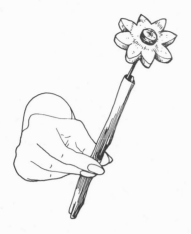

filler foliage like watercress or mint leaves.

Jerusalem Artichoke or Sun Choke

The Jerusalem artichoke or sun choke has a rootlike appearance similar to the

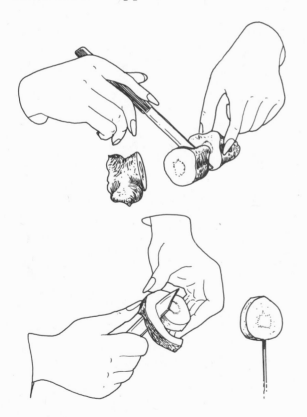

ginger root, yet has the consistency and crunchyness of a nut. The texture and unusual flavor are irresistible and I highly recommend using it in the bouquet. Peel the sun choke, cut into various skewerable shapes, and place in the bouquet.

Bread Sticks

Bread sticks are a particularly appropriate addition to the Italian Antipasto Artistry bouquet. I prefer using the thinner, sesame seed–covered sticks because they're easier to wire. I also make lots of butter available. The addition of bread sticks makes your bouquet look more like a meal than just a floral arrangement, surprising your guests when they discover the delightfully unique way their dinner is being served. They've heard of pot roast in a pot, stew in a kettle, but how many have been served a buffet in a bouquet? Attach one end of each bread stick to a floral pick and distribute them evenly throughout the bouquet.

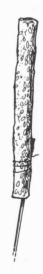

Yellow Crooked Neck Squash

Yellow squash peels can be handled in much the same way as cucumber peels. Because of their fresh yellow color, they can either enhance and brighten a Springtime Bouquet, or add a soft autumn feeling to a Thanksgiving bouquet. Crisp, then place on the cutting board. With a paring knife, peel from the top to the bottom of the squash, making a medium heavy slice (just thick enough so the slice will stand straight on its own). The width of the slice, because of the width of the squash, will be somewhat on the narrow side. Cut these about ½" wide. I usually average about three to four strips per yellow squash, and use about twelve peels in each bouquet. The

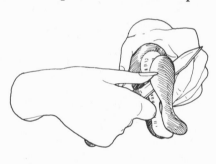

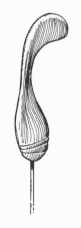

top of the squash has a candy canelike curve, so when this end is displayed with the curves all facing the same way, the color and uniformity make a spectacular sight. Place the slices in ice water for about one hour and watch the ends curve. It is these ends that create such a splendid effect when they pop out of the bouquet.

Sugar Cane

Sugar cane is most appropriate for the Hawaiian Holiday bouquet and is also especially effective in a bouquet for children. From one sugar cane, I am able to get six to eight separate little stalks. They are usually about 5" to 6" long, so I cut the cane in half with the largest, sharpest knife I have. Then I cut down the center lengthwise and repeat this step, cutting each of these in half again. This gives me four little stalks from each half, or eight in all. I then attach them to floral picks one by one and strategically place them in the bouquet along with pineapple spears and anything else edibly Hawaiian I can think of.

Pineapple Spears

I suggest the use of pineapple spears for the Hawaiian Holiday bouquet. The pineapple spears are the easiest to use of all the stickery, since they require almost nothing in the way of preparation other than selection of the greenest and straightest spears. Just cut the top off any pineapple (perhaps the one used as the container for this very bouquet). Wash

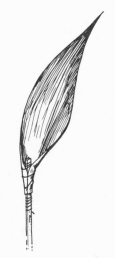

the spears and pull them out one by one until you have the desired number. Attach each to a floral pick by winding the wire around the blunt end and place in the bouquet.

Chives

The chives I have seen most recently come in small bundles in lengths of 3″ to 4″. Crisp and then separate them into very small groups (three to five in each

little bunch). Attach each bunch at one end to a floral pick, leaving the pointed ends free, and place in various spaces in the bouquet.

Artichoke Leaves

This one sneaked in under the heading of stickery, but it is really used as a leaf. Wash and crisp the whole artichoke. Then pull off the individual leaves. Skewer two leaves through the broad end, close to the bottom, so that the sharp ends point outward. Top off with a small vegetable flower.

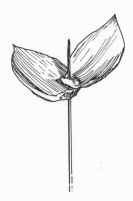

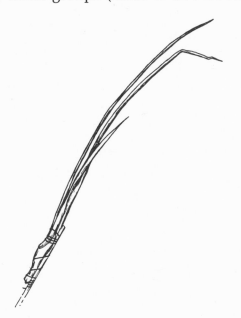

Miniature Artichokes

These are simply small versions of the larger artichoke whose leaves we used

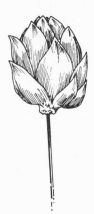

for petals. But the miniature artichokes are used whole. Trim the very tips of the leaves before cooking. Don't overcook; these should be only slightly soft, so they don't fall apart when skewered. Cool first, then skewer the entire artichoke and place in the bouquet. These can be eaten whole; they are tender and tasty.

Potato Knishes

I could not have designed an edible bouquet without including this delightful traditional hors d'oeuvre which has been a part of my cultural heritage. Potato knishes are delicious little potato dumplings wrapped in pastry dough. They can be purchased frozen. To use in the bouquet, bake, cool, skewer, and serve. If the consistency of the knish is such that it slides all the way down the skewer, prop it up with a piece of carrot or red pepper first, then skewer.

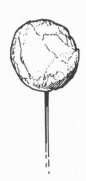

Cherry Tomatoes

Skewer whole cherry tomatoes and place in the bouquet for a dash of color and good taste.

Mushroom Buttercup

Skewer the petal of a small artichoke. Snap the stem off a small, firm mushroom and skewer the cap upside down on top of the petal. Place a carrot spray stamen in the center of the mushroom cap. (See carrot spray stamen, page 129.)

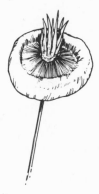

Cranberries

Cranberries are the perfect stickery for a fall or winter bouquet. Skewer five to eight on a skewer and place in the bouquet. These red porcupine quills will add a lovely splash of color and holiday spirit. Another way that I use cranberries is to string them with a needle and thread until I have several yards. Then I

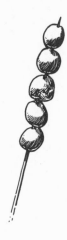

drape them around the special Christmas Condiment bouquet.

Jicima

This vegetable, resembling a very large potato that has been compressed at both ends, makes a most delicious bit of stickery. Slice the jicima into slices ½" thick and cut out shapes with an hors d'oeuvre cutter. Jicima takes very well to coloring and is one of the most popular of the bouquet ingredients. Skewer and place in the bouquet.

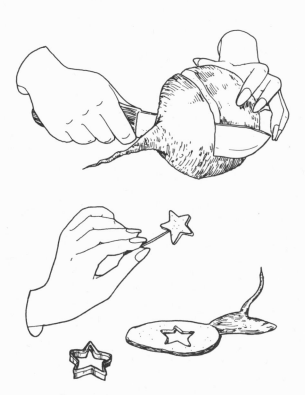

Eggs

Hard boil as many eggs as you can use. Cut them in half crosswise and glaze them, using the method suggested on page 20. Add a tablespoon of condensed consommé for extra flavor. Once the glaze has set, skewer the egg so that the yolk portion will be visible when placed in the bouquet. (Prop up with a carrot disc to keep the egg from sliding down the skewer.) Top with a pimiento olive slice or serve plain.

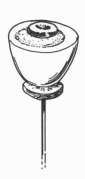

Gefilte Fish

Gefilte fish is not a species of fish, but rather the result of mincing and shaping fish into dainty little balls the size of meat balls. They are used as hors d'oeuvres or in larger portions as an appetizer at a traditional Jewish meal. They are sometimes served with horseradish (guaranteed to leave an internal impression). For the bouquet, skewer a little disc of carrot first to prevent sliding; then skewer the little gefilte fish ball and place in the bouquet.

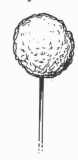

Shrimp

Shrimp is another very popular kind of stickery and is a favorite among bouquet connoisseurs. Select medium to large pre-cooked, peeled shrimp. Wash them thoroughly (being careful to remove any veins) and skewer, going part way through the length of the shrimp, starting at the wide end. The result should be something resembling a shrimp candy cane. Then place in the bouquet.

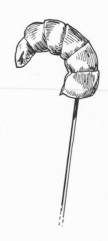

11

Sneaky Sniffery

Surprising additions to create a delightful aroma for your bouquet.

Sneaky sniffery is the addition of hidden little vegetable embellishments designed especially to entice the olfactory sense. Now that we have enchanted the other senses with our spectacular spoof, we mustn't overlook the sense of smell. As your guests move towards the bouquet for closer inspection, they are surprised that these carnations and tulips really do have a fragrance. I call these fragrance enhancers sneaky because they are aromas not usually associated with flowers. This generally adds humor as the whiffers and sniffers among your guests insist that something is blooming, and aren't sure what. To add to our floral fantasy, tulips not only bloom in

November but they emit the fragrance of ginger as well.

Shallots

At times, when I want to add a special emphasis to the theme of the bouquet, I use shallots for whimsical whiffery. The fragrance, unlike other varieties of onions, is not overwhelming, yet adds an

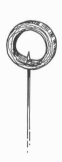

interesting aroma. Peel the little shallots and cut them crosswise, making a slice about ⅛″ wide. Then separate the ringlets and use the largest ones, skewering the side so that you have something resembling an onion lollipop. Five to ten of these ringlets are usually enough, depending on the size of the bouquet. The shallots are particularly piquant and appetizing in a bouquet filled with hors d'oeuvres and condiments.

Mint Leaves

Earlier, I mentioned the use of mint leaves as filler foliage. It is equally effective as sniffery. It is not necessary to use the entire bunch of mint for this purpose, unless you want to. Make five or six separate little bunches of mint, attach them to floral picks, and distribute these among the filler foliage. This adds a refreshing summer or spring aroma to the bouquet and, if you're mixing a variety of hors d'oeuvres, will help prevent a possible collision of food fragrances.

Ginger Root

Ginger root adds an exotic tanginess that makes it a perfect mood setter for the Hawaiian Holiday bouquet. Peel it and cut into several little squares or triangles. Then skewer each one and distribute throughout the bouquet.

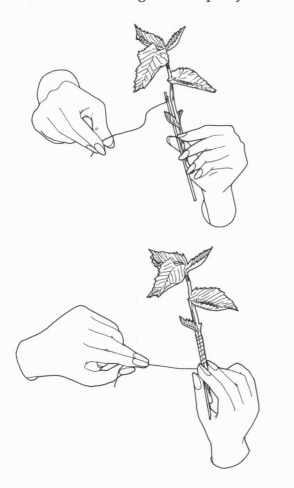

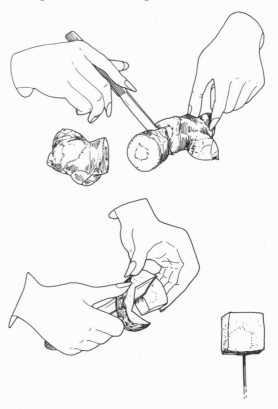

Cinnamon Sticks

I always associate cinnamon sticks with pumpkin pie, hot apple cider, and Halloween. Since the fragrance is delightfully inviting, it is the perfect amplification for a fall bouquet. Wire the cinnamon stick carefully to the floral pick and place gently in the bouquet.

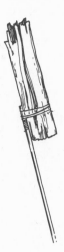

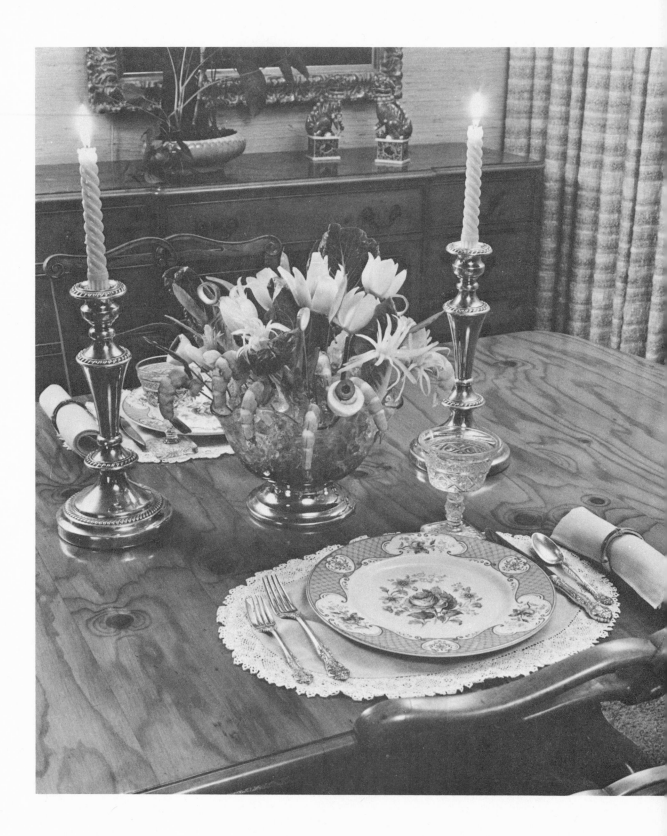

12

Finery Foldery

Linen flowers to enhance your table setting.

Gourmet bouquets take center stage every time you serve them, but the background setting can add a lot to the impact. Whether you are setting a buffet table, a dinner table, or just putting out cocktail nibbles for the crowd, be imaginative with the table decor. Use subtle ideas or splashy ones to create a lively setting for your gourmet bouquet. The bounty of patterned and solid table cloths and placemats with napkins to mix, match, or mismatch gives lots of variety to today's table. There are no rules; just ask yourself, "Do I like it?"

To coordinate a table, begin with the mood you'd like to set. Let the centerpiece, your gourmet bouquet, be the key. Is the mood informal and festive like the Italian Antipasto Artistry bouquet? Then checked gingham, rickrack trim, straw baskets, and candles in wine bottles would be perfect. Try rolling the napkins diagonally from point to point and knotting in the middle. Is the mood quaint and charming like the Springtime Bouquet? Use multicolored ribbons to tie up the napkins. Combine several bright calico prints to carry through the flower theme. Dozens of ideas and schemes can spring from the mood of each bouquet you create.

Sometimes you only need one extra touch. I'd like to introduce a special added attraction: finery foldery. As you may have guessed, this produces not a vegetable or condiment flower but a linen flower. No blooming or cutting is necessary here. Just fold and display. This accent adds the finishing touch to your table. The linen blossoms are all variations on one basic recipe. The first four folding instructions provide the basis for all the flowers. Simply change the last step to produce the desired pattern.

Ingredients A square linen napkin 16" x 16", lightly seasoned with starch

STEP-BY-STEP

1. Fold all four corners to the center and crease. Now we have a square with the folds on top.

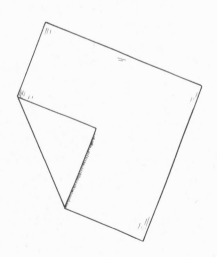

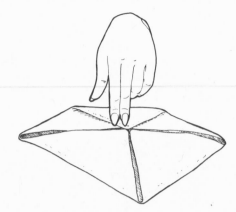

2. Repeat the process, folding the corners to the center once more. Now we have another, smaller square.

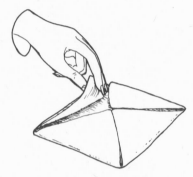

3. Place one palm beneath the folded napkin and one palm on top, making sure that the top palm is holding all four corners in place. Now carefully turn the napkin over, so that the corners are down and the smooth surface is on top.

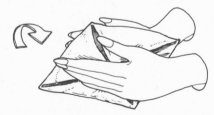

4. Repeat the earlier process of folding all four corners to the center. (The same as step 1.)

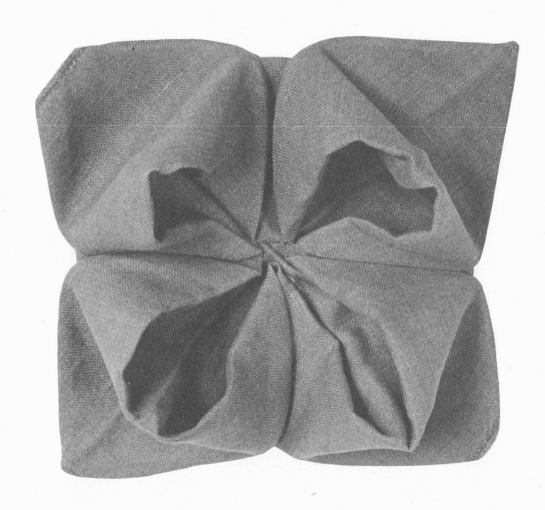

Lotus Blossom

Lift one of the corners and look for the flap hiding beneath. Turn this flap out, causing the corners to peak. Now do the same with the other corners. This will allow the napkin to stand up, producing a lotus blossom.

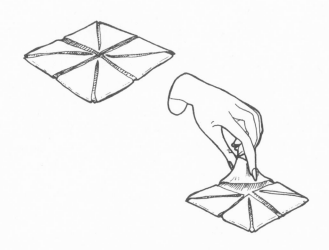

Linen Petal Flower

As with the lotus blossom, turn the flaps out. Now, holding the center firmly with one hand, stretch the petals out. This produces a puckered petal, and you have a linen petal flower.

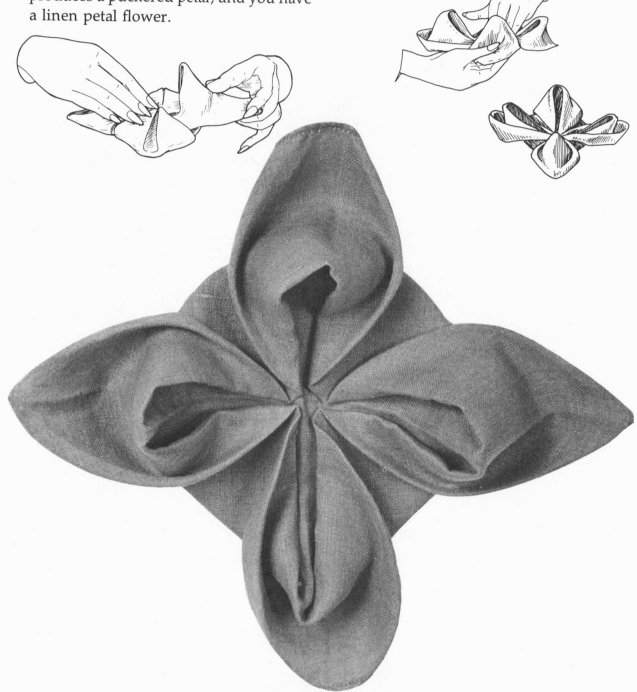

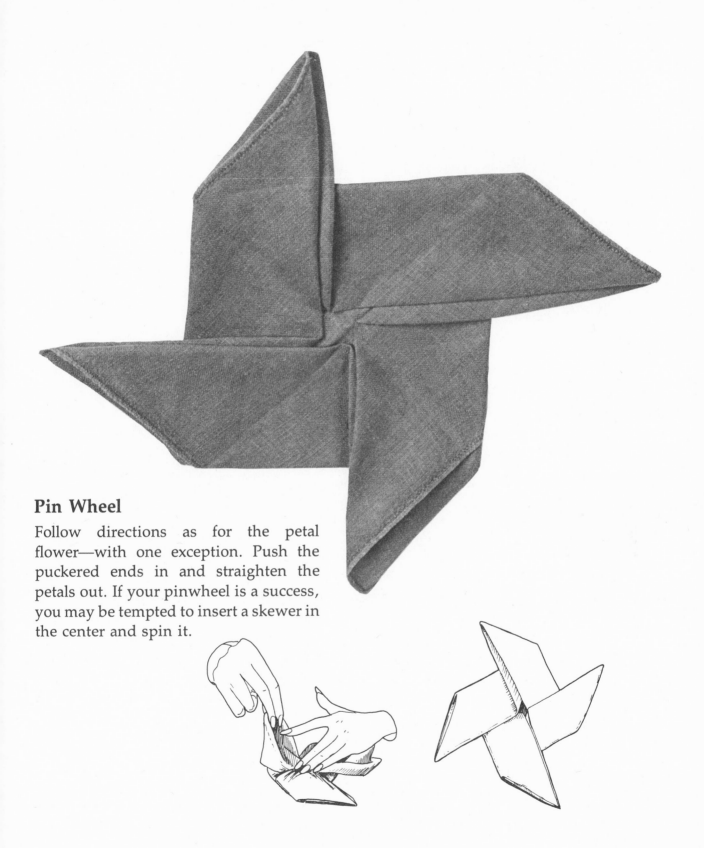

Pin Wheel

Follow directions as for the petal flower—with one exception. Push the puckered ends in and straighten the petals out. If your pinwheel is a success, you may be tempted to insert a skewer in the center and spin it.

Conclusion

Now you have created your own bouquets. I hope you find them pleasing to the eye as well as to the taste. They will give your table an extraordinary air of elegance and style—achieved wholly by your own talent!

Remember, the magic of the bouquet lies not in the creation but in the creator. In a very special sense, the creator grows along with the creation, for the imagination is limitless when free from self-imposed notions like "this is impossible. I can't do it."

This growth is important above all. Not only will you grow in terms of increasing skills and confidence but you will, I hope, grow in a very profound and meaning-ful sense—one that comes of attuning yourself to nature and working with its tools. Accept nature's gifts and let them inspire your imagination; don't become stifled by placing limits on your potential. This process of growth that seems to mirror the very processes of nature itself, is the greatest reward to be attained from creating these Gourmet Bouquets.

I have created one last bouquet—it is the most complex and the most rewarding one of all. This book is the bouquet. I offer it to you.

Lovingly,

Julia

PARTY MINDER

Date	Gourmet Bouquet Served	Additional Menu Notes	Guests

PARTY MINDER

Date	Gourmet Bouquet Served	Additional Menu Notes	Guests

PARTY MINDER

Date	Gourmet Bouquet Served	Additional Menu Notes	Guests

CREDITS

Editors
Evelyn L. Brannon
Carol Castellano

Photographer
Andrew Strauss

Illustrator
Dave Destler